THE LEARNING SOCIETY
AND PEOPLE WITH
LEARNING DIFFICULTIES

Sheila Riddell, Stephen Baron and Alastair Wilson

The POLICY
PRESS

E·S·R·C
ECONOMIC

First published in Great Britain in May 2001 by

The Policy Press
University of Bristol
34 Tyndall's Park Road
Bristol BS8 1PY
UK

Tel +44 (0)117 954 6800
Fax +44 (0)117 973 7308
E-mail tpp@bristol.ac.uk
www.policypress.org.uk

© The Policy Press, 2001

ISBN 1 86134 223 3

Sheila Riddell is Director, Strathclyde Centre for Disability Research, University of Glasgow, **Stephen Baron** is Senior Lecturer, Faculty of Education, University of Glasgow and **Alastair Wilson** is Research Fellow, Strathclyde Centre for Disability Research, University of Glasgow.

Cover design by Qube Design Associates, Bristol
Cover illustration by Jennifer Stevenson
Printed in Great Britain by Hobbs the Printers Ltd, Southampton

Contents

Competing perspectives on lifelong learning and their implications for people with learning difficulties

Introduction

This book explores the ways in which people with learning difficulties experience the Learning Society, drawing on work conducted as part of the Research Programme *The Learning Society: Knowledge and skills for employment* which was funded by the UK Economic and Social Research Council between 1995 and 2000. A central aim of the programme was to understand the diverse constructions of a Learning Society and the implications of placing lifelong learning at the heart of social policy. Our project, entitled *The meaning of the Learning Society for adults with learning difficulties*, explored the range of education, training and employment opportunities available to people with learning difficulties. Our concern was not only to understand the contexts and experiences of this significant minority but also, through the analysis of the group specifically marginalised in a Learning Society, to understand the nature of that type of society more generally.

The research was carried out in two main phases. Phase One was a study of education, training and employment opportunities for people with learning difficulties in Scotland. Documentary analysis of policy texts was carried out and key informant interviews conducted with representatives of a range of agencies (see Riddell et al, 1997a for a report of this phase of the work). The interviews were carried out, mainly by telephone, in late 1996 and early 1997, hard on the heels of regional reorganisation in Scotland, which created 32 unitary local authorities, each with education and social work functions, in place of the 12 regional authorities. Eight authorities were reluctant to be interviewed because they felt that their policies were still in a state of flux. In addition, six of the 22 Local Enterprise Companies declined to be interviewed because they felt that their policies in relation to people with learning difficulties were insufficiently developed. Interviews were also carried out with informants from Further Education (FE), the Employment Service, Careers Service and the Scottish Office (Inspectors of Social Work and Education). Interviews with ten user and voluntary organisations were also conducted. These organisations were selected to reflect a range of service provision and practice with regard to service planning. In particular, People First Scotland is an organisation of disabled people and AccessAbility describes itself as 'disability-led'. The aim here was to understand the perspective of user organisations rather than that of professionals.

In all, 80 semi-structured interviews were conducted, each organised into five domains: the nature and characteristics of services provided by agencies; the groups of people with learning difficulties for which services were intended; the underlying service ethos and the conceptualisation of the target population; the extent to which people with learning difficulties were offered choice and personal progression; the existence of competition between services within a social market. These domains also formed the basis of the analysis that involved summarising responses under domain headings and thematising responses.

The second phase of the study, lasting over 18 months, consisted of case studies of 30 adults with learning difficulties in two local authorities in Scotland (one urban and one rural), drawn from three age groups: the post-statutory education phase (age 16-23), the post-transition phase (age 28-35) and the middle to older phase (age 40+). The case studies were selected to reflect the varied nature of the population in relation to gender, ethnicity, nature of impairment and level of contact with services. Tables 1a and 1b summarise their key characteristics and social contexts, the conduct of the fieldwork and the major life issues facing the individual.

Data gathered in relation to each case study consisted of both observation and interviews. At least ten visits were made to each case study individual. The timing of each visit was carefully arranged to sample varied aspects of the person's life. For instance, the first visit might be to someone's morning placement in a FE college and the second visit to their social club in the evening. In most cases significant others in the person's life (for example, parents, partners or keyworker) were also studied. Field methods ranged from participant observation (for example, mountain biking and muffin making) through semi-structured interviews to the innovative use of visual techniques. The latter included one person making a video about her discharge from a long-stay hospital. Several people were given disposable cameras and

Table 1(a) Case studies from urban area

Pseudonym	Age	Gender	Nature of impairment	Domestic circumstances	Primary responsible organisation	Main daytime placement	Primary context studied	Interviews conducted with significant others	Major issues
Fred	17	M	Communication disabilities	Home: mother	FE	FE college	FE class	Mother – course tutor – keyworker – observation of FE class	Mother withdrew permission for case study to continue. Whole FE class researched while studying Open University module 'Equal People'
Roger	17	M	Heart complaint and non-specific mild learning difficulties	Home: mother–partner and brother	Local voluntary organisation specialist training provider	LEC Skillseekers specialist training provider	Work placement	Voluntary organisation training manager – placement employer	Health problems and difficulties finding employment
Dean	17	M	Autistic spectrum	Home: parents – brother	FE	FE class	FE class – outdoor activities class	College tutors – parents	Need to find niche in which to use considerable IT skills
Reggie	18	M	Non-specific learning difficulties – scarring as a result of an accident	Home – mother and 3 siblings	Local voluntary organisation specialist training provider	LEC Skillseekers specialist training provider	Work placement	Voluntary organisation training manager – placement employer	Continual training – difficulties in finding employment – viewed as suitable for marginal employment only

Table I (a) contd.../

Pseudonym	Age	Gender	Nature of impairment	Domestic circumstances	Primary responsible organisation	Main daytime placement	Primary context studied	Interviews conducted with significant others	Major issues
Kelly	19	F	Muscular dystrophy – non-specific mild learning difficulties	Home: mother – brother and sister	FE	FE class	Home – FE class	Mother – father – course tutor	Serious debilitating health problems – limit engagement with education and work
Martin	23	M	Down's syndrome – moderate learning difficulties	Home: parents and sister	Social work and FE	Adult resource centre/classes at college	FE class – adult resource centre	Mother – keyworker	Difficulties in becoming independent from home and day care
Mick	33	M	Down's syndrome – moderate learning difficulties	Home: elderly mother	Social work	Adult resource centre	Adult resource centre – FE class – dance class	Mother – keyworker	Over full timetable with only 2 hours work – benefits problems
Bobby	39	M	Non-specific moderate learning difficulties	Supported in own home by housing association	Social work and housing association	Adult resource centre and P/T work – via supported employment with job coaching	Adult resource centre – home – work	Keyworker – employer – voluntary organisation manager	Benefits difficulties permitting only 2 hours work per week and supported living difficulties – problems surrounding development of intimate relationships

Table I(a) contd.../

Pseudonym	Age	Gender	Nature of impairment	Domestic circumstances	Primary responsible organisation	Main daytime placement	Primary context studied	Interviews conducted with significant others	Major issues
Clare	43	F	Down's syndrome – moderate learning difficulties	Supported in own home by housing association	Social work	Adult resource centre with P/T work at weekends	Adult resource centre – home – FE classes – dance class – carrera class	Social worker – keyworker – home support worker	Issues around legal status of Incapax preventing increased independence and work – value of employment to increasing social contacts
Ronald	44	M	Non-specific mild learning difficulties	Home: elderly mother	ES	Supported employment – ES wage subsidy scheme	Work	Employer – union representative – manager of specialist voluntary organisation providing ES supported employment place	Rationalisation by employer leading to threat of disciplinary action and certification as disabled with ES intervention
Liam	47	M	Non-specific moderate learning difficulties	Home: brother and brother's family	Social work and voluntary organisation	Adult resource centre/ voluntary organisation specialist training provider work programme	Work – Adult resource centre – FE class – voluntary organisation recreation club	Keyworker – brother – voluntary organisation training manager	Failure of specialist training provider to cope with challenging behaviour

Table 1(a) contd.../

Pseudonym	Age	Gender	Nature of impairment	Domestic circumstances	Primary responsible organisation	Main daytime placement	Primary context studied	Interviews conducted with significant others	Major issues
Fiona	49	F	Non-specific moderate learning difficulties	Supported in her own flat (weekly visit)	Social work and voluntary organisation provided supported living	Adult resource centre/ looking for employment with assistance of voluntary organisation	Adult resource centre – home – FE class	Social worker – support worker	Previously worked F/T now restricted by benefits problems to P/T – social life structured around activities of now deceased mother, need for new social opportunities
Basil	50	M	Non-specific moderate learning difficulties	Home: elderly parents	Voluntary organisation providing supported employment	P/T work via supported employment through specialist training provider	Work – pub – cafe – voluntary organisation disco	Manager voluntary organisation supported employment provider – employer	Social life restrictions – benefits issues preventing increased hours of work
Bryce	55	M	Non-specific mild learning difficulties	Bed and breakfast: social work registered	Social work	Adult resource centre	Adult resource centre – swimming – voluntary organisation recreational activities	Keyworker – landlady	Loneliness – difficulties of living arrangements – cycles of training

Abbreviations: DSS = Department of Social Security, ES = Employment Service, FE = Further Education, F/T = full time, LEC = Local Enterprise Company, P/T = part time

Table 1(b) Case studies from rural area

Pseudonym	Age	Gender	Nature of impairment	Domestic circumstances	Primary responsible organisation	Main daytime placement	Primary context studied	Interviews conducted with signifcant others	Major issues
Chris	18	M	Down's syndrome – non-specific moderate learning difficulties	Home: parents	FE classes	FE	Home – FE classes – work placement	Mother – father – FE course tutor – placement employer	Benefits of FE – limited options post FE – subsequent return to day services
Maureen	20	F	Non-specific severe learning difficulties – severe mobility problems	Home: parents	Social work	Adult resource centre	Adult resource centre	Parents – manager adult resource centre	Ongoing serious health difficulties – problems of diagnosis – day services provision
Jack	21	M	Non-specific moderate learning difficulties	Home then supported accommodation	Social work	Adult resource centre	Adult resource centre	Keyworker at adult resource centre	Allegations of abuse within family resulting move to supported accommodation – death of parent ended case study prematurely
Lois	21	F	Non-specific mild learning difficulties	Home: with mother	LEC specialist training provider	Training for Work programme placement – then unemployed	Home – work – voluntary organisation specialist training provider	Mother – employer – manager voluntary organisation specialist training provider	Cycles of training – failure to gain employment – abusive relationships

Table 1(b) contd.../

Pseudonym	Age	Gender	Nature of impairment	Domestic circumstances	Primary responsible organisation	Main daytime placement	Primary context studied	Interviews conducted with significant others	Major issues
Sally	21	F	Non-specific mild learning difficulties	Home: mother, father and brother	LEC specialist training provider	Skillseeker/ Training for Work/ES supported employment – then unemployed	Work – home – jobcentre	Father – employer – manager voluntary organisation specialist training provider	Cycles of training – sporadic training and support – abusive relationships
Greg	26	M	Serious eczema – non-specific mild learning difficulties	Home: mother and sister	LEC specialist training provider	F/T work – ES supported employment	Work	Father – supervisor at work – manager of voluntary organisation specialist training provider	Successful F/T employment – adaptive employer – benefits of ES supported employment
Imran	27	M	Down's syndrome – non-specific moderate learning difficulties	Residential group home	Social work and voluntary organisation providing residential and day care	Adult resource centre/ voluntary work – 1 morning per week	Adult resource centre – home – voluntary organisation recreational activities	Best friend – keyworker – mother	Dissatisfaction with day services/ difficulties in finding alternatives – depression

Table I (b) contd.../

Pseudonym	Age	Gender	Nature of impairment	Domestic circumstances	Primary responsible organisation	Main daytime placement	Primary context studied	Interviews conducted with significant others	Major issues
Mavis	27	F	Cerebral palsy – non-specific severe learning difficulties	Home: parents and siblings	Social work	Adult resource centre	Home – adult resource centre	Mother – keyworker at adult resource centre – social worker	Allegations of abuse by family – inadequacy of day services provision
Lisa	27	F	Non-specific mild learning difficulties	Home: mother and father	Social work then voluntary organisation specialist training provider	Day services/ES work placement/P/T voluntary work	Home – work placement – voluntary work placement	Parents – keyworker – 2 employers – voluntary organisation (employment support) manager	Withdrawal from inadequate day services – difficulties encountered in accessing ES/voluntary organisation work programmes
Kirsty	28	F	Non-specific moderate learning difficulties	Home: parents and sister	Social work	Adult resource centre	Adult resource centre – home – FE class	Parents – adult resource centre keyworker – course tutor	Increasing independence – lack of differentiated services preventing progression
Doris	33	F	Non-specific mild learning difficulties	Supported in own home by housing association	Social work	Adult resource centre – community education class – voluntary work	Home – adult resource centre – community education class	Boyfriend – community education worker – keyworker – home support worker	Lack of differentiated provision beyond day services to enable increased independence

Table 1 (b) contd.../

Pseudonym	Age	Gender	Nature of impairment	Domestic circumstances	Primary responsible organisation	Main daytime placement	Primary context studied	Interviews conducted with significant others	Major issues
Iona	41	F	Non-specific mild learning difficulties	Home: parents and brother	Community Education	P/T work	Work – community education class	Community education class coordinator and course tutor – employer	Increasing independence
Ewan	46	M	Non-specific mild learning difficulties	Residential group home	Social work and voluntary organisation providing residential and day care	Day services – P/T work	Home – adult resource centre	Keyworker – employer – adult resource centre staff	Restrictions on independence/ employment opportunities imposed by DSS/ social work/ voluntary organisation funding
Kate	47	F	Non-specific moderate learning difficulties	Home: shares with husband	Social work and specialist housing association	Adult resource centre/ looking for P/T employment	Adult resource centre – home	Husband – keyworker	Supported in long-standing marriage and own home

Table 1(b) contd.../

Pseudonym	Age	Gender	Nature of impairment	Domestic circumstances	Primary responsible organisation	Main daytime placement	Primary context studied	Interviews conducted with significant others	Major issues
Maud	56	F	Non-specific moderate learning difficulties	Group home: shares with three others	Social work	Adult resource centre	Adult resource centre	Keyworker at adult resource centre – home support keyworker	Lifetime in training
Ruth	67	F	Mild depression – non-specific moderate learning difficulties	Residential group home	Social work and voluntary organisation providing residential and day care	Day services/FE	Home – FE college – adult resource centre	Keyworker – FE college tutor	Difficulties adjusting to group home following 20 years in institutional setting – long-term treatment for depression – restrictive nature of residential care preventing increase in social networks formed at FE

Abbreviations: DSS = Department of Social Security, ES = Employment Service, FE = Further Education, F/T = full time, LEC = Local Enterprise Company, P/T = part time were asked to photograph what was important in their lives. The photographs were used in later discussion. Symbol cards were used to explore the evaluations of a further education class by non-speaking young adults. The data from each case study were analysed in terms of the theoretical concerns of the project (prior and emergent) and each case was written up into a long pen portrait of some 10-15,000 words.

It is these case studies that provide the data for Chapters 3 to 9. In each of these chapters we focus on those individuals whose life experience best illuminates the particular services under consideration. Twenty-one out of our 30 case studies thus appear at some stage in the book (the other nine have been, or will be, considered in other publications). Four people appear in more than one chapter while other chapters vary from two to eight in the number of people studied depending on the range of experiences in our sample and the depth of insight available from any one particular case study. For example in Chapter 8, eight people appear as this chapter explores the different patterns of social network in our case study group; in Chapter 9 the focus is almost exclusively on one person who shared a particular legal status with perhaps only 30 other people with learning difficulties in Scotland (personal communication, Accountant at Court's Office, 19 October 2000). The form of the data reported in these chapters also varies: some data are transcripts from interviews with our case study people and their significant others; other data are extracts from researcher field notes describing events, where the use of a tape recorder would have been either impossible or inappropriate. In many ways these latter data are the most naturalistic but the former give the reader a better sense of lives in progress.

A particular feature of this research was its commitment actively to include people with learning difficulties in the research process. In addition to the methods outlined above, a formal research group of people with learning difficulties was convened to identify and explore issues relevant to their experience of the Learning Society and to disseminate findings through their networks. While useful in deepening the researchers' understandings of emerging themes, this process did not fulfil entirely the requirements of 'emancipatory research' and became, effectively, a 'focus group' (Riddell et al, 1998a). The lessons of this process are discussed in Appendix 1.

In many ways, people with learning difficulties are positioned at the social margins, educated separately from their peers, often excluded from employment and lacking many of the social and family networks which are essential to psychic and material survival. The central argument of this book is that their experiences of marginalisation through their perceived deficiencies in the core attributes of citizens of a Learning Society exemplify many dystrophic aspects of such a Learning Society more generally, illuminating what the future may hold for a growing group of people at the social margins. At the same time, some of their survival strategies and the development of some progressive services provide insight into ways in which learning and work may be transformed for all in the 21st century, providing opportunities for an inclusive rather than exclusive version of the Learning Society to grow.

In this introductory chapter, we delineate some of the key ideas that will thread their way through this book. We explore the ways in which learning difficulties are understood at the present time, demonstrating the inadequacy of explanations based solely on biological or social constructions. Subsequently, the discussion turns to the multi-faceted nature of Learning Societies. Rather than representing a monolithic construct, we argue that it is possible to discern many versions of a Learning Society, each having particular connotations for people with learning difficulties and wider implications for the future nature of citizenship. Of the various readings of the Learning Society, however, those based on ideas of human capital, social capital and social control are particularly salient for people with learning difficulties.

Who are people with learning difficulties?

Clinical definitions of learning difficulty identify approximately 3.5% of the population as falling into this category. Espie et al (1999), in a review commissioned for the Scottish Executive's Learning Disabilities Review (Scottish Executive, 2000a), commented:

> There is a lack of sound information about the numbers of people with learning disabilities in Scotland. Population registers have been set up in communities in the UK that provide a range of estimates from 1.57% of the population (Wessex, 1963), to 2% in North East Scotland (1966), 3.22% and 3.44% (Leicester 1991 and 1995) (McGrother and Thorp, 1999). A common finding is that prevalence is increasing steadily due to better survival, at least in part, the latest estimate from Leicestershire indicating an annual increase of about 1%. Thus the Scottish population will be between 16,500 (3%) and 18,900 (3.44%). Only a minority of this population will require specialist services. (Espie et al, 1999, p 4)

As well as increasing in number, people with learning difficulties are now much more likely to be living in local communities. The Scottish Executive's Learning Disabilities Review noted:

> In 1965, many people with severe learning disabilities were cared for in hospitals, although the then increasing number in hospital in Scotland (about 7,000) included many people with mild disabilities and some who had no disability. By 1998, less than 2,450 people were cared for in hospitals. The rest, including 90% of those with complex needs, were cared for in the community. (Scottish Executive, 2000a, p 6)

In this book, we adopt an operational rather than a medical definition, so that people are defined as having learning difficulties if they have been labelled in this way by service providers. Accordingly, learning difficulties included those with a background of a Record of Needs and/or special schooling, a small proportion of whom had little or no speech and had spent a significant proportion of their lives in long-stay institutions. In addition, the category included adults who had difficulty with coping skills, oracy, functional literacy and numeracy, estimated by professionals as up to one third of people in areas of social disadvantage (Riddell et al, 1998b). Young people from disadvantaged backgrounds who had missed a lot of school due to accident or illness were also categorised as having learning difficulties.

As noted above, the number of people with learning difficulties in the UK is increasing. From a medical perspective, it is suggested that the increase is due to the greater survival rates of very premature babies, many of whom have complex difficulties in later life. From a sociological perspective, it is argued that the increasing use of the category 'learning difficulties', and 'disability' more widely, is due to high levels of structural unemployment in the Western world. Describing young men as having learning difficulties both explains and justifies the exclusion of many from the labour market (Tomlinson, 1982). Stone (1984) points out that within societies that distribute money largely on the basis of earned income, disability offers an acceptable justification for the distribution of some resources on the basis of need. This results in the expansion of the category of disability, followed by government efforts to tighten definitions, so that it does not become an unmanageable drain on resources, the point of the cycle in which Britain finds itself at the turn of the 21st century.

Irrespective of the definition of learning difficulties that is employed, it is important to recognise that people with learning difficulties represent a significant proportion of those living in poverty in the UK. Disabled people are more than twice as likely to be economically inactive as the rest of the population. Among disabled people, those with learning difficulties are among the most disadvantaged. About 8,300 (rather less than half the total number) of people with learning difficulties attended day centres in 1998. Of these, 93% did not have any paid work. Only 25% of sheltered workshop expenditure is in relation to people with learning difficulties (Scottish Executive, 2000a, p 54). Given this concentration of poverty and worklessness among the population of people with learning difficulties, it is interesting that social inclusion policy pays relatively little attention to this group. For example, the Scottish Executive's social inclusion strategy (Scottish Executive, 1999a) includes only one target specifically relating to people with learning difficulties, and this concerns living arrangements rather than employment (that is, increasing the proportion of people with learning disabilities able to live at home or in a 'homely' environment). A key argument of this book is that the experiences of people with learning difficulties in relation to lifelong learning provide wider insights into the ways in which social exclusion is created and may, in the future, be challenged.

What is the Learning Society?

The rise of interest in lifelong learning must be understood in the context of the rise of global capitalism. Castells (2000), commenting on the emergence of a new economy in the last two years of the 20th century, notes that:

> For the first time in history, the whole planet is either capitalist or highly dependent on capitalist economic processes. (Castells, 2000, p 52)

This new economy has increasingly a number of key features. Firstly, productivity and competitiveness is a product of knowledge generation and information processing. Secondly, this economy is dependent on, and has emerged as a result of, new information and communication technologies, allowing capital to be moved electronically around the globe almost instantaneously, with consequent implications for national, regional and local labour markets. Thirdly, the new economy has the tendency to generate great prosperity for some, but also to intensify the social and economic exclusion of continents, countries, regions, localities and social groups. There are fears that the global markets created by the new technology may be uncontrollable by transnational bodies or national governments.

Social commentators have described the radical changes in individual and group consciousness and life experience arising as a result of globalisation. Beck, for instance, suggests that, whereas in the past an individual's life course was strongly influenced by deterministic social factors such as social class and gender, the new global economy provides new opportunities to exercise agency:

> Increasingly everyone has to choose between different options, including as to which group or subculture one wants to be identified with. In fact, one has to choose and change one's social identity as well and take the risks in doing so. (Beck, 1992, p 88)

This line of argument suggests that individuals are engaged in a process of 'reflexive self-constitution' (Lash and Urry, 1993), enabling them to negotiate and renegotiate their identity and biography with significant others. Other writers (for example, Skeggs, 1997) feel that there is a danger of overstating the potential for individual freedom, and that globalisation tends to reinforce existing patterns of social advantage and disadvantage. Skeggs argues that concepts of individualism tend to legitimate powerful groups and to render other groups unworthy of the designation 'individual' (Skeggs, 1997, p 163).

At European and national level, lifelong learning is regarded as fulfilling a number of central functions which are explored further below. Firstly, lifelong learning is seen as enabling states and individuals to maintain their economic competitiveness by constantly updating their skills and competences, giving individuals a better chance of understanding and controlling information technology rather than being its servant. Secondly, it is seen as bringing people together to engage in a shared endeavour. Thus citizenship, which previously referred to rights to access welfare services, may increasingly rest on an individual's willingness to participate in lifelong learning, thus nurturing social capital and collective identity in an increasingly fragmented and individualised world. Finally, and linked to the previous point, the expectation that all citizens will participate in lifelong learning provides the state with the ability to exercise a degree of social control by promoting values of social cohesion.

Below, we describe some versions of lifelong learning, drawing on work undertaken within *The Learning Society* research programme. Theories of human and social capital are explored more fully in Chapter 8.

Lifelong learning as generator of human capital

Becker (1964) played a key role in the development of the concept of human capital, maintaining that, within Western societies, investment in the education and training of workers was just as important in wealth creation as investment in physical plant. Human capital ideas have dominated official discourse on lifelong learning at global (OECD, 1998), European (EC, 1996) and state levels (DfEE, 1999; Scottish Office, 1999; Dutch Ministry of Education and Science, 1998; DES, 1999). This version of a Learning Society suggests that investment in adult education and training must be commensurate with the generation of future economic prosperity. Investment should thus be targeted at those groups that are most likely to generate the most significant economic returns. Within this framework, there is no self-evident justification for the inclusion of socially marginalised groups in expensive training, since, it is argued, they may prove to be less reliable workers in the longer term. In a world of scarce resources, it is suggested, the outcomes of vocational training should be tightly audited, and funding priorities should be in line with demonstrable economic costs and benefits. As well as in the UK, this approach has found favour in countries like the Netherlands, where it has been used to argue for more flexible routes into vocational and higher education. Powerful critiques of this instrumental approach have been mounted by Flemish writers such as Jacobs and Van Doorslaer (2000), who suggest that a focus on employability will impoverish adults' experience of lifelong learning, thus reducing their overall motivation and enforcing the exclusion of those already at the margins.

It is evident that human capital perspectives on lifelong learning may profoundly disadvantage socially marginalised groups, particularly in countries where there appears to be an oversupply of labour and high levels of structural unemployment. In order for the state to maximise return on investment, it may be argued that the most able should be at the front of the queue for investment. However, the state has not always drawn such simple conclusions from utilitarian arguments. Throughout the 19th century, institutions were established which were dedicated to the training of disabled people in elementary skills for employment. The Egerton Commission of 1889 exemplified such thinking, arguing that:

It is better for the state to expend its funds on the elementary technical education of the blind, than to have to support them through a life of idleness (Egerton Commission, 1889).

This perspective, rooted in philanthropy and utilitarianism, is reflected in a range of education and training establishments in Scotland during the late 18th and 19th centuries. For example, the Asylum for the Industrious Blind in Edinburgh was opened in 1773, followed by Donaldson's Hospital (now school) for the Deaf in Edinburgh in 1850 and institutions for the education and training of 'imbeciles' and 'defectives' at Larbert, Dundee and Edinburgh in the middle of the 19th century. More recently, proponents of supported employment (for example, Riddell et al, 1998a) have used similar arguments, demonstrating that such employment initiatives are cost-effective, once savings on benefit payments and other forms of support such as day centres are taken into account.

To summarise, human capital thinking contains many perils for people with learning difficulties, since it may easily be used to justify investment only in people who need little help in entering the labour market and holding down a job. However, human capital arguments have also been used by the state to justify minimal investment in education and training for people with learning difficulties to relieve the state of a future burden. Such arguments have also been employed, sometimes strategically, by those who believe that social inclusion may only be achieved through participation in the labour market.

Lifelong learning as generator of social capital

Putnam defines social capital in the following way:

Whereas physical capital refers to physical objects and human capital refers to properties of individuals, social capital refers to connections among individuals' social networks and the norms of reciprocity and trustworthiness that arise from them. In that sense, social capital is closely related to what some have called 'civic virtue'. The difference is that civic virtue is most powerful when embedded in a dense network of reciprocal social relations. A society of many virtuous but isolated individuals is not necessarily rich in social capital. (Putnam, 2000, p 19)

One posited negative consequence of the spread of global capitalism is the erosion of social cohesion and relations of trust that are essential to the operation of civil society and to the generation and maintenance of human capital (Coleman, 1988; Putnam, 1995; Fukuyama, 1999). As the labour market fragments and work becomes increasingly deregulated, there is a likelihood that social capital will dwindle with potentially negative economic and social consequences. As an antidote to such fragmentation, lifelong learning that promotes shared values and understandings may take the place of employment in cementing human relationships. Merrill (2000) suggests that in some Northern European countries such as Finland, Sweden and Denmark, adult learning is the norm and has been embedded in popular culture since the 19th century. Castells (2000) describes the way in which Finnish people have "quietly established themselves as the first true information society", using information technology in initial and continuing education in formal and informal settings to foster citizen participation and safeguard civility, supported by both Nokia and a strong welfare state (Castells, 2000, p 72).

The use of lifelong learning to promote social capital also has potentially negative consequences. It has been pointed out that societies high in social capital may base their cohesion on the active exclusion of those regarded as socially deviant. Durkheim (1938) in his work on the creation of social solidarity suggested that societies must have both 'saints' and 'sinners' in order to mark the moral boundaries between the 'normal' and the 'pathological': clearly lifelong learning in a Learning Society may be a powerful mechanism for the maintenance of such polarities. We have pointed out elsewhere (Baron et al, 1998) that social capital was high in Nazi Germany, with disastrous consequences not just for Jewish people, but also for other minority groups including people with learning difficulties.

It may also be the case that some forms of social capital are more useful than others in nurturing economic capital. Putnam, in his book *Bowling alone* (Putnam, 2000), develops the idea of two different types of social capital, bonding and bridging. Bonding forms of social capital "are inward looking and tend to reinforce exclusive identities and homogeneous groups". Bridging forms of social capital are "outward looking and encompass people across diverse social cleavages" (Putnam, 2000, p 22). Exclusive, or bonding, networks tend to reinforce the social status and identity of the particular individual or social group, which may reinforce the privilege of already socially advantaged groups. Inclusive, or bridging, networks may be used to facilitate social mobility and may be particularly advantageous to socially disadvantaged people seeking to 'better themselves'. A major question that we address in this book, and focus on particularly in Chapter 8, is the nature of the social capital to which disabled people have access and the extent to which this reinforces or challenges their social marginalisation.

Lifelong learning as personal and social transformation or as social control

While human capital versions of lifelong learning suggest that participation in education and training is driven primarily by economic self-interest, critics have argued that this view is too reductionist and that people are more likely to be motivated by a desire for self-fulfilment and personal growth (Keep and Mayhew, 1996). Just as workers might have located their identity within their work role, the deregulated labour market, necessitating more frequent changes of employment, means that identity through work becomes increasingly less likely and identity as a learner becomes of greater importance (Rees and Bartlett, 1999).

In the UK, throughout the 19th and 20th centuries, there was a strong tradition within radical, socialist and feminist movements of using lifelong learning to acquire 'really useful knowledge', that is, the sort of knowledge which could be used to challenge social inequality and political oppression as well as leading to personal growth (CCCS, 1981). Such education might be gained through political activism or through self-education, and compensated for the low-level and unimaginative education offered by the public elementary schools. Gradually, organisations like the Workers Education Association emerged, with strong links to trade unions and a mission to organise accessible and relevant education for working-class people. In countries like Spain in the post-Franco era, there has been a focus on Freirian adult education, with an emphasis on popular social movements and education for social transformation. In other European countries such as France and Flanders, the Fourth World Movement, with links to liberation theology, has sought to use lifelong learning to challenge the social exclusion of those in poverty. There are therefore many examples of the use of lifelong learning to advance the position of the socially oppressed, using educational workers as 'organic intellectuals' (Gramsci, 1971) to act as a catalyst for change.

The potential of education and training as a means of achieving social control has already been flagged up in our discussion of the dark side of social capital reflected in an extreme form in Nazi Germany.

Commenting on the findings from the ESRC Learning Society Programme, Coffield (1999) concluded that, rather than generating human and social capital, personal growth or political change, lifelong learning should actually be seen as a means of reinforcing social control. Drawing on the work of Ball and colleagues (1999), he pointed out that the requirement for all young people in the UK to participate in post-16 training was not so much to do with up-skilling the workforce as to prevent this group from engaging in activities that might undermine the social fabric. Courses available for those leaving school with few or no qualifications are generally of low standard and young people are reluctant conscripts, motivated more by the fear of losing social security benefits than the love of learning. Repeated circuits of training with no end point are likely to lead to reduced rather than enhanced employability. The exclusion of socially marginalised people from the labour market may be due to a shortage of jobs resulting from determined efforts to downsize the labour force rather than any skills deficit. The growing reluctance of governments to intervene in the operation of the global free market has led to a growing emphasis on supply-side policies, placing the onus on workers constantly to upgrade their qualifications in order to maintain their 'employability'. Coffield suggests that the 'official list' of skills culled from the traditional rhetoric of lifelong learning, such as information technology, communication skills and teamwork, are unlikely to be effective in helping socially marginalised individuals back into employment. Rather, he recommends a far more critical approach, recognising that lack of education and training, a product of social disadvantage, may be used as a justification for and explanation of social exclusion. Furthermore, the expectation that individuals will participate in learning throughout their lives on pain of losing their jobs has the potential to act more as a form of punishment and control rather than enrichment. Coffield calls for a new emphasis on access to employment rather than training outside the labour market.

Since people with learning difficulties represent a significant proportion of the socially excluded, there is a need to look critically at the type of education and training offered to them. Rather than facilitating access to employment, establishing inclusive social relationships or acting as a source of personal enrichment, this may simply serve as a time-filler, keeping this group in a state of social quiescence.

Conclusion

In this introduction, we have set the scene for the rest of the book, highlighting the fact that, rather than being a simple concept, there are various versions of a Learning Society in play. In the following chapters, we discuss education, training and employment opportunities available to people with learning difficulties, exploring the particular version of the Learning Society that they reflect. Of particular interest are the versions of the Learning Society reflecting human and social capital concerns and the extent to which lifelong learning represents personal and social transformation or social control. In Chapter 2, we discuss further the policy context of lifelong learning, highlighting the range of policy arena involved and, drawing on key informant interviews, to identify the nature and ethos of services provided by a range of agencies. The following chapters draw specifically on the case study data. Chapter 3 focuses on post-school education and training programmes while Chapter 4 deals with the type of education and training available to people with learning difficulties that have moved beyond transitional services. In Chapters 5 and 6, we explore employment-based lifelong learning: narratives of those who are closest to the open labour market feature in Chapter 5, while in Chapter 6 the focus shifts to supported employment. Chapter 7 deals with the wider context of lifelong learning created by the interaction of social security benefits, housing and employment. Access to social capital through lifelong learning is the subject of Chapter 8, where we explore the type of social capital available to people with learning difficulties through lifelong learning and its tendencies to include or to exclude. Chapter 9 returns to the theme of lifelong learning as social control, summarising the ways in which access to education, training, and employment tend to regulate this group in ways which emphasise its separateness from mainstream society. Finally in the Conclusion (Chapter 10) we return to the questions that shape each of the earlier chapters:

- What versions of the Learning Society are reflected in the range of education, training and employment opportunities on offer to people with learning difficulties?
- What are the implications of these discourses of lifelong learning in terms of achieving greater social inclusion or exclusion of this group?

TWO

Policy discourses and lifelong learning

Introduction

In this chapter, we identify the range of social policy fields in which lifelong learning policy for people with learning difficulties is forged and the discourses both of lifelong learning and learning difficulty that underpin them. We also focus on the range of agencies involved in delivery of services and the ethos of these services. In addition to our analysis of official policy documents, we draw on interviews with key informants, who provide insight into how policies work out in practice, sometimes being aligned with original policy intentions and sometimes being subverted or transformed. In the era of 'joined-up policy' (Riddell and Tett, 2001: forthcoming), it is evident that, although the will may be there for policies to reinforce each other, in reality they often pull in different directions. We explore some of these tensions and the consequences for service users.

Community care policy and lifelong learning

Community care policy provides the central backdrop against which lifelong learning policies for people with learning difficulties have developed. We therefore briefly summarise the broad strategy before exploring social workers' perspectives on the nature of lifelong services that they offer. The post-war decades saw an expansion in the number of people with learning difficulties living in residential settings, where they experienced a form of warehousing removed from the mainstream community. Following a number of well-publicised cases of cruelty and exploitation of the inhabitants of such institutions, the justification for the lifetime incarceration of people who had committed no crime was questioned. In addition, there were concerns about the significant amount of health service resource that was tied up in such facilities. The White Paper *Caring for people: Community care in the next decade and beyond* (Secretaries of State for Health, Social Security, Wales and Scotland, 1989) incorporated most of the proposals of the Griffiths Report (1988) and set the framework for a particular model of community care. The key elements were:

- to encourage the development of services to help people to live in their own homes wherever possible;
- to give high priority to the needs of carers;
- to establish proper assessment of need and good case management;
- to promote the development of a strong independent sector along with good quality public services;
- to clarify the roles of the various agencies and improve their accountability;
- to introduce a new system of funding for community care.

The 1990 National Health Service and Community Care Act provided the legislative framework for these principles to be implemented.

It was envisaged that the development of services would include education, training and employment programmes, although local authorities' community care plans focused, at least initially, on social services and health provision. In the context of the new system of funding, money to pay for new places in residential care and nursing homes was transferred from the Department of Social Security (DSS) to social work departments. People whose residential provision was being paid for by the DSS prior to 1993 had 'preserved rights', so that the DSS continued to pick up the bill. As Chapter 7 makes clear, this provision had major knock-on effects in relation to the degree of independent living people were able to enjoy and the possibility of their obtaining employment. Essentially, preserved rights created a perverse incentive against change within the system, since social services had a vested interest in ensuring that the DSS continued to pay as much as possible. The role of social work departments was increasingly defined in terms of purchasing services in addition to making service provision. However, key statutory roles in service provision remained; for example, under the 1984 Mental Health Scotland Act the social work department has a legal duty to provide suitable training and occupation for people with learning disabilities who are over school age.

McKay and Patrick (1995) describe the shifting roles of health and social work. As long-stay hospitals discharged people into the community, provision was made for money to be transferred from health boards to social work departments. The broad idea was that the NHS would provide for people's health needs, while social work departments met people's social needs. However, a number of problems arose. First, the transfer of money did not happen smoothly because the NHS continued to have large amounts tied up in hospitals, even though these were catering for fewer people. In addition, social work departments felt they needed to have services in place before people left long-stay hospitals, but did not have enough money up-front to enable these services to be developed. This slowed down the hospital closure programme (Stalker and Hunter, 1999). Furthermore, there were ongoing disputes about what counted as a health or as a social need. These disagreements were significant and difficult to resolve because whereas NHS services are free, the local authority can charge for services.

The shift from segregated to community-based services for people with learning difficulties, and the importance of inter-agency work in achieving this goal, is underlined strongly in recent policy documents such as the Scottish Executive's *Review of services for people with learning disabilities* (2000a) and Glasgow City Council's joint strategy for people with learning disabilities (2000). The latter document states:

> Substantial investment in a range of providers to develop employment opportunities for people with learning disability in Glasgow will take place. A target of creating 500 jobs for people with learning disability will be set over the next three years. Such opportunities should be available for all, regardless of level of disability or complexity of need. (Glasgow City Council, 2000, p 31)

Official policy documents thus identify education, training and employment services as playing a key role in the achievement of the goals of community care.

Despite widespread agreement that long-stay hospitals did not provide a good quality of life for most people, within the health arena, debates continue about the appropriate balance between specialist and mainstream services. At one level, health resources are being used to support initiatives geared to assisting people with learning disabilities to access employment regardless of "level of difficulty or complexity of need" (Glasgow City Council, 2000, p 31). At another level, there are fears that people with learning difficulties will not be treated well in mainstream primary health care services, where, for example, some GPs allocate four minutes per surgery consultation. The argument is made that there is still a need for some specialist primary care services targeted at people with learning difficulties (Espie et al, 1999). The emphasis on normalisation[1] and inter-agency working has led to a major shift in social work policy, although this has not always been translated smoothly into practice. For instance, key informant interviews revealed a mismatch between stated social work goals and existing services. Most day services in Scotland take the form of traditional Adult Resource Centres (ARCs), each providing a menu of activities geared towards leisure and recreation and often offered in segregated settings. The Scottish Executive's Learning Disabilities Review revealed that only 20% of activity in day centres took the form of education and employment while 28% involves leisure and recreation. However, key informants in social work suggested that the focus of services was to move people out of the centres and into the community. The following comment was typical:

> "Everything people do is aimed at moving them towards greater independence and employment opportunities." (social work manager)

A few respondents were somewhat more sceptical about the actual achievement of services compared with their ambitious goals:

> "[The project] is supposed to provide horticultural opportunities for employment but it has become a big day centre with plants – people don't get paid and they don't move on." (social work manager)

Some managers were extremely enthusiastic about the potential of well-run supported employment programmes:

> "People are seeing how, if you give people with learning difficulties a job, they do it to the letter and they've been so reliable. We had one lad working in McDonald's and he was incredible. The best burgers they had ever seen – the burger in the middle of the bun, the relish in the middle of the burger. He accepts nothing less, nothing sloppy about it. One woman is a cleaner and she is meticulous, keeps the place much cleaner than any of the other cleaners they've got there." (LEC manager)

However, it was also recognised by this manager that shortage of placements and restrictions imposed by social security rules meant that supported employment opportunities were too few and time-restricted to meet demand.

Community care policy has led to a redefinition of roles between health and social work, and a new focus on the range of other agencies, including education and employment, which must work together if people with learning difficulties are to be included fully in communities. However, despite widespread acceptance of this broad policy goal, questions remain about the extent to which inclusive services are being implemented.

Education policy and lifelong learning

To maintain their employability, individuals are called upon continually to update their knowledge, skills and credentials, choosing from a range of competing education and training services. Such policies may be problematic for people with learning difficulties, who may find it very difficult to gain academic or vocational qualifications based on the formal demonstration of skills in literacy and numeracy. In the past, when a much higher proportion of young people left school with no qualifications, people with learning difficulties were able to 'pass' much more easily. In 1998/99, 92% of Scottish young people gained a Standard Grade (1-6) in English and Mathematics. This means that the 8% who failed to achieve this level become clearly identifiable and set apart from the rest of the population. Furthermore, the declining demand for unskilled workers in the labour market over the last two decades has had particularly serious consequences for those lacking basic qualifications. In the following paragraphs, we first review the range of education services available to people with learning difficulties and then consider some of the tensions with other policy areas suggested by key informants' accounts.

Further Education (FE) has a statutory responsibility to 'have regard' to the needs of disabled students under the terms of the 1992 Further and Higher Education (Scotland) Act and premium funding is made available from the Scottish Executive for this. Key informant accounts suggested that colleges, operating as independent incorporated bodies, interpreted this duty differently. However, since there is no clear definition of which students may be regarded as having special needs, there is a perverse incentive for colleges to focus on the most able students with learning difficulties to ensure that they receive the Premium Funding, while avoiding significant expenditure on support for students while they are in college. Because of a shortage of provision, key informants told us that colleges select students rather than vice versa. In the urban study area, the three FE colleges appeared to work closely together, allocating students to colleges in order to maintain viable classes in each. In the rural study area there was only one FE college and therefore no market. There was thus no effective competition among service providers within FE in either of our study areas, although there was fierce competition between FE and Community Education (see below).

Courses for older people with learning difficulties were generally short-term and covered a range of leisure and life skills topics. Here, the supply of courses was not able to keep pace with demand. In FE there was tension between the ethics of personal development and training for work. The perceived low level of 'employability' of people with learning difficulties sat uneasily with the general mission of FE to meet the needs of employers. Key informants told us that people with learning difficulties were almost always taught separately from mainstream students and often used separate rooms and facilities when studying subjects such as home economics or horticulture.

Adult and Community Education services are located within local authority education departments. Whereas patterns of resource allocation in FE reflected human capital understandings, in Community Education services there was comparatively little emphasis on skills directly related to employment but more on personal and social skills delivered in mainstream settings and geared towards social inclusion. Community Education informants felt that, following local government reorganisation in 1996, the service was chronically underfunded and had lost out to FE, whose mission of meeting the requirements of the labour market did not fit comfortably with the provision of quality services for people with learning difficulties. This view of FE from the perspective of Community Education is illustrated below:

> "I think there's a competitive market with the colleges because they're fighting for their lives since incorporation. I'm sure you'll be aware of the colleges, every corner you come to in City B you'll find an FE college. And there's a tremendous amount of in-fighting among themselves ... and they're very protective of what they do.... It means that around the table everyone is not quite open and up-front about what they're doing.... They think they can do everything

and when they're driven by performance indicators that are all about money they say: 'Oh, we can deliver on that', but we know they can't. They've got a tremendous role to play but they haven't got the staff on the ground working with the people on a daily basis.... We've got to be working in the community, doing the confidence building bits, the essential skills bits which colleges can't." (Community Education respondent)

It should be noted that the city referred to by this Community Education respondent was not the urban area in which our case studies were conducted. Whereas in our study area FE colleges operated a cartel, in the city referred to above they appeared to compete with each other for special needs clients. This intensification of competition might reflect the greater number of FE colleges and the precarious financial position of many.

Training policy

Training for people with learning difficulties, particularly in the post–16 age group, is provided by Local Enterprise Companies (LECs, the equivalent of Training and Enterprise Councils south of the Border) through Skillseekers programmes. Training for Work programmes is provided for the older age group. The principal task of LECs is to promote local economic development. Given this raison d'etre, investment in people with learning difficulties may be contentious given that they may be, in perception or reality, less effective workers than their peers. There has been little coordination of LEC and Employment Service training programmes, described below, and as a result there is overlap in provision for people with less significant impairments, while very little provision is targeted at people with higher support needs.

The dominant ethos in the LECs was that of 'employability' – the acquisition of skills, attitudinal and technical, which would make the person an attractive employee. Within this ethos the person with learning difficulties could appear as a poor investment, being more expensive to train and potentially less able to adapt to changing work practices. Key informant interviews suggested that many training programmes, including Skillseekers and Training for Work, which claimed to cater for people with special needs, were in fact targeted at the socially disadvantaged and specifically excluded people with learning difficulties who were seen as the responsibility of social services. The funding regime established by LECs, linking payment to the attainment of vocational qualifications, made this an unattractive area for most private training agencies. A minority of LECs attempted to include people with learning difficulties in their programmes, but often had difficulties in finding a training placement for them. The following training manager explained the basic principle informing LEC activity:

> "Generally speaking, it would be unusual to assist people in sheltered employment because they are the responsibility of the social work department. It's aimed at people who can be economically active. It doesn't need to be full-time, but you have to be able to take up employment outside a sheltered environment." (LEC training manager)

Careers Services have a statutory responsibility to work with young people with special needs after they leave school. Contact was normally initiated at the Future Needs Assessment, about 18 months before the statutory school-leaving age. Careers Services 'endorsed' young people as having special needs for the purpose of participation in FE and Skillseekers programmes. A sifting mechanism operated, whereby some young people were channelled towards programmes leading to the open labour market (mainstream or special needs Skillseekers), while others, regarded as marginal workers, were channelled into FE extension programmes. People with the most significant difficulties moved directly from school into Adult Resource Centres. Young people with learning difficulties had little choice of route or service due to shortage of placements.

Employment policy

Employment and training policy in the UK has a somewhat cumbersome structure. The Employment Service, an agency of the DfEE, has responsibility for employment programmes whereas responsibility for training rests with Local Enterprise Companies (LECs) in Scotland and Training and Enterprise Councils (TECs) in England. From April 2001, the Learning and Skills Council assumes responsibility for post-school education and training in England. Since the advent of the Scottish Parliament in 1999, the situation has become even more complex. Employment is a 'reserved' area of business, with Westminster policy mediated through the Office for Scotland in Edinburgh, while Lifelong

Learning and Enterprise is controlled by the Holyrood Parliament. There is some unease among MSPs about the division between enterprise and employment and the extent to which Westminster and Holyrood policies are aligned.

The Employment Service (ES) has a remit to assist disabled people, including those with learning difficulties, to access the labour market. Disability Employment Advisers, based in Disability Service Teams at jobcentres, assess the training needs of their disabled clients and place them on appropriate programmes, usually delivered by the voluntary sector and private training agencies. Such programmes include the New Deal for Disabled People, Access to Work, Job Introduction Schemes, Supported Employment (formerly known as Wage Subsidy and to which we will refer as Wage Subsidy Supported Employment in order to differentiate it from another type of Supported Employment discussed below) and Work Preparation (formerly known as Job Rehabilitation). Demand for such programmes is growing as more disabled people seek inclusion and support in the labour market. Annual expenditure on ES programmes is rising (for example, government funding for Work Preparation was £8.7 million in 1998/99; for the year 1999/2000 £10.2 million was allocated). However, demand for support, for example through Access to Work, outstrips funding. The ES is forced by the Treasury to report on the effectiveness of its programmes in moving disabled people into sustainable employment. Statistics on programme outcomes do not always support an economic case for expansion, for instance, in Scotland between 1997 and 1999, only 20% of individuals participating in the Work Preparation programme were working 13 weeks after the end of their placement (Wilson et al, 2000).

Many ES programmes were not developed with people with learning difficulties in mind and may not offer enough support and flexibility to meet their needs. For example, job rehabilitation, now known as Work Preparation, arose out of a recommendation of the Tomlinson Report and formed part of the 1944 Employment Act. It was designed to meet the needs of disabled servicemen returning from the Second World War, offering a period of intensive training in Employment Rehabilitation Units. Although Work Preparation now tends to take place in workplace settings, it still only allows an individual 6-8 weeks training and is evaluated in relation to a narrowly defined set of outcomes. Because of the lack of support available both during the training period and in subsequent employment, relatively few people with learning difficulties are included in Work Preparation programmes.

The New Deal for Disabled People (NDDP) outlined in the DSS White Paper (DSS, 1998) was allocated £195 million. Targeted initially at people on Incapacity Benefit (IB), its aim was to move long-term IB claimants back into the labour market. The programme included the following elements:

- personal adviser service to help disabled people and those with a long term illness to overcome barriers to work;
- innovative schemes to explore how best to help disabled people move into or stay in work;
- an information campaign to improve knowledge of the existing help available and to change the attitudes of benefits recipients, employers and the public;
- a programme of research and evaluation.

The DSS work incentive measures, described above, were intended to lubricate the process. Within the context of the personal adviser service, letters were sent to IB claimants encouraging them to contact personal advisers at jobcentres to receive advice on the Single Gateway to Employment (now referred to as ONE, suggesting deification). Although the letters emphasised that participation in the NDDP was voluntary, response by IB claimants was very low at 3.3% (Arthur et al, 1999). Furthermore, despite the promises of novelty, people were directed towards existing and rather inflexible training programmes such as Work Preparation. Evaluation of the New Deal for Disabled People (Arthur et al, 1999) suggests that very small numbers of people with learning difficulties have moved into jobs as a result of the programme and, viewed through Treasury eyes, it may be regarded as less cost-effective than New Deal programmes aimed at lone parents and 18-24 year olds.

Whereas the Employment Service offered no programmes for those with more significant difficulties, voluntary organisations attempted to cater for this group through Job Coach Supported Employment provision (which is different from the Employment Service Wage Subsidy Supported Employment). Funded from a range of sources including the European Social Fund and social work, Job Coach Supported Employment was seen by voluntary organisation key informants as the best means of achieving social inclusion and enhancing social networks. It was also seen as contributing to better health, access to normal living arrangements, and opportunities to develop a range of social relationships. However, proponents of this type of supported employment felt that the market was rigged against them so that there were far too few opportunities available to accommodate the number of people expressing a preference for paid employment. This view is encapsulated below:

> "Most people with learning difficulties tell me they would rather be working than in an Adult Training Centre. The usual primary objective is to get a job. And a lot of the more able people with learning difficulties are voting with their feet – they just refuse to go.... Every one of our supported employment schemes has a unit cost less than an Adult Training Centre placement.... The irony for me is that if there was a proper market we would be inundated with work." (chief executive, voluntary organisation)

Clearly, tensions existed between education, training and employment policies and services on the one hand and those of community care on the other. While the latter emphasised the role of education, training and employment in assisting people with learning difficulties to be included in meaningful community networks, most services were not geared towards people with the most significant difficulties since it was deemed that these individuals were the responsibility of social work. Community education practitioners wished to provide better and more inclusive services for people with learning difficulties, but were prevented by funding problems. Similarly, LEC managers sometimes tried to accommodate people with learning difficulties within mainstream training programmes, but were stymied by the funding mechanism which paid training providers on the basis of the number of trainees in these mainstream programmes attaining Level 2 in the Scottish Vocational Qualification within a specified time limit. The only provision targeted at people with learning difficulties was provided by voluntary organisations running supported employment programmes, and these often operated on the margins of viability.

Social security policy

Our key informants saw social security policy as providing the central framework connecting community care with education, training and employment policies. We have already discussed the significance of shifting funding of residential provision for people with learning difficulties from the DSS to social work in 1993. A further major policy marker was the Green Paper *New ambitions for our country: A new contract for welfare* (DSS, 1998), which expressed a commitment to tackling worklessness and removing barriers to employment arising from the benefits system. Disabled people and those with a long-term illness were identified as being one of the principal beneficiaries of 'rebuilding welfare around the work ethic' (DSS, 1998, p 3). In order to encourage these developments, the Department of Social Security (DSS) introduced personal adviser schemes in pilot areas to advise and assist disabled people in obtaining employment. A number of new work incentive measures were also introduced to counter existing disincentives. A study conducted by some of the authors as part of the National Disability Development Initiative (Wilson et al, 2000) suggested that disabled people were suspicious of any change which might alter their benefits status, and were particularly concerned at having to 'retake' the All Work Test, which determines whether an individual is fit to work or not. One of the DSS work incentive measures, referred to as the '52 week linking rule', was designed to ensure that individuals who entered jobs but left them during the course of a year could return to their original benefits status. Our study of Employment Service programmes (Wilson et al, 2000) suggested that people with learning difficulties and their families simply did not believe that the 52-week rule would be applied fairly and believed that entering employment was tantamount to giving up benefits entitlements.

Another work incentive measure having a particular impact on people with learning difficulties concerned 'therapeutic earnings'. This rule states that individuals on income support with severe disablement allowance are allowed to work for 16 hours a week without losing benefit. Any additional work undertaken may have devastating financial consequences and may threaten the individual's status as permanently disabled. In this way, what is billed as a work incentive measure may act as a powerful disincentive to greater economic activity (see Simons, 1998 for further discussion of the complexities of the benefits system for people with learning difficulties). In Chapter 7, we discuss in more detail the way in which individuals' benefits packages influence their willingness to participate in lifelong learning.

While the government has been explicit about the ways in which welfare to work policies will operate, Townsend (1999) notes that it has had less to say about the ways in which 'security' is to be assured for those who cannot work. In particular, he argues that there is a pressing need for a government report "giving the minimum income and benefit needs of differently constituted families" (Townsend, 1999, p xx).

Conclusion

The brief outline of the policy framework above indicates areas of tension and overlap between the wide range of policy arenas relevant to a Learning Society. As in the rest of the public sector (Deakin, 1994), quasi markets have been established within all service areas, but there is potential for power to remain with service purchasers (care managers) and providers rather than service users, particularly when this group is likely to be poor, inarticulate and lacking powerful advocates. While community care and lifelong learning policies recognise the contribution to be made by a range of service providers, competition among services for control of a particular area may render such cooperation potentially difficult. All agencies emphasise the importance of participation in mainstream society, but most offer segregated rather than inclusive services. While genuflecting towards equal access, resource allocation policies tend to reflect the belief that investment in individuals' education and training must be in relation to their future ability to deliver added value to the economy.

Particular contradictions within present arrangements are apparent within the approach adopted by LECs, social work services and voluntary organisations. For example, whereas LECs claim to offer a Skillseekers course to every school leaver, their special training needs programmes effectively exclude people with cognitive difficulties, since these people are unlikely to gain Scottish Vocational Qualifications at Level 1, the performance indicator for special programmes used by LECs in making payments to training agencies. Most LEC provision focuses on people with social and behavioural problems, because this population is seen as more 'salvageable' than those with cognitive difficulties. Social work provision for people with learning difficulties is similarly fraught with contradictions. Whereas it is claimed that all social work provision is aimed at work preparation, in reality most resources are tied up in Adult Resource Centres where people participate in 'leisure orientated' activities rather than work. Again, there is a stated commitment to person-centred planning and self-advocacy, but little evidence that this is happening to any great degree. Voluntary organisations emerged from our survey as the focus of most innovative practice. Supported employment, work taster and work preparation programmes are all being offered, but shortage of resources and short-term funding mean that many voluntary organisations find that their services, although meeting a real need, are scarcely financially viable. They are critical of social and health services purchasing policies, which favour existing provision in

Adult Resource Centres rather than more innovative forms of provision with firmer roots in communities.

Having set the policy context of the services on offer for the 30 people who constituted our case studies we now turn, in Chapters 3 to 9, to an exploration of the lived experiences of these services. We first turn the provision made for young people on, or shortly after, leaving school.

Note

[1] 'Normalisation' refers to the social policy advocated by Wolfensberger (1972) and O'Brien (1987). Developed in the US and subsequently adopted in the UK, normalisation suggests that the role of services should be to assist people with learning difficulties to 'pass' in mainstream society. Critics of normalisation (for example, Brown and Smith, 1992) suggest that it is conservative in its orientation, maintaining that disabled people must adapt to society rather than vice versa.

THREE

Social justice and post-school education and training for people with learning difficulties

Introduction

As we noted in Chapter 1, the Learning Society is a contested concept. The dominant version of the Learning Society tends to give most weight to human capital principles, underpinned by a utilitarian notion of social justice. The subtitle of the ESRC programme of which this research was part was 'Knowledge and skills for employment' and at the first meeting of the programme the obligatory industrialist commented that he could not understand why research on people with learning difficulties had been commissioned within a programme devoted to economic competitiveness (see Baron et al, 1998, for a discussion of this).

However, rival versions of the Learning Society may be glimpsed both within official policy documents and within radical texts and practices. Counter-hegemonic versions of the Learning Society, rather than seeing education and training as a means of achieving individual and national economic advantage, instead emphasise education as a means of developing social capital. Although the notion of social capital is itself a contentious concept (see Chapter 7 for further discussion), it is generally taken to refer to the networks connecting individuals and groups into a collectivity which provides a sense of identity and purpose for their activities (Baron et al, 2000). The social justice implicit in the idea of a Learning Society based on social capital rather than human capital is very different, giving far more weight to recognising the needs and identities of minority groups.

Education is, by definition, at the heart of the any formulation of a Learning Society, but in addition, various notions of a just society will view education from differing perspectives. Societies based on utilitarian notions of justice are likely to regard education as a good to be transmitted in accordance with the ability of an individual or group to produce a satisfactory financial rate of return on the sum invested. Those based on social capital ideas might, alternatively, regard it as necessary to target additional education and training on those most at risk of social exclusion, on the grounds that this is a good in itself and that the excluded pose a risk to wider social cohesion.

In this chapter, we begin by discussing salient ideas of social justice and their implications for the inclusion of people with learning difficulties. Subsequently, we consider the development of post-war education and training policy for young people in the transition from school to work both in relation to the mainstream population and, more specifically, in relation to people with learning difficulties. Finally, we explore some implication of the experiences of case study individuals with learning difficulties who have been the active recipients of such policies in their post-school years. We argue that training may be seen as a crucible of social values since its distribution transmits powerful messages about who is likely to become economically active and who is to be consigned to some special status of otherness, who is considered salvageable and who is considered unsalvageable. It is also a means of social control, where people are taught to internalise the disciplinary framework of the workplace and understand their position within or outwith it. Finally, we consider which conceptualisations of social justice might hold out most hope for people with learning difficulties in terms of challenging their social marginalisation. In Chapter 4, we consider the types of adult and community education available to people with learning difficulties once they have moved beyond the reach of transitional services.

Utilitarianism and social justice

Utilitarian conceptions of social justice in the Hume–Smith–Bentham–Mill tradition centre on the idea of the 'greatest good'. For an individual this is represented by the rational calculus of balancing different courses of action, in different time frames, with their different expected outcomes so as to maximise overall satisfaction. This model of the calculating individual (taken as universal humanity) is then extrapolated to societal levels where the good of a society can similarly be judged by the net balances of individual satisfactions. The just social arrangements are those that, through the (sleight of) the hidden hand of the market, have the highest net balance of such individual satisfactions.

This conception of social justice, plausible perhaps from the standpoint of a 19th-century British entrepreneur, continues to reverberate through intellectual life in arguments about the moral primacy of the market (Gray, 1992) and, more particularly for these purposes, in arguments about human capital (Carnoy, 1995). This latter position considers the individual as the rational investor in their own human capital, seeking to maximise the personal return through supplying skills that are in demand in the labour market. In recent years this conception has become a central icon of the rapidly changing capitalist mode of production (where every institution is in danger of being prefixed with 'The Learning ...') and of British government policy.

For present purposes three major objections may be made to the classical utilitarian position in terms of people with learning difficulties. Firstly, the individual carefully calculating means–ends as a starting point for social analysis is a conception of humanity and sociality which tends to exclude those with learning difficulties for whom such planning may be difficult or impossible (should this even be a desirable conception of humanity). Secondly, the implicit assumption that people have a variety of means open to them to choose among is necessarily fragile when applied to those with learning difficulties, for whom options are very limited in societies dominated by utility: "Accumulate! Accumulate! That is Moses and all the Prophets" (Marx, 1973, p 654). Thirdly, the vision of the good society as that which maximises the net sum of individual satisfactions has a strong pull to minimise the satisfactions of minority groups that are not consonant with the majority pursuit of happiness. Nils Christie (1992, pp 160-1), in discussing some of the bastard forms of utilitarianism in the 20th century, highlights the potential consequences of the tendency to see non-useful people as less than human and therefore disposable.

The Rawlsian alternative

John Rawls counterposes a neo-social contract conception of social justice to such utilitarian positions (Rawls, 1972). The starting point for Rawls is 'the original position' – a set of hypothetical conditions of equality under which people may rationally agree on a set of principles of justice untainted by knowledge of their actual social interests (the veil of ignorance): "it seems reasonable and generally acceptable that no one be advantaged or disadvantaged by natural fortune or social circumstances in the choice of principles" (1972, p 18). Rawls offers two criteria for inclusion in this primal ethical encounter: capability of having a conception of personal good; capability of a sense of justice (1972, p 19).

In discussing which beings are to be included in the discourse of justice Rawls adopts, and elaborates, these criteria: having a conception of own personal good is "expressed by having a rational plan of life"; capability of a sense of justice is "a normally effective desire to apply and to act on principles of justice, at least to a certain minimum degree" (1972, p 505). These two features constitute the moral personality which is a "potentiality that is ordinarily realised in due course. It is this potentiality which brings claims of justice into play" (1972, p 505). Rawls assumes that this potentiality is possessed "by the overwhelming majority of mankind" and that "when someone lacks the requisite potentiality either from birth or accident, this is regarded as a defect or deprivation ... only scattered individuals are without this capacity" (1972, p 506). Individuals are admitted to Rawls's discourse of justice "once a certain minimum is met ... provided the minimum for moral personality is satisfied, a person is owed all the guarantees of justice" (1972, pp 506-7).

Whether people with learning difficulties can be admitted to Rawls' discourse of justice would thus appear to be in some doubt. As we have suggested above, formulating a 'rational plan of life 'may be difficult or impossible for some people with learning difficulties (as well as the authors) while the capacity to act on abstract principles of justice might similarly be impaired. Currently Scotland is elaborating new procedures formally to declare people with learning difficulties as incapable of just such rational life planning and moral decision making (see Chapter 8). Beyond this formally declared group there is a much larger group of people with learning difficulties whose capacity for life planning and moral decision making is heavily structured by professionals (Baron and Dumbleton, 2001: forthcoming).

Rawls might here retreat behind the notion of 'potentiality', maintaining that people with learning difficulties have the potential for rational life planning and acting on principles of justice, as yet unrealised. This simply pushes the criterion one step back into obscurity and circularity. Without a definition of the 'certain minimum' for admission to the realm of the just, we must assume that at least some people with learning difficulties are among the 'scattered individuals' who due to 'defects or deprivation' are not admissible. While Rawls addresses the moral position of animals ("outside the scope of the theory of justice and it does not seem possible to extend the contract doctrine so as to include them in a natural way" 1972, p 512), he is significantly silent about the status of the 'scattered individuals'. Just as utilitarianism tends to exclude people with learning difficulties from the discourse of justice, so too does the social contract vision of Rawls and, in doing so, both have the tendency to dehumanise people with learning difficulties.

If we assume that, contrary to the above arguments, people with learning difficulties do fulfil Rawls' criteria for inclusion in the discourse of justice, how then do they fare? Rawls elaborates two principles of justice:

First Principle: Each person is to have an equal right to the most extensive total system of equal basic liberties compatible with a similar system of liberty for all.

Second Principle: Social and economic inequalities are to be arranged so that they are both: (a) to the greatest benefit of the least advantaged, consistent with the just saving principle, and (b) attached to offices and positions open to all under conditions of fair equality of opportunity (1972, p 302).

Prima facie this looks more promising for people with learning difficulties, one of the least advantaged groups in capitalist societies. Ignoring for present purposes the First Principle, what are the implications of the Second Principle which directly addresses the potential disadvantaging of minorities in utilitarian 'greatest good' formulations?

Implicit in Rawls' formulation are three assumptions that ensure that people with learning difficulties remain relatively disadvantaged. First, Rawls takes as given that there are people who are "advantaged or disadvantaged by natural fortune..." (1972, p 18), qualities to be suspended in the hypothetical 'original position' but taken as a simple social fact. Secondly, Rawls assumes hierarchies of control to which hierarchies of material reward are attached. Thirdly, Rawls aligns these with his conception of justice through insisting on equality of opportunity so that positions in the hierarchy of control/reward reflect natural talents. The contribution of these assumptions, reminiscent of tautological functionalist attempts in the 1950s and 1960s to prove inequality functionally necessary, ensures that people with learning difficulties remain at the bottom of the hierarchy of control/reward.

New Labour and conceptions of social justice

In 1992, 50 years after the publication of the Beveridge Report, the Labour Party set up a Commission on Social Justice to carry out an independent inquiry into social and economic reform in the UK. The report of the Commission, *Social justice: Strategies for national renewal*, was published in 1994. In terms of its implications for people with learning difficulties, it tends to reflect ideas of a natural hierarchy of control and reward similar to those of Rawls. The following four principles of social justice are identified in the report:

1. The foundation of a free society is the equal worth of all citizens.
2. Everyone is entitled, as a right of free citizenship, to be able to meet their basic needs for income, shelter and other necessities.
3. Self-respect and equal citizenship demand more than the meeting of basic needs: they demand opportunities and life chances.
4. To achieve the first three conditions of social justice, we must recognise that although not all inequalities are unjust (a qualified doctor should be paid more than a medical student) unjust inequalities should be reduced and where possible eliminated.

These four principles leave a number of questions unanswered, in particular, what criteria are to be used to decide what counts as a just and an unjust inequality. Indeed, the meritocracy implied in the provision of equal opportunities and life chances suggests that inequalities will inevitably be created. The extent to which vigorous efforts should be made to challenge these inequalities, and the mechanisms to be employed, are somewhat vague. While the report criticises "fanatics of the market economy, who forget that a market is a social reality which itself requires trust, order, goodwill and other forms of support" (CSJ, 1994, p 19), it is even more scathing of social justice which concerns itself with radical redistribution. This is condemned:

> ... as a subtractive and inhibiting force which busies itself, for reasons ranging from asceticism to sheer envy, in taking away things from successful people and giving them to the unsuccessful (minus the considerable bureaucratic cost of doing so). (CSJ, 1994, p 19)

Within this formulation of social justice, people who are unlikely to compete successfully for reward and control, a group which is likely to include people with learning difficulties, are counted among those who will have their basic needs met, but will not be enabled to enjoy a similar standard of living to their more competitive and successful neighbours. It would appear that to seek equality for people with learning difficulties is to be either ascetic or envious.

Radical notions of social justice: tensions between redistribution and recognition

As we have noted, Rawlsian notions of social justice, reflected in the Labour Party's Commission on Social Justice, while rejecting untrammelled individualism, nonetheless favour only limited forms of redistribution and expect that those who are most successful within a meritocracy will have the greatest power to control redistribution. Over the past decade, attempts by the Left to promote more radical forms of social transformation have foundered on tensions between notions of social justice rooted in 'identity politics' and the recognition of social difference and those rooted in 'social class politics' and the redistribution of wealth. Many on the Left, dismayed by the corruption of Communist regimes in Eastern Europe, maintained that crude forms of economic determinism should be replaced by a recognition of different forms of oppression reflecting cultural identities and experiences of particular groups such as women, black and gay people. Tensions between recognition and redistribution in left-wing politics have been eloquently expressed in debates between two Americans, Iris Marion Young (1990) and Nancy Fraser (1997) and are summarised by Anne Phillips (1997). Fraser maintains that identity politics are potentially damaging to redistributive efforts since they blur class differences: for instance, they assume that once the cultural integrity of disabled people, black people or Scottish people is recognised, all will be well, ignoring the fact that class divisions exist within these groups as well as between groups and that efforts to promote the interests of one group may be at the expense of another, thus undermining the wider struggle against the forces of global capitalism. In support of Fraser's argument, Phillips notes that:

> The radicalism of the new Labour government is far more evident
> in its programme for constitutional reform than in any policies for
> the redistribution of income or wealth. (1997, p 147)

Young, on the other hand, maintains that these apparently competing notions of social justice may be reconciled. For instance, she argues that when African-Americans struggle for a school or university, they are seeking both economic justice and social and cultural recognition. These debates again have particular salience for people with learning difficulties. If social justice is seen in terms of economic redistribution, then this is likely to benefit all disabled people including those with learning difficulties, who are particularly likely to be living in poverty (Beresford, 1996). However, they are unlikely to be in a position to achieve this redistribution for themselves due to their lack of economic power, access to information and control over forms of communication. Similarly, notions of social justice linked to the politics of identity are problematic for people with learning difficulties, partly because of their difficulty in developing a shared sense of identity and solidarity and also because it is not evident that learning difficulties lend themselves to celebration. This contrasts with, for example, the situation of deaf people who have a well-developed culture based on sign language and may see segregated schooling as a source of strength rather than a ghetto. Recently, self-advocacy has been used to assist people with learning difficulties to develop their sense of identity, but this involves the support of non-learning disabled people. Conceptualisations of social justice based on the celebration of difference may thus prove problematic for disabled people, particularly those with learning difficulties. On the other hand, versions of social justice which privilege economic struggles over others may also be in danger of excluding people with learning difficulties, who have often been seen as occupying some special status outwith the social class structure, despite the strong association between disability and poverty (Oppenheim and Harker, 1996).

Thus far we have reviewed a number of theories of social justice and it is evident that those based on utilitarian principles, on ideas of social contract and more radical ones based on either redistribution or recognition may all marginalise people with learning difficulties, consigning them to some limbo-like status outwith the mainstream. We will now look at the nature of post-school education and training policies and their implications for people with learning difficulties.

Training for young people with learning difficulties

The policy context

Training policy and practice for all young people have undergone radical changes since the mid-1970s, when the oil crisis prompted a worldwide recession decimating the youth labour market. Whereas in 1975, 60% of 16-year-olds were in full-time employment, by 1983 only 18% moved into full-time jobs on leaving school. For young people with learning difficulties, the situation was even more dire; whereas in the mid-1970s circa 70% gained employment on leaving school, by the mid-1990s this had shrunk to less than 10%. During the 1950s and 1960s, periods of relatively low unemployment, there had been little state intervention in training. Employers operated apprenticeship schemes and young working-class men 'served their time' before becoming fully qualified in a trade. The rapid decline of heavy industry also led to the collapse of apprenticeship arrangements and the government was forced to intervene. Youth Opportunities programmes, introduced in the late 1970s, were intended to create jobs for those who, if they remained unemployed, might pose a threat to society.

In the early 1980s, these were superseded by Youth Training Schemes, subsequently renamed Youth Training. The ethos of these schemes was different from that of YOPS. Rather than creating jobs, the government redefined the problem to be one of labour supply. Young people were held simply not to be emerging from education and training with the appropriate skills and attitudes and once these problems were addressed the economy would miraculously regenerate (Bynner, 1991). The Manpower Services Commission (MSC), established in the late 1970s, later extended its sphere of influence to schools, funding the Technical and Vocational Educational Initiative so that appropriate work related skills could be developed even earlier and education could be made more 'relevant' to the needs of the economy.

The emergence of Local Enterprise Companies

Yet another rethink of the apparently intractable problem of training took place in the early 1990s. In Scotland, the 1990 Enterprise and New Towns (Scotland) Act established Scottish Enterprise (SE) and Highlands and Islands Enterprise (HIE) and gave them the responsibility for Vocational Education and Training in place of the Training Agency (formerly the MSC), a wing of the Department of Employment. The goal was to operate economic development more effectively by bringing together training and business development. In England, equivalent legislation established Training and Enterprise Councils. Subsequently, a decision was made that arrangements for post-school education and training were cumbersome and tortuous, and the 2000 Learning and

Skills Act creates a Learning and Skills Council (LSC) to replace the Further Education Funding Council and the Training and Enterprise Councils. It is envisaged that the national LSC will work closely with local Learning and Skills Councils and Regional Development Agencies.

In Scotland, Scottish Enterprise and Highlands and Islands Enterprise contract with 22 Local Enterprise Companies (LECs). Over 80% of the SE and HIE budget is devolved to the LECs for a range of training and business development projects. As non-governmental agencies, LECs are not directly accountable through democratic processes and their small self-selecting boards are required to have a majority of members drawn from the senior ranks of the business sector. In practice, despite the increased power of the business sector, the Scottish Executive continues to play a strong role in directing their activities. Fairley (1992) noted that the advent of the LECs was greeted with some suspicion by Scottish local authorities; some officers felt that they were simply a means of bypassing or marginalising local authority influence. LECs were seen as conforming with "... the 1980s Conservative desire to promote solutions based on market forces and so-called 'voluntarism', by means of initially centralising policy development and control" (Fairley, 1992, p 39).

A major role of LECs is to fund and manage the major post-16 training programme, known as Skillseekers, as well as a range of training programmes for adults. Some Skillseekers training programmes are targeted specifically at people with special educational needs, and entry is through 'endorsement' by the local Careers Company. The nature and availability of Special Needs Skillseekers programmes varies greatly from one LEC to another. Such training programmes also take place in a range of locations, but whereas many mainstream Skillseekers programmes are delivered by employers, Special Needs Skillseekers programmes tend to be delivered by private training organisations, by the service delivery wing of voluntary organisations or by FE colleges.

National variation in quality and quantity of SEN Skillseekers' programmes reflects tensions at the heart of the mission of the LECs, which draws on both utilitarian and social contract notions. Their prime commitment to business and economic development implies a human capital perspective: the level of investment in an individual's education and training will be commensurate with their future ability to contribute to the nation's economic prosperity. At the same time, in the 1996/97 Annual Report of Scottish Enterprise, there is a formal recognition of the costs of social exclusion and the need for some form of redistribution:

> Apart from the direct costs of unemployment, economic exclusion has wide-ranging indirect consequences that undermine our efforts to generate jobs, prosperity and an acceptable quality of life. We must therefore work to ensure that everyone is able to realise their potential by overcoming the barriers to their full participation in the economy. (Scottish Enterprise, 1997, p 21)

This statement accords with the Labour government's view that economic prosperity is consistent with promoting the interests of the socially disadvantaged. What is required, it is suggested, is some manipulation of the market to target resources on the most needy, and Scottish Enterprise considers it has "made good progress in responding to the special needs of those with physical and other handicaps" (1997, p 21), although only two examples of good practice are cited. How these special needs are to be addressed in the future is left somewhat sketchy. Key issues identified, we are told, include:

> The changing economic and political context; the requirement to build on existing activity across the network; the need to adopt an integrated approach with all our economic development functions brought to bear; the clear need for new forms of partnership; the need to work with communities; and the importance of a spatial approach and the particular problems of rural communities. (Scottish Enterprise, 1997, p 21)

Essentially, this implies a need to improve the management of what is happening already and ignores the more fundamental question of whether adequate provision for people with learning difficulties is possible within a market framework. The use of ambiguous terms such as 'community' and 'partnership' serve to depoliticise the policy choices implicit in the provision of training and reduce them to what Clarke and Newman (1997) have described as a "series of management imperatives". According to these commentators, throughout the public sector:

> We can see a trend towards major social contradictions and conflicts being experienced at the frontline of service delivery organisations. This is uncomfortable for those working there, but more importantly it points to the limitations of the capacity of new organisational regimes to cope with these problems. (Clarke and Newman, 1997, p 159)

Such a sense of discomfort is evident in some of the accounts of LEC training managers who were interviewed during Phase One of the research. The majority indicated that clear distinctions were drawn between people with higher support needs, who were unlikely to make a significant economic contribution no matter how much training they were given. These people were seen as the responsibility of social work:

> "Generally speaking, it would be unusual to assist people who are in sheltered employment because they are the responsibility of the social work department. It [the Skillseekers programme] is aimed at people who can be economically active. It doesn't need to be full-time, but you have to be able to take up employment outside a sheltered environment." (LEC manager)

A minority, on the other hand, challenged the conception of a person with learning difficulties as unable to make a significant economic contribution:

> "Just because someone has learning difficulties does not mean that they are not going to be very capable employees. I think probably the opposite may be the case – they may be a more capable employee and would certainly give the employer a loyal member." (LEC manager)

However, including people with special needs was difficult within a target-driven regime where any additional support had to be identified and requested formally from the outset:

> "We no longer pay a standard rate [for people with special needs] you know. There used to be a sum extra we paid for people with special needs. Now we don't do that. The needs have to be identified in the training plan and costed." (LEC manager)

Within this climate, LEC managers observed that training organisations dedicated to meeting the needs of young people with special needs were finding it hard to compete with organisations aimed at mainstream clients:

> "The difficulty with that sort of organisation [Enable, Remploy], nothing against them, they find it hard to survive the competitive jobs-driven market. The way we pay them, they're hit one by one.

They're struggling. They're not getting the same outcomes as others."
(LEC manager)

If gaining employment continued to be a key performance indicator in the assessment of Skillseekers programmes, then special training needs programmes would, it was felt, continue to be regarded as failures because employers were almost invariably going to choose a non-disabled person to employ given the choice, no matter how sympathetic they might be to the position of people with learning difficulties. Individual LEC managers appeared to be struggling to reconcile their desire to widen access to training opportunities for people with learning difficulties with the constraints of a market-driven financial regime. Before turning to case studies of young people with learning difficulties, we consider the role of FE in the delivery of post-school training for people with learning difficulties.

Further Education colleges

Most FE colleges in Scotland were founded in the latter part of the 19th and first part of the 20th centuries. Their curriculum and working methods were geared towards equipping young people, mainly young men, for work in traditional industries, particularly heavy manufacturing industry in the central belt. Until the early 1990s, the responsibility for funding FE lay with local authorities. During the 1970s and 1980s, FE colleges changed, becoming geared towards the emerging service sector of the economy and including women and people with special educational needs. Modularised National Certificate programmes catered for growing numbers of part-time students. The 1992 Further and Higher Education (Scotland) Act marked a radical change in colleges' development. In line with the Conservative government's desire to introduce the discipline of the marketplace into the public sector, FE colleges became incorporated, each operating as an individual enterprise. The implications of the change were two-fold. Firstly, the duty of providing the FE service was transferred from local authorities to the Secretary of State for Scotland. Secondly, new Boards of Management assumed responsibility for strategic decision making, college finances, property and personnel, and a much more business management style was adopted. There were fears that the newly acquired independent status of FE colleges would lead to a neglect of equal opportunities issues and a number of stipulations were made about colleges' responsibility to meet the needs of their local communities, and not simply provide the courses that would be most lucrative. In particular, with regard to their planning of provision, colleges were obliged to 'have regard' to the needs of disabled students.

The Scottish Office underpinned this obligation by providing additional funding for students identified as having special needs by the careers service. Currently, this premium funding stands at 1.8 times that of a regular place. This flat rate encourages colleges to accept students who have special needs but are not the most expensive to educate. For instance, if a post-school extension course catered extensively for students requiring transport to college, the finance section might start to raise objections. There are also issues in terms of the hypothecation of funding. At the moment special needs funding is not ring-fenced, and colleges may use this funding to support some of their other provision. There continues to be an extreme shortage in Scotland of provision for young people with profound learning difficulties. Some of the costs for personal assistance should be met by social work, but FE colleges avoid protracted wrangling with multiple departments, preferring to cater for those whose needs are covered adequately by Scottish Executive funding.

In the two fieldwork areas, it was evident that few choices were available to young people with learning difficulties and that they were allocated to college places rather than choosing between different options. This was particularly evident in the urban area, where the three colleges were each allocated a limited number of premium-funded places by the Scottish Executive. Each year, a meeting was held when it was decided which students should be offered a place at a particular college. The rationale for this was to avoid competition between colleges for scarce resources, but it clearly ran counter to the notion of consumer empowerment within an incorporated FE sector.

Post-school destinations for young people with special educational needs

In Scotland, just over 1% of the school population is educated in special schools or units, and this proportion has remained constant for at least 20 years (see Riddell et al, 1999, for further discussion of Scottish policy of the education of children with SEN). When young people leave school, further divisions take place that re-emphasise the distinction between mainstream and special populations. These divisions emerge clearly from data provided by one careers company that compare the post-school destinations of young people from special schools and others. These data are not broken down by nature of impairment, but Scottish Executive statistics drawn from school census data confirm that the majority of these children have learning difficulties as a primary or secondary impairment.

Table 2 comparing post-school destinations of young people leaving mainstream and special school illustrates that while a significant proportion of the former move into employment or higher education, a far smaller proportion of the latter find work on leaving school and virtually none enters higher education. By comparison, a far higher proportion of special school leavers enters FE, with a smaller proportion moving directly into an Adult Training Centre. On the face of it, such data might indicate that young people with SEN are doing relatively well in attracting a significant share of public investment in their post-school training. However, as the following case studies make clear, the type of training they receive does not have a significant positive impact on their labour market position, enhancing neither their human nor their social capital.

Table 2: Mainstream and special school leaver destinations, 1999

Careers Company I	Mainstream school leavers	Special school leavers
Employment	2,752 (39%)	18 (10%)
Training (Skillseekers)	634 (9%)	16 (9%)
Further Education (following a full-time programme at a college of FE)	1,177 (17%)	70 (41%)
Higher Education (following an advanced course at a university or college)	1,845 (26%)	1 (0.6%)
Adult Training Centre	0 (0%)	9 (5%)
Day Centre for adults with a physical disability	0 (0%)	3 (2%)
Unemployment	266 (4%)	23 (13%)
Unavailable (due to severe disability, illness or pregnancy)	102 (1%)	13 (7%)
Unknown	216 (3%)	18 (10%)
Total	**6,992**	**171**

Case studies of young people

In the following sections we focus on two young people whose post-school experiences exemplify the different routes taken by those accorded special status. Kelly had learning difficulties in association with a genetically transmitted muscular disorder. She attended a special school and at the time of the research was participating in a Lifeskills course aimed at students with severe learning difficulties in an urban FE college. Reggie, in the same urban area, attended a mainstream school where there was no official identification of learning difficulties. Due to a domestic fire, he incurred serious injuries and missed a lot of school. As a result, he left with no qualifications, but this was not related to cognitive impairment. He was identified by the Careers Service as having special needs and attended a special Skillseekers course, subsequently progressing into part-time, and highly marginal, employment. Each case is discussed in more detail below.

Kelly

Kelly was of medium height and build, had pale skin and shoulder length hair tied back in a ponytail. In her late teens, she was in the first year of a two-year Lifeskills course at a local college. Her speech was quite clear and she was markedly keen to communicate with lecturers and students, although she also had periods of withdrawal and silence. Although the Lifeskills course was intended for young people with severe/moderate learning difficulties, all the young people in the group were reasonably articulate and independent travellers. In order to attend the college, Kelly undertook a fairly long bus journey from the other side of the city.

Kelly's family consisted of her father, a retired armed services man, her mother and an older and younger brother. Both her siblings and mother had similar physiological conditions. The elder brother attended an Adult Resource Centre and the younger brother was at a special school for children with severe and profound learning difficulties. Mrs F's condition had recently deteriorated and breathing and swallowing difficulties had necessitated a tracheotomy. A bed had been installed in the sitting room, and it was clear that, although very ill, Mrs F fulfilled a pivotal role in the family, overseeing the work of the carers and the details of her children's lives. The local authority flat where the family lived appeared to be a very busy place, due to the presence of carers and other professionals. The family appeared to have a range of social networks in the surrounding community and Kelly felt safe going to the shops or walking into the city centre.

Kelly's mother, a highly articulate woman, had fought hard for the type of services necessary for the family's survival. She explained that at one point social services believed that she was no longer able to look after the children and planned for them to live with foster parents. She objected and as a result carers were provided to attend to her physical needs and undertake domestic work such as cooking the evening meal and cleaning. Kelly's mother was also proactive in choosing the Resource Centre for her elder son. She visited a range of centres and was shocked by the conditions of some, saying that you wouldn't wish to leave a dog there. She kept in close contact by telephone and post with the college and alerted them to concerns over Kelly's progress. She was very keen for her daughter to live as independent a life as possible, recognising that she is much more able than her brothers. Employment and an independent home were seen as desirable.

The Lifeskills course attended by Kelly focused on the development of social and independent living skills and is described as 'non-vocational'. A great deal of emphasis was placed on independent travelling. The course was oversubscribed and the college was able to select students who, while labelled as having severe learning difficulties, were a relatively able group. Some mainstream lecturers taught on special needs courses, but many seemed to regard this as an entirely separate enterprise. On occasion, special needs students used different facilities from mainstream students, for instance, they were taught catering in a separate location rather than within the main department. Whereas most college students had a clear departmental base at one of the college's campuses, the special needs students travelled between all three campuses for different classes. One of the campuses, a former secondary school, was used almost exclusively for special needs extension and Skillseekers programmes. Movement between campuses was seen as enhancing students' abilities as independent travellers, but also contributed to the feeling that they were marginal to the main activities of the college. It was noticeable that although friendships had developed between individuals in the Lifeskills class, there was very little contact with other college students. Friendships within the class were difficult to maintain because students were drawn from a wide geographical area.

Within the Lifeskills programmes, learning targets in each curricular area were identified for students and Kelly's tutor believed she was doing well in achieving the learning goals identified. However, there were concerns that she sometimes appeared anxious and tearful or else quiet and withdrawn. There was speculation that Kelly absorbed, but could do little about, a range of tensions within the family. She was clearly concerned about her mother's and brothers' health and her own future prognosis, but there was little time to address these issues in the college setting. Kelly referred to one of the young men in the group as her boyfriend and hoped to have children in a few years' time. College staff believed she had received no counselling about her inherited genetic condition and its implications. While they felt able to provide some emotional support, they felt unqualified to address the wider health issues that confronted Kelly.

At the end of the Lifeskills course, the normal pattern was for students to move into an Adult Resource Centre. The course tutor believed that Kelly was part of a particularly able group, but that their future prospects were not good. In the absence of adequate supported employment opportunities or Skillseekers programmes, Kelly and her peers were likely to be placed in an Adult Resource Centre where their progress was unlikely to be sustained due to the segregated setting and the lack of stimulating daytime opportunities. Thinking about her own future, Kelly expressed a wish to work with young people and her parents' view was that she would be ideally placed in a local sheltered workshop which ran a bakery and coffee shops. They were definitely opposed to the idea of an Adult Resource Centre placement:

> "She's going to leave college and go down to the Adult Resource Centre and she's going to be taken up and back and forth all the time. Now that to me, that's not a life. You've got to give your children as much independence as you can." (Kelly's mother)

Indeed, the likely post-college outcome was regarded as so depressing by the college that it was simply not discussed at all with the students.

Reggie

Reggie, aged 18, lived in a socially disadvantaged urban area with six children in his family, of which he was the youngest. He had five siblings and was the youngest child. His mother worked as a cleaner at the airport and his father had recently died of bronchial pneumonia. He had been badly burnt in a house fire as a child and had very bad scarring on his face and hands. He was a friendly young man who had close social networks within the local neighbourhood, going fishing, to the local pub and, occasionally, to a disco with his friends, brothers and cousins at the weekend. He also had an interest in breeding budgies. At the time of the research, Reggie was participating in a special needs Skillseekers programme. Staff at the private school where he was placed confirmed that he was easy-going, had a pleasant personality and they were quite unaware that he might have learning difficulties. Because Reggie was working as a general labourer, an ability to respond to verbal instructions was required, but literacy and numeracy were not important.

Reggie attended a mainstream Catholic secondary school, taking Standard grades in English, Maths, German, Woodwork, Accounting and Finance, Craft and Design. Due to absence from school, he failed to obtain certificates in a number of these subjects and, following an interview with a careers officer, was 'endorsed' as having special needs and was put in touch with a private training agency funded by the Local Enterprise Company to provide Skillseekers programmes for young people with SEN. The training workshop, located in disused army barracks, was founded in the mid-1970s as a result of alarm at rising levels of youth unemployment, which had particularly negative consequences for young people leaving school with no qualifications. The workshop offered some in-house training (printing, painting, office work) as well as work-based placements.

As noted above, Reggie's placement was in a private school where he initially attempted to develop joinery and painting skills. It was felt, however, that he lacked the required manual dexterity for these tasks and he was transferred to general duties, helping to shift furniture, tidy the grounds or mow the lawns. According to the training officer, Reggie was well suited to a job that was repetitive and intellectually unchallenging, giving him few anxieties and leaving him free to enjoy his social life. A major challenge had been to persuade Reggie of the importance of turning up to work regularly and phoning in when sick.

At the end of the two-year Skillseekers programme, the school employed Reggie as a part-time sessional worker at £3.00 per hour. This represented a drop in income compared with the training programme, where Reggie had received an allowance of £40 per week in addition to bus fares. He continued to work for the school for a number of months after the end of the programme, but was eventually laid off due to the seasonal nature of the work and his apparent unreliability.

Discussion and conclusion

In this chapter, we began by reviewing a range of discourses of social justice, in particular those informing post-school education and training for young people with special educational needs. It appeared that the utilitarian model of justice informing LEC and FE provision, albeit overlaid by social contract principles, had the effect of marginalising people with learning difficulties. Attempts to manage the market by targeting additional resources on people at the bottom of the meritocratic hierarchy were insufficient to redress their labour market disadvantage while at the same time removing them from the mainstream and according them special (and inferior) status. For people in this category, the supposed benefits of the market in post-school education and training provision did not apply due to the shortage of provision and the continuation of paternalistic attitudes that had little place for consumer power. The practical and ethical conundrum of attempting to provide meaningful education and training opportunities within a system based on market principles was left to people at lower levels to resolve.

Kelly and Reggie, the case studies presented in this chapter, illustrate some of the problems within post-school education and training policy for people with learning difficulties, although both were regarded as having successful outcomes by training providers. Although Kelly's Lifeskills course provided opportunities for personal growth and development, it nonetheless perpetuated the segregated education regime of the special school, allowing few opportunities for contact with her mainstream peers. Her major achievement during the FE course was the development of her skills as an independent traveller, able to navigate her way around complicated bus routes in the city. However, at the end of the programme it seemed unlikely that she would be able to put these navigational skills to good effect, since placements in the sheltered catering firm were few and far between. In the absence of supported or sheltered employment, she was likely to move into an Adult Resource Centre, with little access to stimulating daytime opportunities. Kelly had already been identified as particularly prone to anxiety and depression, and yet it was clear that these were likely to be caused by fears surrounding the inherited condition affecting her family. In particular, her mother's ill health evidently caused her major concern, but there was no agency able to provide help in the form of information and counselling. Kelly's experiences suggest that investment in post-school education for young people with severe learning difficulties will have few long-term positive effects unless it is accompanied by effective employment measures and attention to the emotional well-being of young people in the context of their families.

Reggie provides insight into the consequences of extending the label of learning difficulties to a widening group of young people who do not have cognitive impairments, but experience economic and social disadvantage. Tomlinson (1982) suggested that pathologising working-class young men as having employability deficits, often described as learning difficulties, conceals high levels of structural unemployment and the disappearance of traditional areas of manual work where they might previously have worked. The special educational needs Skillseekers programme introduced Reggie to the world of work, but it was clear that at the end of the training period the employer was unwilling to pay a wage to a worker whose labour could easily be defined as surplus to requirements. Reggie, finding himself worse off after a two-year period of training, decided to opt out of economic activity. Reggie's experience raises questions about what conditions might have been necessary to sustain him in employment. An ongoing subsidy to the employer might well have encouraged the school to retain him, and longer-term support might have helped him to improve his reliability. It is evident, however, that in a highly competitive labour market young people experiencing social and economic disadvantage as well as those with learning difficulties are likely to find themselves squeezed to the margins. This has implications for current labour market policies, which are increasing intervening on the supply side by attempting to enhance employability, rather than intervening on the demand side, by altering the underlying conditions of the labour market in which people compete for employment.

If models of social justice based on utilitarian and social contract principles are likely to exclude people with learning difficulties, the question remains as to what versions of social justice might prove more inclusive. We suggest that much bolder redistributive policies are required, which recognise that people with learning difficulties are oppressed not only in terms of social class, in the same way as others on the margins of economic and social activity, but also in relation to their impairment, which limits access to information and communication, and, in a culture valuing intellectual dexterity, produces a damaged social identity. As Young (1990) maintains, policies based on both redistribution and recognition are required. This is not to ignore the inherent problems with identity politics highlighted by Fraser (1997), that more articulate groups may privilege their claims over others. Recognition for people with learning difficulties is dependent on redistribution, since the development of group consciousness requires the resource-intensive process of a non-learning disabled person working as a supporter alongside people with learning difficulties. A more critical approach to self-advocacy for people with learning difficulties may also be needed. Associated with normalisation theory (O'Brien, 1987; Wolfensberger, 1972) rather than the social model of disability (Oliver, 1990), self-advocacy may be used to help people with learning difficulties make individual choices about their lives with a view to becoming more like the non-disabled population, thus blurring the boundaries of their own identity. It also has the potential for more radical use in the development of a sense of solidarity with other learning disabled people and the disability movement more widely. In the context of training, a dual focus on redistribution and recognition might allow people with learning difficulties to play a much more active role in deciding what form of training is provided and the forms of employment to which this leads. This is particularly important in the context of New Labour's Welfare to Work programme, where an extreme form of utilitarian social justice might dictate that those who cannot work are provided with the means for subsistence but are denied access to citizenship predicated on economic activity.

In this chapter we have focused on the notions of social justice implicit in, and the experiences of young people with learning difficulties of, education and training provided to smooth the transition from school to work. In the next chapter we explore the experience of older people with learning difficulties of 'lifelong learning'.

FOUR

Lifelong learning for people with learning difficulties

Introduction

In Chapter 3, we focused on post-16 training opportunities for people with learning difficulties. Our argument was that, due to the dominance of human capital thinking, young people with learning difficulties were marginalised in training programmes. While participation in post-16 education and training was high, with many special school leavers moving into full-time education or training, a low proportion of young people progressed into employment at the end of their training programmes. The majority of post-school programmes were designed to enhance social skills and maturity and were not directly vocational. Within FE, such programmes were often in segregated settings where young people with learning difficulties had very little contact with their mainstream peers. The minority of young people with learning difficulties who undertook vocational, employer-based training often found themselves with insufficient support to sustain them in work at the end of the training programme. There was evidence of definitional drift, so that places on training programmes designated for young people with special needs were taken up by young people experiencing social disadvantage rather than cognitive difficulties. In this chapter, we consider the nature of post-transitional educational services for people with learning difficulties. These services may be seen as part of the lifelong learning policy agenda which is being promoted increasingly within the UK and other European states. We begin by considering the current rationale for lifelong learning, in particular its status as the prime means of challenging social exclusion as well as enhancing economic productivity. Subsequently, we discuss the way in which lifelong learning has become a major player in the world of 'joined up policy', associated with diverse fields including employment, urban regeneration, housing and health.

Subsequently, we discuss the range of agencies delivering lifelong learning to people with learning difficulties in the context of their service ethos and *modus operandi*. Finally, we consider the ways in which a range of services are experienced by people with learning difficulties and, in particular, the extent to which these services actually enhance their social inclusion.

Throughout Europe, educational policies to combat social exclusion and poverty have tended to focus on initial education and training systems, where efforts have been made to prepare school leavers for the labour market. However, there is a growing emphasis on the idea that acquiring knowledge and skills does not stop when a person leaves school, and that employability is dependent not only on the development of skills adaptable to the changing needs of the labour market, but also on appropriate social attitudes and competencies. In a period of rapid technological and economic change throughout Europe, lifelong learning is identified as the means whereby states can both retain their competitive economic edge, but also achieve social cohesion and stability, essential pre-conditions for growth and prosperity. These messages are to be found in a range of documents emanating from the European Community, Organization for Economic Co-operation and Development (OECD) and individual countries (EC, 1996; OECD, 1998; Scottish Office, 1998a; DfEE, 1999).

The veneration of lifelong learning as a means of challenging social exclusion has, not surprisingly, been challenged. It has been pointed out, for instance, that social exclusion is the product of powerful structural forces and that lifelong learning in itself will not produce social inclusion unless it is accompanied by wider economic changes (Levitas, 1996). In the face of Western governments' sense of powerlessness to intervene in the demand side of the labour market, they instead attempt to exert influence on the supply side, enjoining workers to enhance their employability or suffer the consequences. In addition, it is suggested that lifelong learning for the socially excluded may be seen as a means of social control. In the absence of employment, with its powerful disciplinary mechanisms, lifelong learning may be seen as a means of promoting appropriate behaviours and attitudes among those who might otherwise be regarded as a threat to social order (Coffield, 1999). The growing importance of lifelong learning in a range of social policy arenas is documented in the following section.

Lifelong learning: a policy catch-all?

Until recently, education tended to exist as a relatively isolated area of social policy, attracting little attention from social policy analysts (an exception was Finch, 1984). Research attention focused on the business of teaching children in the classroom, and the political message taken from the school effectiveness research movement, which enjoyed a vogue in the 1980s, was that individual schools and head teachers were of critical importance in determining educational outcomes, irrespective of the wider social environment. Sociologists recognised the persistent link between social class background, educational outcomes and life chances and argued that measures such as early intervention and the reorganisation of schools along comprehensive lines were likely to interrupt the transmission of social inequality (Ford, 1969). The Labour government elected in 1997 identified education as perhaps the most effective means of moving towards the type of social justice identified in the Commission on Social Justice (1994), which depicted a society free from some of the socially based determinants of future health and prosperity. In pursuit of these policies, the New Labour government invested in a range of early intervention strategies and expressed a commitment to increasing the funding of compulsory schooling. At the same time, a new emphasis was placed on widening and equalising access to post-school education. This approach was exemplified in the Forward to the Green Paper *The learning age* stated:

> To cope with rapid change and the challenge of the information and communication age, we must ensure that people can return to learning throughout their lives. We cannot rely on a small elite, no matter how highly educated or highly paid. Instead, we need the creativity, enterprise and scholarship of all our people.... What was available only to the few can, in the century ahead, be something that is enjoyed and taken advantage of, by the many. (DfEE, 1998, p 7)

At the same time as access to lifelong learning was being seen as the means of achieving greater educational equality, other policy fields were identifying education as the means of achieving fairer social outcomes more widely. These policy expectations on education are discussed below.

Health, social capital and lifelong learning

Over the past decade, there has been a clear shift of emphasis in public health policy in terms of its goals and definitions. Following the general framework set in *The health of the nation* policy document (DoH, 1992), health came to be defined not just as the absence of illness or disability, but a general sense of well-being and enjoyment of a high quality of life. During the 1980s, the Conservative government favoured individualised explanations of sickness and health. According to this thinking, poorer people had worse health because they made poor lifestyle choices, consuming the wrong sort of food, abusing tobacco and alcohol and failing to take exercise. The suggested remedy was to educate the public about healthy lifestyle choices; if this advise was ignored then individuals deserved to suffer the consequences.

Medical sociologists such as Macintyre (1999) demonstrated the social and economic factors shaping individual choices. Thus in poorer areas shops had less fresh produce available and it was more expensive. There were less sport and leisure centres in poorer areas and unsafe public spaces discouraged people from walking or jogging. Arguments about the social structuring of health outcomes was reflected clearly in the *Independent Inquiry into Inequalities in Health* (Acheson Report) (DoH, 1998). While it was recognised that individual lifestyle and age, sex and constitutional factors were implicated in health outcomes, far more powerful were general socio-economic, cultural and environmental conditions. Whereas health care services were seen to play an important role in improving health outcomes, other agencies and settings were seen as equally important. These mediators of health included education, employment and lifelong learning (work environment, living and working conditions, unemployment, education, social and community networks). Evidence given to the *Independent Inquiry into Inequalities in Health* by Whitty et al (1999) maintained:

> Education may be hypothesised as having both direct and indirect effects on health outcomes. Existing research on health and educational inequalities suggests that disadvantage is cumulative and health opportunities are heavily skewed towards the disadvantaged. (Whitty et al, 1999, p 143)

Whitty and colleagues pointed out that the causal relationships between educational experiences and health outcomes are not well understood. However, evidence to the *Independent Inquiry into Inequalities in Health*

(Whitty et al, 1999; Wilkinson, 1999) pointed to the importance of social capital in improving educational and health outcomes (see Chapter 8 for further discussion of social capital in relation to the experiences of people with learning difficulties in the community). Whitty et al draw on Putnam's definition of social capital, defined as:

> Features of social organisation, such as trust, norms and networks, which can improve the efficiency of society by facilitating coordinated actions. (Putnam, 1993, p 57)

Although poverty is likely to impede the generation of social capital, it is suggested that investment in education and the nurturing of social networks in disadvantaged areas will produce benefits in health and education, notwithstanding the negative effects of poverty. Wilkinson (1999) postulated that societies that have greater levels of inequality also, and as a direct result, have lower levels of social cohesion and this produces a range of negative effects for poorer people, including higher rates of morbidity and mortality. The relationship between social capital and poverty is thus regarded somewhat differently by Whitty et al and Wilkinson. Whereas Whitty and colleagues argued that social capital might overcome some of the negative effects of poverty, Wilkinson represented social capital as a direct function of economic inequality. Whether social capital is seen as a dependent or an independent variable, it is evident that educational processes and outcomes and health are interconnected. This relationship is likely to be particularly important for people with learning difficulties, who are likely to represent some of the poorest people in the community.

Employment and lifelong learning

Just as lifelong learning is seen as having strong direct and indirect effects on health outcomes particularly for socially disadvantaged groups, so employment policy is increasingly linked with lifelong learning policies. Audit of Employment Service programmes often identifies participation in education as a key success measure. This is the case, for example, in relation to the ES's work preparation programme in Scotland, where successful outcomes include employment or participation in a further employment programme, a training programme or education. The New Deal for Disabled People similarly regards participation in education as a successful outcome indicator.

In the context of current reviews of services for people with learning disabilities by the Scottish Executive and by local authorities, it is evident that both education and employment are seen as valuable daytime activities, and sometimes work is regarded primarily as therapy rather than a chance to earn money. This perception is further enforced by benefits regulations, which enable disabled people to earn up to £58 a week as 'therapeutic earnings'. Recently, as noted above, there has been a tendency to shift health and community care policy into the domain of education and employment. The Glasgow Strategy for People with Learning Disabilities (Glasgow City Council, 2000) expresses a commitment to the development of 'an employment or meaningful activity service', which should aim to provide long-term placements/jobs/voluntary work for 15% of present day service users over the next five years. In addition:

> A target of creating jobs for people with learning disability will be set over the next three years. Such opportunities should be available to all, regardless of level of disability or complexity of need. (Glasgow City Council, 2000, p 31)

For the majority of the population, education and lifelong learning are seen as the means of enhancing chances of getting and retaining employment but for people with learning difficulties, there appears to be a blurring of the distinction between education and employment. Education is seen as an index of successful participation in an employment development programme, and employment is valued for its educational and therapeutic, rather than financial, benefits.

It is evident that health, community care and employment increasingly venture in to the domain of lifelong learning and there is a tendency to suggest that health or employment outcomes are determined by education and lifelong learning, rather than policies and practices pertinent to that particular domain. On the positive side, this may be seen as recognition of the interconnectedness of policy. On the negative side, it may be seen as a shifting of responsibility for social outcomes into another policy domain, in response to recognition of the complexity and difficulty of recurring problems. In the following section, we consider the range of agencies that are active in delivering lifelong learning to people with learning difficulties.

Agencies and locations

Adult Resource Centres

Most educational and leisure opportunities for people with learning disabilities are concentrated within Adult Resource Centres (ARCs). According to the Scottish Executive's Learning Disabilities Review *The same as you?* (Scottish Executive, 2000a), provision in this area has gradually increased, partly in response to the closure of long-stay institutions. There are currently about 150 ARCs in Scotland:

> The number of people with learning disabilities going to social day centres has grown from 4,400 in 1980 to 8,300 in 1998.... Only 20% of activity in day centres takes the form of education and employment, while 28% involves leisure and recreation.... Most people using services as part of our user and carer survey described day centres as boring and lacking in direction. (Scottish Executive, 2000a, p 54)

Barnes (1990) provides a useful overview of the development of day centres. From the 18th century onwards, there was a growing tendency to incarcerate those regarded as social deviants within long-stay institutions, including prisons, workhouses, hospitals and asylums. Stone (1984) suggests that failure to provide adequate home-based support was one of the fallouts of the industrial revolution that was gathering pace. Simultaneously, the expanding empire provided revenues essential to the construction of grand-scale buildings to accommodate the growing number of those categorised as infirm in body, mind or moral character. Segregation continued throughout the 20th century, but there was a gradual move to seek ways of accommodating people with learning difficulties in the community. The 1913 Mental Deficiency Act, for example, contained provision for voluntary and statutory provision of the 'mentally handicapped' in the community and the 1930 Mental Treatment Act recognised a growing movement for the provision of outpatient clinics. The Royal Commission on Mental Illness and Mental Deficiency of 1954-57 recognised the problems arising as a result of outdated mental hospitals and the stigma attached to in-patient treatment. Subsequent official documents emphasised care in the community and this policy was given official imprimatur in the Griffiths report (Griffiths, 1988) and the White Paper *Caring for people* (DoH, 1989).

While the demise of the long-stay institutions is generally welcomed, this has not led to the disappearance of segregated provision. Adult

Resource Centres have developed steadily since the 1950s, fulfilling slightly different roles at different times. In the 1950s and 1960s, it was commonplace for individuals to undertake basic tasks such as envelope filling, which would bring some money to the local authority and centre and might result in the individual being paid a small weekly allowance. During the 1970s, there was concern about the potential exploitation of individuals undertaking these tasks, and activities in day centres became more recreational. The new focus, in the language of the Warnock report (DES, 1978) was on 'significant living without work'.

Little research has been conducted on ARCs, signifying their lack of social salience. Barnes, in his study of day centres for young people with physical impairments, suggests that they are perceived as the 'dumping grounds' for people who are excluded, because of impairment, from the normal economic and social life of society. The Scottish Executive's Learning Disabilities Review points out the range of possibly conflicting interests surrounding ARCs:

> Most people using services who were interviewed as part of our user and carer survey described day centres as boring and lacking in direction. However, they did value the chance to access health services and to meet friends.
>
> Carers' perspectives may be different. Day services give them valuable opportunities to follow other interests, education or work. Carers are understandably concerned at any suggestion that services might be taken away, and their own opportunities restricted. It would be pointless if new developments place heavier burdens on carers.
>
> Many day services for adults are not focused enough on continuous learning and development. Day care is not seen as a stepping-stone to new experiences or to employment. It does not challenge and stimulate each person enough. (Scottish Executive, 2000a, p 54)

The Learning Disabilities Review suggested that in the future, services need to be more flexible and enable people with learning difficulties to interact more with the wider community. At the same time, it was recognised that structured day services would continue to be required by those multiple and complex difficulties, including those with autistic spectrum disorders.

Interviews with key informants from social work suggested that existing services were geared towards leisure and recreation and tended to retain adults within the centre rather than enable them to venture into the wider community. The following was a typical description of activities:

> "In the Adult Resource Centre we have a community education input and also a therapeutic type of training and education, things like music therapy. Also we have some skills training, some computer work, home skills etc to help identify people who may go into catering." (social work respondent)

There were clear aspirations to move towards person-centred community based provision, but most respondents agreed there was a gap between aspiration and reality:

> "In day care we are trying to move away from the traditional day centre model guided by the policy of inclusion. Centres are just a base for people to move out of, a resource rather than a centre and should be seen as a community resource, as an attempt to bring people into the centre rather than the centre coming into the community. We are trying to get the centres to find their own community location as well as diversifying the range of day provision." (social work respondent)

Further Education

As we noted in Chapter 3, provision for young people with learning difficulties in FE colleges has gradually increased since the 1980s. The 1992 Further and Higher Education (Scotland) Act placed a responsibility to include the needs of disabled students within the college's planning process. Patterns of funding have produced very uneven levels of provision for students with different support requirements and within different age groups. Post-16 extension courses are funded relatively generously, although numbers are limited and places restricted to those who require little personal assistance. Provision for older students with higher support needs tends to be far more ad hoc and reliant on short-term funding for specific initiatives. Such provision is often funded by social work and questions have been raised about whether it replicates ARC practice or offers something radically different. These issues are pursued further within the case study data presented below.

In Chapter 3, it was evident that young people with learning difficulties in FE colleges might find themselves within the same building but have virtually nothing to do with students on mainstream vocational programmes. Such problems may be even more acute for older students with higher support needs who are attending college on a part-time basis. Recent government sponsored reports on further education have suggested that the prime educational principle should be that of inclusion, and this involves a general ethos rather than presence in the same learning environment. The Tomlinson Report (FEFC, 1996), for example, noted that provision for students with learning disabilities/difficulties had trebled in the decade between 1985 and 1995, although provision for young people with emotional and behavioural difficulties, adults with mental health problems and people with multiple and profound difficulties was still inadequate. Tomlinson suggested that decisions on how to teach each student should be based on an assessment of learning requirements. Issues to do with interaction between students were thus sidestepped. The Beattie Committee (Scottish Executive, 1999b) adopted Tomlinson's notion of inclusiveness, considering how it might be applied across the lifelong learning sector. The report stated:

> The key to inclusiveness is that the learning environment should match the learner's needs, abilities and aspirations. An inclusiveness approach, does not, therefore, remove the option of a separate learning environment where it is offered in response to the needs of the individual. But a separate learning environment is not justified on the grounds that it fits better with the institutional infrastructure or organisational practices. (Scottish Executive, 1999b, p 9)

A further justification of separate provision has been offered by Maudslay and Dee (1995). Drawing analogies with the strategy of the women's movement to organise separately for a period of time, they suggest that people with learning difficulties may draw strength and a sense of identity from being educated together:

> Our belief is that a model in which total inclusion is seen as the only way forward can deny the specific identity, and hence undermine the dignity, of people with learning difficulties and disabilities. Much has been stated about the importance of people with learning difficulties having the right to choose to integrate into the mainstream. This is a choice we would strongly advocate. However, less is articulated about the right of people to choose to spend time and receive education with a peer group of people with similar educational

needs as themselves. We feel that if a choice is only one way it does not constitute a real choice. (Maudslay and Dee, 1995, p 84)

Maudslay and Dee's defence of separate provision ignores the paucity of choice for people with learning difficulties in any direction. In addition, the analogy with the women's movement is difficult to sustain in the light of our findings that people with learning difficulties generally do not identify themselves as a distinctive group (Riddell et al, 1998a). Despite these defences of the Tomlinson notion of inclusiveness, it has been strongly criticised as a smokescreen for segregation. Whittaker (1995), for example, evaluated the special needs provision of five FE colleges in the North West and offered the following commentary:

The colleges could be compared to a Social Services 'mini' Day Centre. The enrolment of students was commonly through a 'Special Needs' section that started a process of segregation away from the mainstream of the college and rapidly developed into noticeable isolation. The locations where students would congregate were often identifiable and described by mainstream staff and students in disparaging ways, 'That's the unit where they go' or 'That's where the handicapped go' or 'That place is for that sort of student'. (Whittaker, 1995, p 76)

Booth (2000) suggests that the increasing adoption of the term 'inclusion' in preference to the former term 'integration' may be regressive, in that it allows social arrangements within colleges to be ignored. Booth is particularly critical of the notion of inclusion used by Tomlinson, defined as "matching the resources we have to the learning styles and educational needs of the students" (FEFC, 1996, p 193). He comments:

It carries no implications for shared participation with peers, even to the extent of presence within the same college, and is contrasted in this respect with *integration*, which is seen to require shared learning experiences. (Booth, 2000, p 88)

Despite the expansion of provision in the last two decades, there remain many live debates about the nature and quality of provision for people with learning difficulties in FE colleges. If such institutions introduce new forms of segregated provision under the guise of inclusiveness, then it could be argued that they represent little genuine progress on previous, ostensibly segregated, provision.

Community Education

Whereas the raison d'etre of FE is to serve the needs of the economy by producing appropriately trained workers, Community Education has very different origins, often rooted in ordinary people's desire for personal growth, self-improvement and political change. During the 19th century, workers organised self-help learning groups to acquire 'really useful knowledge', thereby compensating for the inadequacy of state or Church funded elementary schooling. At this time, some people with learning difficulties would have had access to basic vocational training, but not to education for personal growth. Ideas from community education percolated into state provision during the post-war period through the development of village colleges, serving the needs of the entire community in rural areas (Baron, 1989). The idea of community schools, encompassing provision for pre-school children and adults, subsequently spread to urban areas, although these schools rarely included people with learning difficulties in their provision.

During the 1970s, concerns with high levels of functional illiteracy led to the growth of the Adult Basic Education (ABE) movement. In its radical early form, the ABE movement adapted ideas from Freire, who suggested that in developing countries the attainment of literacy could be coupled with a project of politicisation. Initially targeted at those experiencing social disadvantage rather than learning difficulties, ABE came under increasing pressure to include people with learning difficulties as clients. It has been suggested that as ABE moved into a social work setting, it gradually lost its power to act as a consciousness-raising tool. Emphasis on community participation gradually gave way to a new focus on literacy and numeracy, focusing on individual deficit and reinforcing power relationships between clients and professionals.

Interviews with key informants in adult and continuing education revealed a commitment to inclusion of people with learning difficulties within mainstream provision, coupled with an uncertainty about how this might actually be achieved in practice. An idealistic view of community education as a generator of social capital for people at the social margins was reflected in the view of one Community Education respondent:

> "Everybody should be allowed to participate in the community, should be involved in making choices, encouraged to develop their abilities, be treated with respect and have a valued social role, so that

people develop relationships and grow up in a society as a valued member."

However, the mechanisms of achieving inclusion were only vaguely sketched and within most authorities there appeared to be no additional support available:

"People with learning difficulties can enrol for classes of their choice and just join in if they're happy enough to do that. If they require support, social and personal support, then it's a requirement of the carer or the referring agency to provide that ... if somebody, for example, can't go to the toilet on their own then they're not going to be walking down the street and coming into the building and joining a class anyway ... if they need help, that help is not appropriate for an educational tutor to provide, it's appropriate for a friend or a support worker or a carer to do that." (Community Education respondent)

Another respondent was more sceptical about the possibility of including people with learning difficulties into community education provision:

"It's actually not impossible but exceedingly difficult to meet the needs of people [with learning difficulties]. We have had to be much more realistic and say, 'This is what we can realistically provide'. Because there's so many factors to make things work – there's the venue, there's the transport and then the key is the number of individual helpers or volunteers needed to help a class or project go ahead. There's also the quality of the tutor and their availability." (Community Education tutor)

There was dissatisfaction with the perceived colonisation by social work that appeared to happen when community education workers operated within ARCs:

"Our educational input in the new resource centre run by social work tends to be determined by social work, what the needs are, and most of these are sort of maintenance skills rather than new skills, although we are operating two classes this year where we are doing some work on skills leading to people being discharged into the community for independent living, so we do offer that." (Community Education organiser)

In our discussion with community education workers, it was evident that they regarded FE colleges as somewhat aggressive competitors who were 'cornering the market' in adults with learning difficulties:

> "You've got colleges, which are offering modules on basic skills, and I'm beginning to be suspicious, if that's the word, that they run these courses to boost their funds. They're paid on a per capita basis and they all have targets to meet and therefore sometimes I feel they're getting the people simply to justify their funding and they're not wholly looking at the individual." (Community Education respondent)

> "I think there's a competitive element with the colleges because they're fighting for their lives since incorporation.... They think they can do everything and when they're driven by performance indicators that are all about money they say, 'Oh we can deliver on that, but we know they can't. They've got a tremendous role to play but they haven't got the staff on the ground working with the people on a daily basis.... We've got to be working in the community doing the confidence building bits, the essential skill bits which colleges can't do." (Community Education respondent)

In the future, it is evident that Community Education is envisaged as playing a role of growing importance in provision for people with learning difficulties (Scottish Executive, 2000a). At the time of writing, local authorities were drawing up community learning plans that were obliged to take account of the needs of people with learning difficulties. However, the extent to which additional resources were likely to be channelled in the direction of people with learning difficulties remained uncertain. As a non-statutory service, Community Education experienced constant funding reductions during the 1980s and 1990s, which accelerated following the creation of unitary authorities in 1996. The Convention of Scottish Local Authorities estimated that, in the four years following local government reorganisation, the sector sustained an average reduction of 20% in its budget; in some areas, funding reduced by 50%. The service was being asked to play a key role in many aspects of Community Education and regeneration, but respondents were clear that, in order to be able to achieve this, major reinvestment would be required. At the time of writing, the future of Community Education continued to look uncertain. Its distinctiveness continued to lie in its ethos of raising the political consciousness of disadvantaged communities, empowering people to engage in social action through the transmission of 'really useful knowledge'. A recent report on the future of Community Education in Scotland (Scottish Office, 1998b) underlined its importance in stimulating lifelong learning, combating social exclusion and promoting active citizenship. While reiterating that sufficient funding had to be found, both reports were vague as to the source of the additional resources.

In addition, while attesting to is significance, the reports simultaneously deny that Community Education should be regarded as a distinctive sector with an independent budget, casting doubts about its future financial viability.

To summarise, this review of lifelong learning agencies and sectors catering for people with learning difficulties confirms that there was great diversity in the location of services (ARCs, FE colleges, the community), the ethos of services and their sources of funding. This reinforces the view expressed by Hancock and Sutcliffe (1995) that:

> The map of continuing education is not a well-ordered landscape such as the schools system or higher education, but a diverse network of providers. (Hancock and Sutcliffe, 1995, p 75)

Most resources were tied up in ARCs run by social work, where people often spent a large part of their week within the centre. FE was an increasingly important player, but questions emerged as to whether this provision was distinctively different from that which was already available in ARCs. Finally, Community Education was the service that subscribed most overtly to including people with learning difficulties in its programmes, whether these were classes or one-to-one tuition. However, this area appeared to be hit hardest by lack of adequate resourcing.

People with learning difficulties and experiences of lifelong learning: evidence from case studies

In the following section, we explore how continuing education, further education and ARC provision are experienced by specific individuals. The case studies illustrate the potential of lifelong learning to enlarge the social capital of people with learning difficulties and provide them with opportunities for personal growth. At the same time, the experiences described here point to the limitations of lifelong provision linked both to funding shortages and limitations in conceptualisation.

Iona

Iona was a 41-year-old woman who lived in the family home, an old stationmaster's cottage near a small rural town. She was slightly built with short curly blonde hair and a freckled friendly face. She was contacted through the Community Education service, where she had attended a class for over two years. She also worked part time as a kitchen assistant in a home for elderly people where her employer regarded her as a competent and hard worker. Iona lived at home with her brother. Her other siblings, two sisters and three brothers, all lived locally. Louise, the Community Education coordinator, described her thus:

> "She is very interesting – I don't know how I can describe her adequately. I think she is much more capable than she appears to be. I think that if you sat down with Iona you would have this impression of this little mouse that really couldn't do anything at all. But actually I know from the work she does with us, and her knowledge base of other things, and her recollections from childhood and from her work situation that actually Iona is quite a capable person. But superficially I think that you get the impression that she is not. That is the impression that she gives."

As a child Iona attended a village primary school where she learnt to write but not to read. Subsequently, she moved to the area secondary school where she was very unhappy, feeling picked on and bullied. She left school with no qualifications and moved straight into employment in a textiles factory. She later moved to another factory job and then to her current place of employment. The owner of the nursing home noticed the discrepancy between Iona's reading and writing abilities and, with her agreement, contacted the local Community Education service.

Within the rural area, Community Education operated an Adult Basic Education service on an outreach basis. There were three area teams each covering a wide area. The service had recently changed its name to Adult Education to avoid any danger of stigma and catered for people with very different needs, ranging from those with basic literacy difficulties to those needing support in working towards degree level qualifications. People with learning difficulties represented about 30% of the client group, which also included people with mental health problems. In addition to literacy skills, the team offered assertiveness training programmes and an adult guidance service. Tutors also recruited and trained volunteers, thus increasing the number of individuals able to receive one-to-one support. Of the people who come to her for educational courses, the Community Education organiser felt that the majority have had poor learning experiences rather than cognitive impairments. Working relationships between Community Education, the Careers Service and Further Education were sometimes fraught. The Community Education service had been located on the campus of the FE college but had been forced to move following incorporation. A bid for funding to conduct guidance services had been construed as encroachment by the Careers Service. Despite tensions between principal officers of the services, workers close to the grassroots enjoyed reasonably congenial working relationships.

Iona had attended Community Education for almost two years now and was very committed to her class, although the underlying reasons for her reading problems remained unresolved. The Community Education tutor believed that she might have a form of dyslexia that had been masked by her learning difficulties. An assessment by an educational psychologist was required, but it appeared that this would have to be paid for by Community Education because Iona was not covered by the statutory services.

Most of Iona's classes were with a volunteer tutor, who felt that Community Education offered her an opportunity to get out and meet people as much as improving her literacy skills. Her own role had subtly changed during the course of the two years:

> "Well officially I am a tutor, because she has very grave difficulties with reading, but since her difficulties are so great, I think I'm turning into a kind of a friend. I mean, a lot of it seems to me to be bringing her out of herself a bit and making her talk a bit more." (Community Education voluntary tutor)

Progress with reading skills seemed to be very slow and sometimes it felt like 'plodding on'. Iona's employer and the Community Education coordinator had a more positive view. Even if Iona's literacy skills had not improved a great deal, her confidence appeared to have grown. Overall, there was a feeling that if Iona was to make a significant breakthrough, a better understanding of her problems and more intensive tuition were required.

Jack

Jack was 21 at the time of the study and, at the start of the research, lived with his parents outside a small rural town. He was full of energy and talkative but his conversation was somewhat disjointed and he was sometimes perceived as aggressive, shouting and swearing a great deal. He was tall and slender with dark hair and dark eyes. Both Jack and his elder brother had a genetic disorder and the brother lived in supported accommodation run by a religious order. During the course of the research, a crisis arose in Jack's family life. His keyworker believed he was being physically and emotionally abused at home and finally, with the support of staff at the resource centre, he decided to move into temporary supported accommodation. Shortly after the move, Jack's mother died and contact with other members of his family, including his father, have been lost. As a result of this, Jack has become dependent for all his social contact on people in the group home and the ARC.

Jack spent a significant part of his week at the local ARC and his week was organised according to the following timetable:

Monday:	Centre all day – plays pool
Tuesday:	At group home all day
Wednesday:	In centre – works in garden in afternoon
Thursday:	Works in a sheltered employment unit making woodwork items
Friday:	Member of a hill-walking group – sometimes taken out for a hike
Sat/Sun:	At home: likes to watch football on TV

Observation of Jack at the centre suggested that a great deal of time was spent moving restlessly from one activity to another. He watched television briefly but rapidly moved on to something else such as looking at a bird table. Jack's eating at the centre was also quite chaotic. He snacked a great deal, eating crisps, biscuits, chocolate and drinking cans of Coke. Jack participated with interest in the Centre Meeting, sitting quietly and paying attention. Previously, he had participated in a first aid course at the local FE college but, at the time of the research, was not involved in any new courses. His memories of the first aid course were rather vague; it seemed that he could recall some key words such as 'emergency' and 'bandage', but there had been no subsequent reinforcement of what he had learnt.

One day a week was spent at a sheltered workshop run by a religious organisation where he made a range of wooden objects such as boxes and bird feeders. These were sold through the resource centre and Jack made about £10 a week in this way. The money was kept by a worker at the centre and given to him over a period of time so that he did not spend it too rapidly. Jack's keyworker believed in the importance of employment but felt it should be meaningful and of financial value to the person:

> "I'd say it is important and I mean it would be absolutely brilliant if people could just go out and get paid jobs on a scale like ourselves, but I mean at the moment that's obviously not going to happen. What I see as being important is getting people out there and giving them work experience ... and getting their benefits at the same time.... If you're going to give somebody a role than make sure it's a valued role and it's a worthwhile thing. You know, I mean there would be nae point if Jack knocking a couple of bits of wood together unless it's saleable at the end of the day, you wouldnae be daein' Jack any favours you know. So I'd say valued and recognised roles. You're no just shovin somebody in a corner and saying 'Right, carve buttons all day'." (adult resource centre keyworker)

Jack was encouraged to save his money for things like haircuts, but he also used it for what he described as 'sweetie money'.

At the time of the research, there were clearly aspects of Jack's life that he found enjoyable and meaningful. Time spent at the sheltered workshop was valued for a range of reasons, including the small amount of money earned. The ARC provided some degree of structure in his life and the opportunity to spend time with professionals who were able to offer emotional support, but activities tended to be repetitive and failed to hold his attention. Time spent in the group home was possibly the least enjoyable part of Jack's week. Even though he was meant to be looked after in his present accommodation, his rather grubby appearance gave the impression that he was somewhat neglected. His time at the home was spent passively watching television rather than engaging in any meaningful activities. Jack's keyworker was concerned that independent living arrangements for him, which were being discussed, might lead to even further isolation.

Ruth

Ruth was a woman with moderate learning difficulties, in her mid-sixties. She had lived in residential care for at least 30 years with the majority of that time being spent in institutional care with a religious order. She went to live at the convent when her father became seriously ill and her mother was no longer able to look after her. The institution was closed down a decade earlier and Ruth was moved into community based supported accommodation. At the time of the research she lived in 24–hour supported accommodation run by a religious order in a country town with four other women. Because the women spent a great deal of time in each other's company, there were recurring tensions between them.

Ruth was an enthusiastic and vibrant person and the impression she gave is of a woman who has found a new freedom. In sharp contrast to many other older people with learning difficulties, Ruth was encouraged in her learning and was increasing her independence if only by a small degree. Her keyworker at the group home explained:

> "Over the last year she [Ruth] can go to the local shop on her own. We're working on her sort of getting public transport to the college and things like that. But I mean she used to do this years ago but she would do silly things and folk would take away that independence, now it's just like building up her confidence but she can dae these things. And there's a big trust thing as well. We say to her, 'We are trusting you to dae this so dinnae mess it up, ken, this is your chance'. So it's trying to get that through to her an' all. And working on sort of leaving her in the house for maybe quarter of an hour, half an hour herself, because ultimately that's her goal."

Ruth also understands these changes:

Ruth: "Well I sometimes go into the town."

Researcher: "You've started going to the shops."

Ruth: "I've started to go down to the wee shop an then come right up again to the house."

Researcher: "You're doing really well with that."

Ruth: "Aye."

Researcher: "Would you not have done that before?"

Ruth: "No and now I'm getting brave at doing that now."

Researcher: "We're kind of working towards you getting the bus to college."

Ruth: "Getting the bus to college."

Researcher: "You're getting a lift just now. Why do you think you can do those things now?"

Ruth: "I've just got to try and learn."

Researcher: "Well before when you didn't go out by yourself, were you scared to go out or?"

Ruth: "No I wasnae scared, I just thought about it. I'll try and go down to the wee shop for some things, messages ... an right back up again."

Ruth attended the local college two days a week on a Lifeskills course. The class, made up of 15 people, was a mixture of ages and abilities with some of the group being in their early- to mid-twenties and very able. The college was generally respected in the community for its work with people with learning difficulties and the Lifeskills course seemed to have been created as a result of some community consultation. The course had been particularly valuable to Ruth and had made a significant difference to her life. Prior to this, she had undertaken a number of morning or afternoon courses but these had been too short to have major impact. The course tutor felt that Ruth had benefits in the following ways:

> "She [Ruth] does learn. I mean I think she's learnt to be more organised. She does know a bit more about how to use a computer. She still finds it difficult because her reading skills are very poor but even she can learn to use the mouse and to switch it on and use various programmes that we've got and she learns to work as part of a group. You know when they go away on the residential together they plan it as a group, they do things together ... what other things they do, they learn how to use the video camera and make a wee video film about themselves. Oh there are a lot of new things."

Ruth herself was particularly excited about the course having found it both challenging and rewarding:

Researcher: "So how did you find out about the college course?"

Ruth: "Well I went, I was working here and I went for my interview."

Researcher: "How did you find out about the interview?"

Ruth: "… it was Julie that telt me – you've to go for your interview. Well I was working here an got a phone message from [the college tutor] saying 'How would you like to come and start in the college?' an I said I would like that fine."

Researcher: "So you weren't sad at leaving here for a few days a week?"

Ruth: "No I was glad to go there, I said I'm going to go and try it and see how I get on and I got on all right. But when I passed them aw … oh that was great."

Researcher: "Did you not think you would?"

Ruth: "I said I don't think I would pass when I was with [the course tutor] told me I'd passed it I said 'oh great' I was happy."

Researcher: "Oh that's great, well done. So when did you get your certificate, did you have to go in to the college and get it?"

Ruth: "Yeah, and I got a photo frame and Marie's man to put it in the photo frame for me an put it up at the wall."

Researcher: "That's great."

Ruth: "So my cousin can see it again when she comes down."

The staff at Ruth's home also felt the college had been a very positive experience:

> "I think her confidence has improved…. She's no as feart to be away from the staff. Like going to the canteen or stuff like that. She will use the canteen, she chooses not to use it a lunchtime as her pal disnae but I think that that is a definite choice she makes because her pal's not wanting to have lunch." (keyworker, group home)

The FE course was arranged along similar lines to those described earlier, being taught separately from the colleges mainstream programmes. The course tutor commented how virtually all of the classes for people with learning difficulties were located outside the main building in a series of Portakabins. Observation of the class revealed the difficulties in teaching a number of adults with learning difficulties, each with specific difficulties, in an open session. For example, a shopping expedition to a local supermarket revealed that some students' difficulties were in the area of literacy and/or numeracy, while others had problems with social aspects of the activity. It was difficult for the tutor to address each person's individual difficulty.

The social aspect of the course had been particularly valuable for Ruth, allowing her to meet teaching staff and adults with learning difficulties from a wide geographical area. However, the course was soon to finish and there appeared to be no opportunities for further development beyond it. It would also be difficult for Ruth to maintain the new set of relationships due to lack of opportunities for travel and difficulties in using the telephone:

Researcher: "But next year, has the college got anything you can go to?"

Ruth: "Naw."

Researcher: "You don't know?"

Ruth: "But when I do finish up, I'll miss it."

Researcher: "Yeah.... What will you miss about it?"

Ruth: "Well I like going.... I've met all my friends.... There's Susan, there's Anne. Susan started to speak to me and she said to me 'Ruth will you mind if I be your friend' an I said 'Naw' an that's how we got together."

Researcher: "You didn't know Susan before?"

Ruth: "Nope."

Researcher: "You just met her on the course?"

Ruth: "Aye and now she's my friend for life."

Researcher: "Has she been to see you out here, or do you just see her at college?"

Ruth: "No ... well ... it's too far away to ask her to come up."

Researcher: "So you wouldn't maybe see her then once you leave college?"

Ruth: "She leaves too."

Researcher: "Right. So you won't see her very much then."

Ruth: "But she said 'I can give you my address Ruth, my phone number. You can phone up and see how I am'. I said 'aye'."

Researcher: "Uh huh ... so you'll probably just give her a ring then, but it might be hard to go and see her?"

Ruth: "Aye."

Researcher: "Can you get a bus over from here?"

Ruth: "Aye well I could but I didnae ken where about in the town she stays an...."

Researcher: "Aye."

Ruth: "[The home keyworker] was always saying that we should ask her up but, well, where she stays it would be too far away."

Despite the positive college experience, it was evident that Ruth's future development was likely to be impeded by the limited future learning opportunities available to her.

Discussion and conclusion

We began this chapter by exploring the diverse, and sometimes competing, agencies and locations involved in the delivery of lifelong learning opportunities for adults with learning difficulties. The case studies provide insight into the strengths and weaknesses of the available services. All the adults whose stories are presented here gained from participating in lifelong learning both in terms of practical skills and social capital. For all three, however, it was clear that their enhanced social networks were dependent on continuing contact with key individuals within a learning context. In general adults develop and sustain social networks by spending a great deal of time with people either through participation in further and higher education programmes or work. Most people find it difficult to sustain these relationships if they leave a work situation. In the general population, women at home with small children and unemployed men in socially disadvantaged groups are particularly likely to experience depression and anxiety (Goldberg, 1999). It is not surprising, therefore, that people with learning difficulties find it problematic to sustain relationships developed in educational settings, since they are more likely to have difficulty making social arrangements and having access to transport. Furthermore, the type of courses available are likely to be short-term and disconnected from earlier learning experiences. This is an issue, of course, not just for the maintenance of social networks, but also for the retention and reinforcement of knowledge and skills.

A further major issue concerns the extent to which adults with learning difficulties in different settings are included in mainstream provision. While all services identified social inclusion as a major priority, Community Education appeared to be the only service to include people with learning difficulties in mainstream provision, albeit without devoting resources to removing barriers to access. ARCs catered only for people with learning difficulties and many clients spent a significant part of their week in a centre building. Such experiences were not without value, for instance, Jack had access to a keyworker who was able to offer him emotional support in the absence of family networks. However, there was ample evidence from this study and others (Stalker et al, 1999a) that, while valuing contact with their friends, people with learning difficulties do not find centre-based activities sufficiently interesting and demanding. FE appeared to be particularly culpable in terms of segregating people with learning difficulties from mainstream students within the same institution. The orthodoxy of inclusiveness, which states that the individual student's learning needs must be of paramount importance, completely ignores the importance of the social context in which learning takes place. In particular, there appeared to be a total lack of awareness of the micro-political significance of space. Students with learning difficulties were often taught in separate (and inferior) premises from mainstream students even in the same subject area. Thus those with learning difficulties taking a catering or horticultural class were unlikely to be taught by the mainstream tutors in these areas or to use the same facilities. They had virtually no academic or social contact with their mainstream peers. We agree with Booth (2000) that this appears to be a distortion of the term 'inclusion' and that the term 'integration' might be preferable, since it at least acknowledges the political and social salience of physical location.

Finally, the funding of lifelong learning for people with learning difficulties remains a highly contentious issue. Community Education, the service with the greatest overt commitment to social inclusion and active citizenship, has been starved of money particularly since local government reorganisation. The requirement to produce community learning plans paying attention to the needs of people with learning difficulties will be a meaningless exercise unless it is adequately resourced. FE provision, by way of contrast, has undergone a massive expansion since the early 1990s following incorporation and the implementation of the 1992 Further and Higher Education (Scotland) Act (Closs, 1993). However, service provision is driven by financial imperatives. Full-time courses for post-16 students with moderate learning difficulties are relatively generously funded, but provision for those with higher support needs and for older people is far patchier. There is currently pressure to move adults with learning difficulties out of ARCs and into mainstream daytime opportunities. There is a danger that incoherent and badly organised activities, which represent the worst features of ARC provision, may be reproduced in a new FE college setting. An additional negative effect would be the short-term nature of such courses, which would prevent people with learning difficulties from sustaining enduring relationships.

The avowed outcome of most of the educational and training provision for people with learning difficulties is gaining and maintaining employment. It is to policies for, and the experiences of our case study people in, the open labour market to which we now turn.

FIVE

Access to the open labour market by people with learning difficulties

Introduction

This chapter considers the position of people with learning difficulties in relation to the open labour market. Access to employment is critical to the achievement of social inclusion and access to lifelong learning, since, in addition to the financial benefits of working, many people derive their social networks from their workplace. This is also the site for much formal and informal learning (Coffield, 1999, 2000). Whereas 62% of the total working-age population are 'economically active' (either in employment or unemployed according to the Independent Labour Organisation definition used in the Labour Force Survey[1]), only 40% of the total disabled population of working age are economically active. According to Sly's (1996) analysis of Labour Force Survey data for winter 1995, only 28% of people with severe or specific learning difficulties and 15% of those with long-term mental illness are economically active. Of the 60% of the disabled population who are economically inactive (for example, on long-term Incapacity Benefit or Income Support with Severe Disablement Allowances) a very high proportion have learning difficulties. Access to mainstream employment opportunities with its financial and social benefits is thus a pressing concern for people with learning difficulties. This chapter concentrates on the minority of individuals within our case study sample who were employed, with or without support, within the open labour market, exploring the barriers they had encountered, the circumstances which supported their ability to work and the unintended consequences of these support mechanisms.

While some aspects of the New Labour government's Welfare to Work programme has attracted censure because of its coercive elements, the New Deal for Disabled People has had a generally positive reception from the disability movement. This is largely due to the disability movement's understanding of employment that tends to support the government's emphasis on employment as the chief route out of poverty. Having outlined some theories of disability and employment, the paper describes post-war employment and benefits policies and their impact on the employment status of people with learning difficulties. Subsequently, the evolution of the Employment Service's Wage Subsidy Supported Employment scheme is considered. This programme is particularly significant because it reflects clearly the shifting direction of post-war employment policy for disabled people. In the immediate post-war period, governments believed they had a duty to intervene in the demand side of the labour market on behalf of disabled people, particularly those who had been wounded during the Second World War and to whom a social obligation was felt. The Quota System and the Wage Subsidy scheme were the strongest expressions of this commitment to intervention. During the 1980s and the 1990s, there was a marked shift away from attempts to intervene in the demand side of the labour market towards supply side measures, and changes in the Wage Subsidy Supported Employment scheme exemplify this shift. Finally, we use case study data to explore experiences of the Employment Service's Wage Subsidy Supported Employment programme.

Disabled people and work: the historical context

The logic of industrial capitalist social relations is towards disabled people working if at all possible rather than becoming a burden on the state. The foundation of the Asylum for the Industrious Blind in 1773 reflected the view that the acquisition of basic educational and vocational skills would prevent blind people from sinking into a life of penury to which their impairment would otherwise condemn them. In the 19th century schools for children with learning difficulties equipped them with manual skills such as the ability to cobble shoes or undertake laundry work and young people often moved into sheltered workshops on leaving such institutions. The relatively low level of investment in their training reflected the view that they would never be highly economically productive and therefore subsistence and social control were the ultimate goals.

In the second half of the 20th century, an increasingly complex system of welfare developed. The collapse of manufacturing industry and the growth of youth unemployment in the 1970s, coinciding with the election of a Conservative government, produced an acceptance that work was no longer an option for many sectors of the population. As Stone (1984) noted, within societies which distribute wealth on the basis of work, tensions arise when deciding how to support those who are unable or unwilling to work. Children and retired people may be regarded as putative or former workers, but the status of those not active in the labour market is uncertain. Disability may become a catch-all administrative category used to justify benefit payments to a very wide group of people, but its elasticity is likely to cause economic and political tensions, ultimately leading to attempts to define disability more rigorously, thus rationing the number of people claiming to be disabled.

The expansion of the category of disability which took place in the 1980s and 1990s served the dual function of masking levels of unemployment and of justifying the distribution of resources to people on the basis of need not work (Drake, 2000). In the UK, considerably more people are registered disabled than unemployed. According to Department of Social Security (DSS) statistics, 2.8 million people of working age are claiming incapacity benefits or disability benefits, 1.3 million people are on Job Seeker's Allowance and 1 million single parents are in receipt of Income Support. In areas where traditional industries have disappeared the proportion of the population in receipt of Incapacity Benefit (IB) and Income Support with Severe Disablement Allowance (IS with SDA) is higher. For example, in some areas up to a third of the male population is in receipt of IB and IS with SDA (Beatty et al, 1997). In the Green Paper *New ambitions for our country* (DSS, 1998), there is an unequivocal statement of the government's commitment to reducing rather than broadening the category of disability and ensuring that that smaller group who continue to be categorised as such should be targeted for significantly greater support. The following two of the eight key principles guiding the programme of reform pertain directly to disabled people (DSS, 1998):

• the new welfare state should help and encourage people of working age to work where they are capable of doing so;
• those who are disabled should get the support they need to lead a fulfilling life with dignity.

To achieve these goals, the government declared its intention to strengthen the rights of disabled people by establishing a Disability Rights Commission, which came into being in 2000, and implementing the remaining provisions of the 1995 Disability Discrimination Act. At the same time, access to Incapacity Benefit has been restricted by abolishing

Severe Disablement Allowance and by reforming the test criteria so that no one will be declared unfit to work for life. The focus of the new medical test of incapacity, referred to as the Capability Test, is to establish what work a disabled person is able to undertake and, at least in principle, what support they will need to do this. The rolling out of the Personal Adviser scheme, piloted as part of the New Deal for Disabled People, means that in future all those in receipt of Income Support will be required to attend for interview to establish an individual work or training plan. Effectively, the boundaries of disability are being redrawn to include a much smaller proportion of the population, with the expectation that those not encompassed within the new definition will find paid employment.

The disability movement and theories of disability and employment

Perceived elements of coercion within the New Deal programme have been criticised by those who believe that they represent a form of punishment for people in geographical areas where traditional industries have disappeared. The New Deal for Disabled People is different from the other New Deal programmes, in that it operates on a voluntary basis, but nonetheless some disabled people have assumed that all New Deal programmes operate on similar lines. Perhaps surprisingly, there has been little resistance from the disability movement to government attempts to encourage disabled people into employment. This apparent acceptance is in contrast to hostile reactions to earlier efforts to scrutinise the validity of claims made by those on disability benefits, in particular the Disability Integrity Project. The reason for this acceptance of active labour market policies may lie in the dominance of two particular theories adopted by the disability movement, the social model of disability and normalisation, both of which regard employment as a central means for disabled people to challenge their marginalised social status. In the following sections, we explore what each of these theories has to say about disability and work.

The social model of disability and employment

The social model of disability as developed by Finkelstein (1980), Abberley (1987) and Oliver (1990) draws on Marxist theory and envisages a central role for employment in terms of determining the status of disabled people. Finkelstein (1980) described a three-stage process in the development of the status of disabled people in the labour market. In Type 1, comprised of pre-industrial societies, disabled people would be integrated into the largely domestic production process. Type 2 societies in Finkelstein's typology emerged with the advent of the Industrial Revolution. As production moved from the home to the factory, adopting disciplined timetables and tightly regulated processes, disabled people became far less easily accommodated. With the gradual emergence of welfare, disability became recognised as a category for needs-based rather than work-based distribution (see above), thus becoming a group distinct from others within the underclass. Within Type 3 societies, the final stage envisaged by Finkelstein, disabled people are once again integrated through the provision of 'necessary appliances', of which new technology represents a major part.

The role ascribed to employment in Marxist theory is actually much more complex than Finkelstein allows. Within capitalist economic relations, employment was envisaged as innately exploitative and alienating, but also as the only source of economic power accessible to the working class. In the post-revolutionary period, work is envisaged as occupying a central means of personal fulfilment that would absorb and inspire a vast amount of creative energy. In the 1857-58 *Grundrisse*, Marx maintains:

> Really free working is at the same time precisely the damned
> seriousness, the most intense exertion. (Marx, 1973, p 611)

In the new social order Marx was convinced that the old divisions between mental and manual work would disappear and, in place of class divisions, would emerge a society in which each individual is free to develop as they wish. However, within this utopia, the position of those who are unable or unwilling to work is unclear. Indeed, a close reading of Marx suggests that, in the context of his critique of capitalist society, disabled people are seen as a visible expression of the ravages of capitalism. Marx offers the following example of the callousness of the employer in exposing workers to the risk of impairment in pursuit of profit:

> It is a well known fact that during the last twenty years the flax
> industry has expanded considerably, and that, with that expansion,
> the number of scutching mills in Ireland has increased.... Regularly,

in autumn and winter, women and 'young persons', the wives, sons and daughters of the neighbouring small farmers, a class of people entirely unaccustomed to machinery, are taken from field labour to feed the rollers of the scutching mills with flax. The accidents, both as regards number and kind, are wholly unparalleled in the history of machinery. In one scutching mill at Kildinian near Cork, there occurred between 1852 and 1856 six fatal accidents and sixty mutilations.... Dr W White, the certifying surgeon for factories at Downpatrick, states in his official report, dated 15 December 1865: 'The serious accidents at the scutching mill are of the most fearful nature. In many cases a quarter of the body is torn from the trunk, and either involves death or a future of wretched incapacity and suffering'. (1976, p 610)

For Marx, once societies were free from the scourges of capitalism and the impairments it produces, people would be free to find self-fulfilment through work. While agreeing with Marx that the social creation of impairment is to be condemned, Abberley (1998) rejects the view that impairment should be seen as something which could or should be erased. Similarly, he objects to the elision of a person's identity with the work they do. He comments:

While other needs can be met for impaired people, and this can perhaps be done in a non-oppressive manner, the one need that cannot be met for those unable to labour is the need to work. (1998, p 87)

Abberley suggests that feminism may offer a way of valorising the lives of those who do not participate in paid employment. However, this argument too is problematic because, while feminists have insisted that domestic work, childcare and care of the sick and elderly is of value, they have done so on the grounds that this too is labour and contributes, albeit indirectly, to economic accumulation (Hartmann, 1981).

Despite these reservations about aspects of the Marxist construction of work and disability, nonetheless it is evident that many disabled people continue to support the view that, if at all possible, disabled people should work because dependency on benefits will produce neither social equality nor a decent standard of living. Ultimately, a Marxist perspective on employment suggests that alienated labour is better then unemployment, since economic power through the wage offers workers the possibility of developing a collective consciousness which will ultimately lead to the overthrow of the capitalist system.

Recently, some disability theorists who support the social model have pointed out its limitations for those disabled people who may be unable to work because of the extent of their impairments. Barnes (2000), drawing on the work of Castells (1996), suggests that a broader understanding of the nature of work is necessary to escape these tensions. Increasingly, theories of work in late capitalist societies emphasise not only the value of production, but also of consumption. People with learning difficulties, in particular those with significant impairments, contribute to the economic whole by creating employment for others. Increasingly, people with learning difficulties may act as employers, receiving direct payments from social services to employ personal assistants. Barnes suggests that recognition of the inter-relationship between production and consumption may dispel the idea that only those in work make a valuable economic contribution. This development of the social model avoids the tendency within traditional Marxist thought to insist that social recognition can only be achieved through labour power.

Normalisation, work and supported employment

While the social model of disability is the *lingua franca* of the disability movement, the theory of normalisation is commonly employed by those advocating for people with learning difficulties. Developed in the US by Wolfensberger (1972) and O'Brien (1987), normalisation is defined as the provision of normative social and cultural roles for those who would otherwise be at the social margins because of their cognitive impairment.

For Wolfensberger (1983), the social roles people occupy are the key to defining their social status. Thus to improve the social status of a particular group it is necessary to establish them within 'normal' society, rather than seeking to change the attitudes of others as to what is to be valued. According to O'Brien, services for adults with learning difficulties should be community based, allow choice, encourage the development of a range of skills, afford respect and ensure social participation. Critics of normalisation (for example Brown and Smith, 1992) object to the emphasis on behavioural adjustment and suggest that it leads to a conservative, authoritarian and conformist approach to services for people with learning difficulties.

Wolfensberger has been criticised for ignoring the power of political and economic factors and assuming that changes to the surface of people's appearance will make a major difference to the way in which 'normal' people respond to those with learning difficulties:

> Cosmetic surgery can often eliminate or reduce a stigma, and can be as effective in enhancing a person's acceptability as teaching adaptive skills, changing his context or working on his feelings. (Wolfsenberger, 1972, p 34)

Because work is one of the central means by which people in Western societies gain social valorisation, normalisation provides a strong underpinning for participation in employment.

Both the social model of disability and normalisation emphasise the importance of work for disabled people, although for different reasons. The social model of disability suggests that work empowers while benefits are likely to disempower. Normalisation places great value on the accomplishment of work, but as a means of gaining acceptance within mainstream society where work is highly valued. In the following sections, we consider the development of the Employment Service's Wage Subsidy Supported Employment programme in Scotland. Subsequently, by examining the experiences of two individuals who participated in this programme, we discuss its relevance to people with learning difficulties at the margins of the labour market.

Post-war employment policy and wage subsidy supported employment

The Second World War drew on a number of 'reserve armies of labour' and disabled people may be seen as one such group who had previously been regarded as unemployable but whose services were suddenly regarded as essential. Nearly half a million disabled workers were drafted into the labour force at various levels in support of the war effort (Lonsdale, 1986; Humphries and Gordon, 1992) and at the end of the war some effort was put into sustaining this employment due to what was regarded as a 'social obligation' (Thornton et al, 1995).

The 1944 Disabled Person's (Employment) Act adopted a medical model of disability, identifying individual disability or deficit as the main reason for high levels of unemployment among disabled people. Training for individuals to overcome or circumvent their problem was seen as the most immediate priority. However, direct intervention in the labour market was also seen as appropriate. The 1944 Act provided the first comprehensive employment enhancement provisions for disabled people and was in part a response to the labour market shortages that followed the Second World War. Aimed primarily at the war injured (Barnes, 1991, pp 68-9; Lonsdale, 1990, pp 46-8), the 1944 Act provided for:

- the establishment of a Quota Scheme whose aim was to ensure that at least 3% of the workforce of all non-governmental organisations with more than 20 people were registered disabled people;
- the setting up of a national network of industrial rehabilitation units to rehabilitate disabled people and the establishment of sheltered workshops and factories (termed at the time 'factories fit for heroes');
- the development of a service to help disabled people find employment.

Although radical in its conception, the Quota System in the UK was always limited in its application. For example, people with mental health problems were not included, and it was never enforced (there were only ever ten prosecutions for failure to comply). In the mid-1990s it was quietly dropped.

The longer-term effects of post-war employment policy were influenced by the social security benefits measures that were put in place at the same time. Although at least some aspects of employment policy encouraged disabled people into the labour market, the creation of long-term 'out of work' benefits tended to reinforce exclusion from paid employment (Hyde, 2000, p 328). Whereas these benefits were intended to offer support and security to disabled people (DSS, 1998), they have been criticised from two quite separate perspectives. Treasury concerns with a rising social security bill led to criticisms that these benefits placed an undue burden on public finance (DSS, 1998). Members of the disability movement argued that they failed to tackle poverty (Disability Alliance, 1991) and justified the exclusion of disabled people from the labour market (Barnes, 1991). Hyde (2000) and Barnes (1991) both concluded that the operation of post-war employment and social security policy was ultimately negative. The level of social security benefits failed to lift disabled people out of poverty, but the unskilled work, which was often their only option in the labour market, meant that they were worse off in employment than on benefits.

To summarise, in the immediate aftermath of the Second World War, a positive action employment programme was put in place to counter some of the problems experienced by disabled people in the labour market. These attempts were undermined, however, by adherence to an individual deficit view of disabled people, the instigation of segregated systems of training and the creation of perverse incentives to remain on benefits rather than enter employment.

The Employment Service's Wage Subsidy and Supported Employment schemes

The supported employment programme put in place by the Employment Service after the Second World War was geared to providing jobs for disabled people who:

> ... because of the nature or severity of their disability, are unable to work without this type of support. Providers/employers receive assistance to offset the additional cost of employing a disabled person who is not fully productive at work, but who is able to make a significant contribution to the employing organisation. (Employment Service, unpublished)

Jobs are provided either in supported factories or with mainstream employers. Remploy, a company set up be the Secretary of State, is the biggest provider of supported employment. Supported employment placements with mainstream employers are generally managed by local authorities and voluntary organisations. Contractors identify suitable jobs for eligible people referred to them by the Disability Employment Adviser (DEA) and the contractor sets up a separate agreement with the 'host' company. This agreement covers the responsibilities of the employer and the contractor towards the disabled person and the levels of support to cover the cost to the employer of the individual's reduced productivity because of the nature of their disability. To be eligible for this Wage Subsidy Supported Employment programme, the individual's output should be between 30-80% of a non-disabled employee doing the same or similar work. No one can enter the Supported Employment programme without being assessed as eligible by the DEA.

The Supported Employment programme is by far the largest and most costly of the Employment Service's disability programmes. For the year 1999-2000, the budget was £155.1 million, providing over 22,000 jobs through Remploy and 22,000 jobs managed by voluntary organisations and local authorities. This compares with a budget of £19.6 million allocated to Access to Work and £10.2 million allocated to Work Preparation for the same period. The government has become concerned at the size of the budget and the fact that people working within the Supported Employment programme rarely move into open employment. The fact that the budget for the programme is capped means that there is a long waiting list for supported employment placements. For example, an internal Employment Service document stated that in 1998 there was a potential demand of 100,793 supported employment places compared with 22,838 actually available. In Scotland the gap between supply and demand is less acute than in other parts of the United Kingdom. In 1997/98, 11,434 people were eligible to participate in the Supported Employment programme, and 2,655 places were funded. This is in contrast to London and the South East, where 29,413 people were eligible, but only 3,720 places were available.

A consultation on the future of the Supported Employment programme was conducted in 1999, seeking views on programme aims, entry criteria, ways of increasing progression for supported employees, the future role of supported factories and businesses, and quality standards. Most respondents expressed dissatisfaction with the productivity criteria, feeling that a much wider group of disabled people should have access to the Supported Employment programme and that a range of additional supports, such as job coaches, should be available. There was also consensus that, if in a mainstream placement, the disabled person should be employed directly by the host employer and not by the contracting local authority or voluntary organisation. Most respondents were in favour of enhancing progression into open employment, but there was strong resistance to the idea that sheltered factories should be phased out. Respondents referred to the inevitable tensions between running a viable commercial enterprise and fulfilling the desire of disabled people for employment.

In spring 2000, a ministerial statement on modernising the Supported Employment programme was released by Margaret Hodge, Minister with responsibility for disability and employment. The Minister announced a reform in the criteria for access to supported employment, currently dependent on being assessed as less than 80% productive compared with a non-disabled person. Future eligibility criteria would include the following groups:

- former supported employment employees who lose their jobs in mainstream employment within two years of progressing;
- people on incapacity benefit; or

• people with disability on Jobseekers Allowance for 12 months or
more.

It was also stated that 'demanding targets' would be set for numbers
moving into mainstream employment from both supported factories
and work based placements. The future expectation would be that the
majority of disabled people should spend only two years within a
supported employment placement prior to progression into the labour
market. This clearly marks a radical shift in the conceptualisation of the
supported employment programme. While few would argue with the
ambition of facilitating access to mainstream employment, many
questions remain concerning employers' willingness to retain a disabled
employee at the end of a two-year period where the majority of the
cost of employing the person has been met by an outside agency. For
many, the temptation might be to 'let the person go' and take on a new
individual under the same programme. Certainly, the evidence from
the Special Needs Skillseekers programmes is that employers are reluctant
to offer long-term employment to individuals at the end of a
government-subsidised initiative. One policy option would be for the
government to require employers to take on a disabled employee at the
end of a supported employment scheme. However, since the demise of
the Quota System, there has been little evidence of the government's
willingness or ability to intervene in employers' recruitment policies.
Government preference seems to be to rely on employers' good will
rather than enforcing a social obligation.

The reform of the Supported Employment programme encapsulates
many features of new directions in employment policy. Direct
intervention within the labour market, a key feature of the post-war
period, has been replaced by supply-side measures, focusing on enhancing
employability, with the implication that employee deficit is the
fundamental problem to be tackled. The Wage Subsidy Supported
Employment programme clearly failed to move disabled people into
open employment. However, this was justified on the grounds that,
given the choice between a disabled and non-disabled employee, an
employer who is fundamentally concerned with maximising profit is
likely to employ the latter. Accordingly, the only hope that disabled
people have of accessing the labour market is if labour market conditions
are tilted to some extent in their favour. In the following sections, we
consider the experiences of three case study individuals in mainstream
employment, two supported through Employment Service programmes.

Experiences of open employment and the Employment Service's supported employment programme

Iona

Iona was the only case study individual with learning difficulties in open employment. Her only contact with statutory services was with community education that we analysed, together with her life circumstances, in Chapter 4.

Since leaving school, Iona has had three long-term jobs, two in clothing factories, driving between home and work on a small motorbike. In her present place of work, she is judged to be a very good cook and is well integrated into the social life of the old people's home. Her employer, Annette, resists the label of learning difficulties, seeing it as far too broad to be of any use:

> "I don't like the term – I know that it is politically correct. I am a highly intelligent woman but I have a learning difficulty if you throw maths or physics at me. But I wouldn't like to think that I was on anybody's list as a person with learning difficulties. But they are applying that term to people with Down's syndrome. I just don't approve of the term – it is too big an umbrella. I wouldn't have classed Iona as having a disability of some sort. Using the old term I would not call her mentally handicapped at all. I have got difficulties with the term. I don't know who dreamt it up and what it is supposed to encompass really – it covers anything that they have not got another label for really. That is my personal opinion." (Iona's employer)

Annette felt that Iona had not yet achieved her full potential and that she would eventually take over as chief cook in the home. Her main problem, she felt, was not to do with a cognitive impairment but was a simple lack of confidence that could be overcome.

> "I am hoping to groom her as a replacement for Jean, when she retires, but Iona doesn't know that, because if I told Iona that she would worry about it. So, I suppose, careful handling is needed. But anything that seems official frightens her. So I try to be very casual with her and not do like formal reviews like we do with the

carers. It is quite important with the carers. Iona would be totally
intimidated by it, so I try to keep it all low key." (Iona's employer)

As far as Annette was concerned, Iona was no different from any other
employee, working for the same reasons as others and gaining similar
satisfactions:

"She gets her wages, she gets companionship, she enjoys the company,
and she is good with the residents." (Iona's employer)

As noted earlier, despite lacking basic literacy skills, Iona had managed
to avoid the learning difficulties label by attending mainstream schools
where she was regarded as a fairly typical rural girl who would survive
in life without formal qualifications. Although known to community
education as a person with learning difficulties, to her employer and
others in her social network she was simply an unmarried woman,
working and keeping house for her unmarried brother. Had the label
of learning difficulties been attached to her earlier, she might well have
received special education and have pursued a 'special' route into later
life, bypassing any possibility of mainstream employment. Iona acts as a
useful reminder that the receipt of special services may entail negative
connotations, diminishing the social status of those at whom they are
aimed, becoming a self-fulfilling prophecy. It is to two such cases that
we now turn.

Ronald

Ronald was aged 44, of medium height and heavily built. He worked
as a cleaner in the offices of a public utility, moving around the building
very purposefully and deliberately. He had a large bunch of keys attached
to his waist and these were employed, along with a swipe card, to open
many of the doors in the workplace. There was very little in his
appearance to distinguish Ronald from any other middle-aged cleaner
managing an often dirty, manual day's work.

Ronald gave no immediate impression of having a learning difficulty
and indeed the basis of this categorisation was not entirely clear. He
travelled to work independently and could read and write. Ronald
lived with his mother, his father, a serviceman, having died some 12
years ago. He travelled widely in his childhood, living in several different
places including Africa. Ronald had many stories about his past but

talked little very little about his present life, and it was evident that he socialised very little. His job was clearly of central importance to him.

Ronald had amiable but superficial interaction with colleagues but he had particularly close contact with the union representative who had played a key role in defending his position in the workplace. He appeared to be very polite, making a point of greeting colleagues by name. The union representative gave this impression of him:

> "I think half the time there's nobody here that makes a menace of him you know, that, you know, is cheeky wey him, takes the micky out of him or anything like that. Where he might have got that other places ... but here, no, they all respect him. They aw like him, have a good laugh with him and they know what he is, When I say that I didnae mean that in a bad way. They know that he's got learning difficulties but they accept it, it's no a problem." (Ronald's union representative)

Ronald worked through the morning and did not take a tea break with the other cleaners. At lunchtimes he sat with the other cleaners and joined in the conversation.

After leaving school, Ronald attended a government training centre which was a "... sort of preparation course although they didn't really train you for anything unless you were 18..." (Ronald). He then worked as a car washer and subsequently had a job filling up cigarette machines. Ronald was unemployed for about three years before taking up his present job. At the time of the research, he had been in the same post for 18 years. Ronald was initially employed on the same terms, conditions and pay as any other cleaning worker. Five years ago a new manager was appointed with the mission of streamlining the workforce to increase efficiency prior to possible privatisation. When Ronald's work rate was examined, it was decided that he was too slow and he was given the choice of disciplinary action or an interview with the staff doctor. The union representative intervened at this point and arranged for Ronald to be assessed for an Employment Service Wage Subsidy Supported Employment programme. As a result, Ronald was assessed as capable of doing 50% of the job, and the employer was compensated for the deficit by the Employment Service.

The extent to which Ronald had genuinely become less productive was disputed by the Wage Subsidy Supported Employment programme contractor:

"I think Ronald was doing OK, but, because of the restructuring, and the accountability for people's performance and everything, it was identified, look here we've got somebody here that's really, he's not really fully effective."

The union representative was even more sceptical that the problem lay with Ronald:

Union representative: "I don't know about the other cleaners, they aw seem to get on fine with him. And they all understand about Ronald. He disnae do any worse a job than anybody else or indeed probably any better a job. But ... we just like to look after him but we don't see a problem with Ronald."

Interviewer: "Did you see any need for the SEP to get involved?"

Union representative: "Not particularly, I've got to say. Because I think that the manager was just wanting to try to get rid of him."

Ronald clearly found the threat to his job deeply disturbing and was unhappy about having his status changed from that of an ordinary worker to a supported employment worker. At the time of the assessment, he felt he had been doing the equivalent of two jobs and the manager was unfair in claiming that he was slow. He was conscious that his employer was now the Employment Service via the supported employment contractor and this made him feel different from his workmates. Because of these dissatisfactions, he had thought about moving jobs, but his new status as a supported employee meant that his chances of gaining a new post were much lower. The Wage Subsidy Supported Employment scheme may have helped Ronald retain his job, but it also contributed to a sense of damaged identity and of being trapped in the current workplace.

Greg

Greg was 25 years old and lived at home with his mother and sister in a small rural town where he worked in the knitwear factory as a cleaner. Greg attended a special unit within a mainstream school where he was identified as having specific learning difficulties. These difficulties may be connected with medical problems. He was born with heart defects which required extensive medical intervention over a period of years and this was complicated by the fact that he had meningitis when he was three. His father felt that Greg's learning difficulties were not attributable to his illnesses, but to the fact that he missed a lot of schooling.

Greg's father made it clear that he was opposed to his son being labelled as having learning difficulties:

> "They decided to put him in the special unit and I was dead against it.... A couple of my pals were in it, ken what I mean, and they treat them like lepers.... The teachers decided if he were at the special unit he'd get a one on one sort of thing. But they got parried [treated the same] with the Mongols and they got different play times and they got different lunchtimes and ken so he was never mixing with normal kids and then all the boys that he used to be in the class wi' just, every time he went out in the playground, they'd say, 'Oh you're a Mongol, ken you're wi' the Mongols, and ken ... he just wouldnae go ast." (Greg's father)

When interviewed at work, Greg expressed the view that he had learnt very little at school:

> "I never learnt anything at school. I learnt everything here. Joined up writing, well we learnt that at home.... But everything I've learnt is basically from here [work] and nothing else, school I learnt nothing because I didnae get a chance to." (Greg)

Greg had been employed in the same knitwear factory since leaving school, initially within the Youth Training programme. According to his supervisor, Greg found the work difficult:

> "We actually tried him in the factory in a production scenario. It was actually fold-down bagging but there were very quickly difficulties there and Greg just wouldn't be able to hold a job at fold-down bagging. Which meant folding a garment, eh ... to a correct size and putting it in a bag and doing that over and over again. But he had a target of an hour and [if] he was two garments short instead of putting them in the bag he would hide them under the table and say they were done. Of course at the end of the shift there were all these garments hidden under the table." (Greg's supervisor)

A letter was written terminating Greg's employment but the supervisor was persuaded by several of the engineers in the company to keep him on until the end of his placement. At the end of the placement, the Youth Training assessor suggested that Greg would benefit from a Wage Subsidy Supported Employment placement and this was duly arranged. At the same time, he was moved from industrial work to maintenance.

Greg's supervisor at work felt that his main problems were in concentrating and remembering tasks. His work output was assessed at only 30% of that of other workers:

Supervisor: "To do the toilets it would probably take somebody ... it takes John say 25 minutes. It takes Greg about an hour, an hour and a half. To do the cardboard it would take John probably about 20 minutes, it takes Greg about an hour and a half."

Interviewer: "So he's always running about a third behind?"

Supervisor: "He's always running about a third. To sweep the yard with the petrol sweeper it would probably take John about 40 minutes, Greg can spend up to about three hours on it. To cut the grass, eh ... John would take probably 30 minutes ... he would take maybe a whole afternoon."

Greg was described as 'easily stressed' at work, developing a painful skin rash. The twice-yearly visits by the voluntary organisation supported employment contractor made him particularly anxious, since he was never sure when these were going to take place.

For Greg, the Wage Subsidy Supported Employment programme appeared to offer particular benefits. He received a wage of £165 a week for a 44-hour week, 30% of which was paid by the employer and 70% by the supported employment contractor. Given this heavy subsidy, the supervisor was able to argue that it was cheaper to employ Greg than hire contract cleaning staff. However, the woollen industry had been in recession for several years and many of Greg's friends had lost their jobs. Since he was judged to be a less efficient worker than most, Greg would almost certainly have lost his job if left to compete in the open labour market. Even with the benefits of the Wage Subsidy Supported Employment programme, Greg felt that his future employment was uncertain.

Discussion and conclusion

As we noted at the start of this chapter, the disability movement has generally supported the stated intentions of the New Labour government to assist disabled people in their attempts to access mainstream employment. Both the social model of disability and normalisation have as their central tenets that social inclusion depends to a large extent on participation in paid work. Social model thinking suggests that benefits are unlikely to provide enough money to sustain a truly independent life and normalisation asserts that in Western societies the status of worker represents a highly valued social role that disabled people must embrace to be accepted.

We then considered the direction of post-war employment policy. In the immediate aftermath of the Second World War, Keynsian economic policy suggested that it was both possible and desirable for government to intervene in the labour market. Demand side policies were pursued which meant that employers were required by law to recruit a given proportion of disabled workers, sheltered factories were created and wage subsidy schemes introduced. These positive action measures meant that disabled workers were given some advantages in competing for jobs with their non-disabled peers.

Since the 1980s, demand side policies have fallen out of favour and there is a renewed emphasis on enhancing disabled workers' employability rather than tilting the labour market in their favour. Proposed reforms to the Employment Service's Wage Subsidy Supported Employment programme exemplify this shift to supply side measures. Particularly significant is the new stipulation that after two years of wage subsidy a worker must progress to the open labour market.

The case studies presented here illustrate the characteristics of people with learning difficulties who have managed to find mainstream employment. Such individuals are highly unusual, since the majority of people with learning difficulties are economically inactive. It was evident that these people were, relative to other individuals with learning difficulties, very able. Their problems, which tended to be described as specific learning difficulties, often stemmed from lack of opportunities to learn due to social disadvantage, frequent changes of school or health problems rather than cognitive impairment. There was also a resistance to accepting the label of learning difficulties by the individual themselves, their parents and, in Iona's case, her employer.

The two participants in the supported employment programme illustrated both its strengths and shortcomings. Both felt somewhat stigmatised by the special status it conferred and were anxious about their future. In both cases, however, it was evident that, in the absence of the scheme, ongoing employment was unlikely. Both were victims of the restructuring of the labour market within post-industrial societies. Rodney's employment was called into question as a publicly owned utility prepared itself for privatisation by shedding staff. Greg was employed in part of the manufacturing sector that had shrunk rapidly and was likely to disappear altogether. Workers deemed to be less efficient than others are clearly the most vulnerable to cuts in the labour force.

The experiences of these individuals raises questions about plans to impose a strict time limit on future participation in Supported Employment and tight productivity targets on sheltered factories and workshops. For both men, the end of the two-year allotted period of support would almost certainly result in their becoming economically inactive rather than moving into the open labour market. Hyde (1998), in his study of disabled workers in sheltered and supported employment placements, underlined this point, commenting:

> Disabled workers who are faced with the prospect of moving into open employment feel apprehension about the prospect of more intensive working conditions and greater job insecurity. Many disabled workers in sheltered and supported employment are reluctant to take up the option of 'progression'. (Hyde, 1998, p 212)

Although the goal of helping people with learning difficulties achieve mainstream employment is highly commendable, it may be damaging if it fails to take account of the structural barriers that prevent this group competing with non-disabled workers on equal terms. Access to open employment, even of the special terms of the Employment Service Wage Subsidy scheme, was available only to a minority of our case study individuals. A further small group had access to the labour market through a different type of supported employment, the Job Coach Supported Employment projects offered by voluntary organisations. It is to these that we now turn.

Note

[1] The 'unemployed', according to the International Labour Organisation definition used in the Labour Force Survey, are those aged 16 and over without a paid job who said they were able to start work within the next two weeks

and who either had looked for work at some time during the four weeks prior to the interview or were waiting to start a job they had already obtained. 'Work limiting disability' refers to those in the LFS who answer positively to both of the following: Do you have any health problems or disabilities that you expect will last for more than a year? Does this health problem affect the kind of paid work that you might do?

SIX

Participation in supported employment

Introduction

In the previous chapter, we discussed the operation of the Employment Service's Wage Subsidy Supported Employment programme that is underpinned by statute and is aimed at disabled people judged to be almost 'work ready'. Whether ability is measured in terms of relative productivity or benefits status, participation in the Wage Subsidy Supported Employment programme is contingent on being able to survive in open employment with little ongoing support. This chapter explores the operation of a quite different form of supported employment that has developed from grassroots movements and lacks statutory or central government financial support. This version of supported employment, Job Coach Supported Employment, reflects the principle that all citizens have the right to work since this is the key aspect of social inclusion in Western societies. Every individual, it is argued, is capable of working if they wish to do so. However, particularly for individuals with more significant impairments, it is recognised that a considerable amount of support will be required, not just in the initial stages of mastering a job, but possibly on a long-term basis. It is acknowledged that supporting individuals with complex difficulties in a work placement will be expensive, but other forms of support, for example in day centres, are also expensive. In this chapter, we first outline some central principles of Job Coach Supported Employment and then discuss some recent findings on its position in the UK. Subsequently, we use case study material to explore experiences of Job Coach Supported Employment by people with learning difficulties.

Principles of Job Coach Supported Employment

In general, most Job Coach Supported Employment agencies adopt a 'place, train and maintain' model. A supported employment placement generally begins with a period of assessment or profiling, so that the keyworker understands the individuals within their social context. The work-related goals of individuals will be placed within their broader life aspirations and their strengths and weaknesses are identified. The person will then be 'marketed' to an employer, with whom the person's support needs will be discussed. A keyworker will conduct an analysis of the job to be undertaken and systematic instruction techniques may be used, breaking the task down into component parts and encouraging the person to practice each micro task until it is mastered. This form of instruction is informed by a mixture of behaviourist psychology and mastery pedagogy, both of which have the faith of the educator that if instruction and practice time are adequate, most people can accomplish most tasks to a satisfactory standard. Recently, emphasis has been placed on the use of natural supports within the workplace, based on the recognition that work is a social activity. In order for a person with learning difficulties to sustain employment, it will be necessary for them to understand the culture and the unwritten rules of the workplace. Such understandings are at least as important as mastering the mechanics of particular activities (Mank et al, 1997).

A key aspect of Job Coach Supported Employment is that workers should be paid the going rate for the job and should thus be removed from a negative state of benefit dependency. Within the US context, it has been maintained that individuals increased their annual earnings by up to 500% through participation in supported employment (Kregel, 1997; Kregel et al, 1989). Wehman and Kregel (1995), for example, argue that supported employment has provided severely disabled individuals with the opportunity to undertake a real job in their local community as opposed to meaningless work in a segregated setting for poverty wages. However, the picture of success is not entirely unalloyed. Wehman and Kregel point out that Job Coach Supported Employment must face the challenge of converting day programmes to supported employment, increasing programme capacity, expanding consumer choice and promoting meaningful employment outcomes. They suggested that in the US, Job Coach Supported Employment has reached a plateau, whereby future developments require a resurgence of energy and commitment, perhaps by harnessing the power of consumer choice (Parent et al, 1996).

The development of Job Coach Supported Employment in the UK

In the UK, Job Coach Supported Employment has developed rapidly since 1985. Beyer, Kilsby and Shearn (1999) undertook a survey of supported employment agencies on behalf of the Employment Service in 1996 and in the following section we draw on findings from this work. Whereas the Wage Subsidy Supported Employment programme is funded by central government, Job Coach Supported Employment agencies were often established by voluntary organisations or parental action groups, frustrated at the lack of opportunity for many people with learning difficulties to participate in mainstream employment. Beyer et al found that the largest sources of funding were local government social services departments (58%), followed by health authorities (15%) and the European Union (12%). Only 4% of the total budget came from the Employment Service. Agencies were generally small, with an average budget in 1994/95 of £86,395. The majority of workers (41%) were in the 25–34 age group and two thirds were male.

The most common areas of work were the following: domestic/laundry (20% of all jobs), kitchen helper/waiter (15%), shop work (15%), grounds keeping (10%), clerical (9%), manufacturing (8%) and warehouse assistant (8%). Only 21% of Job Coach Supported Employment workers were employed for 36 hours or more, the traditional full-time pattern of work in the UK. Fifty per cent were employed for 16 hours or less a week as a result of 'therapeutic earnings' regulations (see Chapter 7 for a further discussion of this). In brief, people on higher levels of disability benefits are only permitted to work for a limited amount of time before their benefits are encroached upon. At the time of the research, the therapeutic earnings limit in Incapacity Benefit and Severe Disablement Allowance was £15. From April 1999, this limit has been raised to £58 per week to allow people carrying out therapeutic work to benefit from the national minimum wage, which is currently set at £3.60 per hour. For those people whose earnings were not distorted by therapeutic work regulations, Beyer et al found that the average hourly rate of pay was £3.50, considerable below the average hourly rate of £4.95 for non-manual occupations but close to the national minimum wage. Most supported workers increased their income by entering employment, but one third experienced no change in income due to employment and 10% were not paid any wage at all, raising questions about the possibility of exploitation if a supported employee is working for a long period of time in a voluntary capacity while all other workers are being paid.

As we noted above, US researchers have presented an optimistic view of Job Coach Supported Employment as an overwhelmingly successful service that is likely to enjoy future expansion. In the UK, the picture looks rather different. Job Coach Supported Employment has no statutory underpinning and little central government support. Most agencies are small and survive on often short-term grants mainly from social services and health. Beyer et al (1996a) characterised UK Job Coach Supported Employment as an innovation with a fragile root system. Rather than becoming more secure, they argue that supported employment remained a vulnerable service.

Supported employment is justified ultimately through the opportunities it provides for a valued social role and interaction with other members of the workforce. The nature and quality of interactions with non-disabled people have been studied in ARCs and Job Coach Supported Employment placements (Beyer et al, 1996a). Such comparisons suggest that Job Coach Supported Employment provides a higher degree of interaction and social engagement and time on meaningful activity. However, US research (Lugnaris-Kraft et al, 1988) suggests that people with learning difficulties may experience different inter-personal interactions than their non-disabled peers, receiving more commands and spending less time discussing work-related topics. Furthermore, they missed out on informal aspects of work culture, being less involved in teasing and joking.

In the following sections, we first draw on interviews with key informants in Job Coach Supported Employment agencies to understand their perceptions of the way in which schemes were operating, before considering the positive and negative ways in which such supported employment was experienced by three of the people with learning difficulties who constituted our case studies.

The perspective of Job Coach Supported Employment agencies

Forms of Job Coach Supported Employment have been in existence in Scotland for less than a decade and draw directly on US models informed by normalisation. Funded by local authorities, urban aid and the European Social Fund, Job Coach Supported Employment agencies were located within voluntary organisations. The views of representatives of the two largest service providers are presented below.

One Job Coach Supported Employment scheme run by a large voluntary organisation was based at a city council plant nursery, where workers were trained and assessed prior to moving into the open labour market. The director of this voluntary organisation described them as 'the leader in the field', pioneering Job Coach Supported Employment in Scotland. The only principle of supported employment with which he quibbled was the idea of open choice of job:

> "To talk of free choice is nonsense. It couldn't be more than in the employment field, you know, try as they might, they're not going to be a brain surgeon or an airline pilot. They can do the same as other people and that means they can get a job, but not everybody can be an airline pilot or a brain surgeon." (voluntary organisation manager)

The ultimate justification of supported employment was:

> "To help their self-esteem, bring them into the mainstream with other people and make them feel ordinary. I think feeling ordinary is very important when you've been made to feel as if you're extraordinary." (voluntary organisation manager)

However, a proper job may not be a full-time one, as long as it gives meaningful engagement and reward. In some parts of Scotland there appeared to be a reasonable balance between those seeking supported employment placements and their availability. However, if a welfare market were to operate effectively, there would be an overwhelming demand for the service:

> "Most people with learning difficulties tell me they would rather be working than in an Adult Training Centre. The usual primary objective is to get a job. And a lot of more able people with learning difficulties are voting with their feet – they just refuse to go.... Every one of our Supported Employment schemes has a unit cost less than an ATC placement.... The irony for me is that if there was a proper market we would be inundated with work." (voluntary organisation manager)

This respondent felt that social work departments and ARCs would, in the future, have to make much greater efforts to provide employment opportunities, requiring a major change in focus.

Our second respondent in this area represented another major provider of Job Coach Supported Employment services. This organisation had been in existence for about two decades, founded by parents of young adults with learning difficulties who were concerned about the lack of support for independent living. Job Coach Supported Employment was a more recent service development and was clearly founded on principles of normalisation:

> "Any services that are provided must be within the community, to give people the opportunity to be included. It's all about the valued relationships between people with disability and the rest of society. It's about real choice and that people have the opportunities to develop real skills and abilities and be treated with respect." (voluntary organisation manager)

The principles underlying Job Coach Supported Employment, drawn from the organisation's wider mission, were the following:

1. Jobs must be integrated.
2. We're not involved in work teams or enclaves and jobs must be valued by the employer.
3. It must be paid at the going rate for the job.
4. People should have the opportunity to develop skills through work.
5. Services must be client focused.

There was concern within this agency that social services were encouraging a shift towards work experience rather than real work:

> "'Work experience' involves no training and support and no pay – it could be someone working 25-30 hours a week for nothing.... People with learning difficulties may not learn transferable skills ... that's the underlying principles of training and systematic instruction – you actually have to train the person in *that* job with *that* dishwasher with *that* group of workmates. Someone who can work in McDonald's may not be able to manage in Burger King. So work experience services may be to meet the needs of professionals – not of people with learning difficulties." (voluntary organisation manager, emphasis in original)

The agency emphasised constraints on service development including the benefits system that prevented most people with learning difficulties from earning the going rate for the job. In addition, the crisis in funding following local government reorganisation meant that little money was available to support people with the most significant difficulties. Finally, there was a sense of resistance from ARCs to the further expansion of Job Coach Supported Employment programmes. The closure programme of long-stay hospitals brought with it the prospect that more able users of ARCs would be replaced by people with challenging behaviours and much higher levels of need. Faced with this prospect, managers of ARCs were left to see it as in their interests to discourage more able people from taking up Job Coach Supported Employment placements and in looking for employment in the open labour market. It is worth noting that organisations running supported accommodation might also wish to dissuade their clients from taking up mainstream employment, since to do this might entail the loss of housing benefit, essential to meet the high costs of this type of housing. This point is discussed more fully in Chapter 7.

To summarise, both voluntary organisations saw their versions of Job Coach Supported Employment as informed by principles of normalisation and there was a sense that five years earlier their activities might have been regarded as extremely radical and innovatory. However, although the idea of employment for people with learning difficulties was now widely accepted and featured prominently in the rhetoric of FE colleges and ARCs, there was a sense in which its future development was being stymied by a range of structural factors and the existing pattern of service delivery. If decisions about funding were made purely on cost-benefit assessments to the state and to the individual, then Job Coach Supported Employment providers were in no doubt that demand for their services would mushroom. However, it was very hard to move the inertia within the system that was highly resistant to further change.

Case studies of supported employment participants

In this section, we present three case studies of people on supported employment schemes to illustrate the diversity of the programmes and the way in which they are experienced by participants in relation to their objectives of achieving social inclusion.

Basil

Basil was 50 and of slight build. He wore glasses and when not at work, he dressed conventionally in polyester trousers and an anorak. At the supermarket where he was employed his overall was neat and clean. Basil was soft spoken and uses language in a very deliberate way. He was very well mannered and made a point of opening doors for people. He was described as a quiet private person who made few demands on people and was thoughtful and methodical. Basil travelled all over the city where he lived and to other nearby cities using public transport. He lived with and cared for his elderly parents and also had occasional contact with a sister in London. He was a good reader.

After leaving special school, Basil worked in a biscuit factory, but this closed down and he became unemployed. Failing to get another job, he was given a place at a day centre and hated it, describing it as 'doing jigsaws and sticking things in all day'. He chose to take up a place at a training centre where he did paving, woodwork and fencing. Subsequently he went to another training centre for people with learning difficulties run by a voluntary organisation and based at a council nursery. He found gardening work was very much to his taste but despite many applications to the city council was not given a job since their equal opportunities policy demanded that all applicants were treated the same, making no allowances for a learning disabled applicant. Basil became very depressed at his failure to find work.

In 1992 the voluntary organisation's Job Coach Supported Employment scheme was implemented and Basil was one of the first people to find work through it at a supermarket. Basil felt extremely grateful towards the voluntary organisation, commenting: 'If it wasn't for that place I'd still be waiting to get a job'. His main reason for wanting to work was 'to get a little bit more money'. As one of the first successful Job Coach Supported Employment workers in Scotland, Basil was something of a celebrity. The voluntary organisation had made a video about him and he featured in both the local press and the supermarket in-house publications, who described their commitment to supported employment as evidence of their community responsibility.

Basil's job was to gather together trolleys on the roof of the supermarket and bring them down in the lift to the supermarket shop floor. This produced headlines such as: 'Life is just jolly for trolley Basil'. The reality, however, was slightly bleaker, involving hard physical labour in all weathers. Basil was initially assisted at the start of his placement by a supported employment worker, who helped him to understand the tasks that were required and worked alongside him for several days. Six weeks after his placement began, some problems arose, mainly because Basil had difficulty in communicating with customers and got flustered if there was a backlog of trollies. It was decided at this point that his working week would be reduced to three days. Since then, Basil had impressed the supermarket with his dedication and, according to his supervisor, was regarded as a model employee.

> "You don't need to go after him and say: 'Basil, have you remembered to do such and such?' The only time is, if it gets really busy he hasn't got the mobility of some other staff members. So all we do if it gets very busy is say to someone, 'Will you go and give a hand to Basil'. He never panics, but he can be a bit abrupt with customers some time. He's got a routine and if they try and break that routine he's quite abrupt with them.... But he really needs no help at all. He works really hard and he's very organised.... The job he does he's out in the open quite a lot in all weathers, but he never moans. He has his own set of waterproofs but he never complains like some of the young ones on a Thursday and Friday, who say: 'It's absolutely freezing'. He never complains – that's why I say he's an ideal employee." (Basil's supervisor)

It was clear that Basil took his job extremely seriously, making careful note of his shifts. In addition to his wage, he received Disability Working Allowance and Disability Living Allowance. He was assisted in his claim for Disability Living Allowance by a worker in another voluntary organisation, who explained that in order to claim DLA he had to establish his inability to cook a full three course meal for himself using fresh ingredients. If this criterion for qualification were removed, then Basil would no longer be better off by working.

Work was the centre of Basil's social life, although in the staff canteen he communicated very little with other workers. He exchanged routine greetings but tended to sit with a small group of other supported employees. His supported employment worker emphasised that Basil was included in all workplace social activities and was invited to staff parties. Basil corrected her that there was only one party to which he was invited. Outside work, he attended a number of social clubs run for people with learning difficulties, but apart from this he led an isolated life.

Bobby

Bobby was a tall, heavily built man in his late thirties. He talked effusively and often cracked jokes, enjoying being the centre of attention. He had significant problems with time, dates and money and anxieties about losing money or being defrauded. After special school, Bobby was placed at a resource centre catering for large numbers of people with learning difficulties. Group activities such as games took up most of the day. Bobby's keyworker described it as very old fashioned and felt that Bobby's development was held back significantly by staying there for many years. He was now based at a more progressive ARC that attempted to place people in Job Coach Supported Employment. Bobby appeared to have been subjected to physical abuse at home by his alcoholic father and lived for some time in a hostel before moving into his present supported accommodation. Supported employment occupied a relatively small amount of his week and his timetable was as follows:

	Daytime	Evening
Monday	Supported employment	photography club
Tuesday	Training – chores in flat all day	
Wednesday	Adult Basic Education class	social club
Thursday	Art class at ARC	
Friday	ARC – watch videos	social club
Saturday	At home	social club
Sunday	At home	

Bobby was interviewed by the Job Coach Supported Employment manager at the Adult Resource Centre and it was decided that he should attempt some limited work (not more than 16 hours classified as therapeutic earnings, giving him an additional £15 a week). His first placement was at a Church of Scotland café that he did not enjoy, feeling that he was not treated with respect:

> "The other job I had they were bossing me about, telling me I'm not doing my job. 'I cannae rush, I'm no machine' I told her. She said, 'You get on with it, stop walking about'. I said, 'If you're going to tell me what to do, I'll just walk out.' And I told the supervisor. She said, 'It's a good idea just to walk out if they boss you about'."
> (Bobby)

He was also outraged that someone had walked across his newly washed floor, paying no heed to the energy he had expended:

> "I told her twice to stay off the floor … she just listened to me …
> she just walked right onto the floor." (Bobby)

Bobby's second placement was at a café near to the university. He was both excited and anxious about the new job and described working in the confined space of the basement kitchen:

> "Well it does get busy when I can't get moving about. It's like … it's
> like being crushed in a prison." (Bobby)

The importance of attitudes appropriate to the status of being employed was emphasised:

> "I'm a staff now … I do what I'm told. If I don't do what I'm told
> I know what happens: 'Out the door and don't come back'. I don't
> want that to happen." (Bobby)

Bobby worked in a kitchen under the café alongside two junior cooks and another dishwasher. His main task in the two and a half hour shift was to wash the used milk jugs, coffee pots and containers from the previous evening. This job was usually done by a young man who felt that Bobby worked well and needed little help, although he was not convinced that Bobby was actually needed. Bobby appeared to have friendly interactions with the staff, who made an effort to include him in banter and jokes. He received more instructions than other members of staff.

Bobby had difficulty understanding basic number values and at the start of his employment had no idea how much he was going to earn. He received the following benefits:

Disability Living Allowance		
Mobility component - lower scale		£12.90 £12.90
Income Support - includes		
supported accommodation costs		
(£211.58)+ pocket money		(£13.75) £225.33

For three hours work in the café, he was paid £3 an hour. In his previous job, he worked 12 hours per week and as a result lost his

Severe Disablement Allowance. In his present situation Bobby decided with help from his keyworker that he would be more financially secure if he restricted his earnings to £15 per week to protect his Income Support benefit. In order to benefit from the £15 a week 'disregard', he applied for and received 'therapeutic earnings' status. This required him to have been certified by a doctor as having a debilitating condition that would be helped by gentle employment. In addition he was reapplying for his Severe Disablement Allowance, as this would ensure that his supported accommodation would continue to be met. If Bobby remained on Income Support, he could be moved to the Jobseekers Allowance that would require him to attend job training and interviews.

In the past, Bobby had been left to manage his own financial affairs and had got into financial difficulties. Now, most of his bills were paid by direct debit and, despite having a reasonably large income, very little of this was his to be spent as he chose. By far the largest part of it was used to meet the costs of supported accommodation. However, Bobby maintained that he would rather be living more independently. He disliked the location of his flat, which was near a busy road, and was upset by the intrusion of the housing keyworker, who told him off because of his liking for unhealthy fried food. Bobby was also banned from visiting another resident within the supported accommodation apartment block because it was alleged that he had been harassing her. Overall, Bobby was prevented from working longer hours and living more independently by the complexities of his particular benefits package. The way in which social security arrangements shape wider aspects of the lives of people with learning difficulties is discussed further in Chapter 7.

Lisa

Lisa was a 27-year-old woman who lived at home with her parents outside a small country town. She had meningitis at the age of five and subsequently attended special school before entering an ARC. After ten years in the centre, where her parents felt services had been very poor, Lisa was given the opportunity of participating in a new employment initiative. Lisa was one of the more able people among our case studies. She could hold a conversation easily, although her literacy and numeracy skills were limited. The family was determined that, despite her learning difficulty, Lisa was able to make a significant contribution to society. Her post-school placement in the ARC was against her father's 'gut feeling'. As an only child, much of Lisa's social life centred on her family.

In the late 1990s, a pilot Job Coach Supported Employment scheme was launched in the rural area, which previously offered few mainstream daytime opportunities to people with learning difficulties. A voluntary organisation was contracted by social services to provide a pilot Job Coach Supported Employment scheme to feed into an extra seven Employment Service Wage Subsidy Supported Employment placements that were made available. Other Employment Service programmes were to be tapped into as appropriate, including the Work Preparation programme that offers short placements (usually 6-8 weeks) to assist disabled people back into the labour market after a period of economic inactivity. The plan was to use the Job Coach Supported Employment funding from the local authority to provide job coaching for people for three months, after which they would move into the Employment Service programmes if they were able. As we noted earlier, the Employment Service Wage Subsidy Supported Employment programme is aimed at individuals who are able to survive in the open labour market with little support. It was therefore evident from the start that there was a degree of mismatch between the Job Coach Supported Employment service run by the voluntary organisation, aimed at people requiring relatively high levels of support, and the Employment Service Wage Subsidy Supported Employment programme, aimed at individuals requiring very little support.

It was decided that Lisa would commence a placement in the geriatric unit of the local day hospital on the Employment Service Work Preparation scheme. However the placement was deemed to have failed after 9 weeks. The hospital expected Lisa to perform the job as competently as other auxiliaries and particular problems arose due to her inability to read and write. This prevented her from noting tea and coffee orders and delivering them promptly, one of the key tasks of the job:

> "She needed to be very closely supervised at all times. There were quite a number of the core tasks that despite a lot of job coaching input she still needed to be repeatedly instructed and prompted about doing them; em one of the things that we trying to get her to do more or less independently was making tea for patients in the morning but she could forget between the sitting room, the day room and the kitchen whether somebody took milk and sugar or indeed whether they asked for tea or coffee.... She tended to spend a lot of time

running back and forth and double-checking things. And she just didnae seem to be grasping that at all.... Just because of the short-term memory and the retention of all of it." (Lisa's job coach)

Mealtimes presented the same difficulty for Lisa, as patients meals were labelled with their names. In general, the hospital was cautious about retaining Lisa and felt that she was not sufficiently able to participate in the Wage Subsidy Supported Employment programme. A member of staff in the day hospital, although confident that Lisa had a lot to offer in some areas, felt that a permanent placement was simply not possible because of time pressure:

> "It's like today, just look at the place; it's like a bombsite.... She was great when it came to baths and things; 'cause then there was always two.... As long as there was two, it was fine, but we're not in that position where we can always spare two folk to do something." (Lisa's supervisor)

Health and safety was also mentioned as an issue. The hospital manager felt she would be held responsible if Lisa had an accident herself or was involved in causing an accident. By the end of the placement, both the hospital staff and the supported employment contractor were convinced that it had been an inappropriate choice.

After the failure of the Work Preparation placement in the day hospital, Lisa was given the opportunity to undertake voluntary work in an old people's home. Despite some tensions with another member of staff, Lisa appeared happy with the placement:

Lisa: "Yeah it's all right, I have my good days and my bad days. I get my upsets and that you know, but this week it's been good, but sometimes it's terrible."

Interviewer: "Was it just 'cause you didn't enjoy it or did something go wrong?"

Lisa: "Just 'cause I didn't enjoy it, there's one person she isn't in just now and I'm quite pleased about that 'cause I don't get on with her."

Interviewer: "What's her job?"

Lisa:	"Kitchen, she's too bossy, she tells me what to do an stuff, she won't leave me alone so she gets me upset an that when I go home, it's terrible."
Interviewer:	"What, are you in the kitchen all the time?"
Lisa:	"Uh huh, now I am. When I first started I was in the bedrooms but now I'm in the kitchen a lot now."

In contrast to the lack of support that Lisa received in the hospital, her placement in the old people's home has been much better managed. The care manager had considerable experience of working with adults with learning difficulties and she was able to set up a structured routine for Lisa, initially expecting her to work for only two days a week. The manager explained that she had briefed staff on recognising that Lisa might require prompting to finish a task. Some initial job coaching was provided to enable her to settle into the new work environment and understand aspects of the workplace culture. Lisa was unlikely to move into paid work, but nonetheless she was deriving satisfaction from her present level of involvement.

Discussion and conclusion

At the start of this chapter, we outlined the framework of the type of Job Coach Supported Employment programme that is funded predominantly by social services and delivered largely by voluntary organisation contractors. Such schemes are aimed at individuals with more significant difficulties who are currently not included effectively in Employment Service Wage Subsidy Supported Employment provision. In the US, it is claimed that individuals participating in supported employment are far better off than they would be on benefits. In Scotland, the economic gains were only marginal. Among our case studies, only Basil, who was spending 60% of his week in supported employment, was significantly better off. Neither Bobby nor Lisa benefited from participation in supported employment and Bobby had lost his entitlement to Severe Disablement Allowance by working for more than 16 hours per week. At the time of the research, Bobby had restricted his work to three hours per week, but this was insufficient to allow him to develop work-based social networks. Lisa was undertaking supported employment on a voluntary basis, which appeared to benefit her but raised questions about potential exploitation.

In addition to the financial benefits of employment, it is suggested that supported employment provides opportunities for individuals to enhance their social capital by developing their social networks. The work undertaken by Basil and Bobby is repetitive and Basil's job, gathering trolleys on the roof car park of a supermarket, is physically demanding and isolated. Bobby's job is more sociable but too short-term to allow him to develop the type of social relationships which might carry over into non-work time. Lisa's unpaid supported employment has the greatest potential to provide enriching social relationships. The work undertaken by Bobby and Basil also leads to a considerable degree of surveillance. As marginal workers, they constantly have to demonstrate that their presence in the workplace is justified and their employers claim credit for behaving in a magnanimous fashion by taking them on. Both Basil and Bobby are encouraged to be grateful for their employment and are unlikely to make a fuss over their conditions of employment.

Lisa acts as a reminder of the potential dangers of moving people from ARCs into employment with insufficient support. The hospital's expectations were too high for her to fulfil even with support from a job coach. As a result, she was seen to have failed, although the supported employment agency had probably been over optimistic in their assessment of her existing levels of competence. As we noted in Chapter 5, the inbuilt assumptions of Employment Service programmes are that disabled individuals will be able to slot into the open labour market with little support and accommodation. If these programmes are to be extended to a much wider group of disabled people, then more realistic assessments of support needs will be required. As we saw in the case of Bobby, the regulations connected with one form of support may vitiate the actions of another form of support. It is to the nature of 'traps' that we now turn.

SEVEN

Community care, employment and benefits

Introduction

In earlier chapters, we explored the various positions occupied by people with learning difficulties in relation to lifelong learning in education and the labour market. For the general population, lifelong learning programmes are funded from personal education and employment budgets. For people with learning difficulties, however, lifelong learning is often funded by social or health services. To understand the shape of lifelong learning for people with learning difficulties, it is therefore essential to understand the operation of local social care markets. This, therefore, is the focus of the present chapter.

Current community care policy places a strong emphasis on the principles of normalisation (Stalker et al, 1999b), including an opening up of mainstream daytime opportunities (Scottish Executive, 2000a). In addition a "Close and harmonious working within social work, with other statutory agencies, with the voluntary and private sectors..." is advocated (Scottish Office, 1999, p 9). In this chapter we first analyse community care policies as they developed over the last decade. The nature of contracting arrangements between service purchasers and providers is then explored to identify the locus of power. We finally question the extent to which social care markets are delivering choice and diversity of provision, empowering service users to exercise control over their future life course, through case studies of three adults with learning difficulties in a market town in our rural study area.

Social care markets: purchasers, providers and contracts

The 1990 NHS and Community Care Act placed the responsibility on local authorities to assess individuals' care needs, design an appropriate package of care and ensure that this was delivered. In the policy guidance document *Caring for people* (DoH, 1989) the government indicated the way in which local authorities were to effect change. Central to the process was transforming the role of local authorities from service provider to service purchaser. Local authorities were required to stimulate the growth of the independent, voluntary and private sectors, thereby creating a market in service provision that would increase consumer choice, provide better value for money and higher quality services[1]. However, what was created was not an open or pure market but a 'quasi market' of care provision (Le Grand, 1991). According to Barnes (1997) the key differences between quasi-markets and pure markets operate on both the demand and supply side of the equation:

> On the supply side there is competition between providers, but not all providers are motivated by profit maximisation. Providers compete for customers, although not necessarily for all types of customers, but increasing the number of customers does not necessarily equate with increasing the resource base. On the supply side money does not directly change hands at the point of service delivery. Purchasers may make either block or spot purchases from providers and such purchases come from a budget allocated from public funds for the purpose. Secondly, the decisions about where such purchases will be made are not up to the direct consumer. (Barnes, 1997, p 31)

Taylor and Hoggett (1994) differentiate the quasi-market into two distinct forms of market; the *producer market* that is primarily inter-organisational and the *consumer market* in which the individual consumer personally engages in a transaction with the service provider. The quasi-market constructed around community care is primarily a producer market in which the key agent is not the consumer of the service but the local authority social work services purchasing manager. It is the purchasing manager who decides what the demands and needs of individuals and groups of consumers are. Furthermore, it is the purchasing manager who then, on behalf of groups of consumers, negotiates the terms of the contract with the selected service provider.

Where services are to be purchased on the behalf of large numbers of individuals, the construction and terms of the negotiated contract are particularly important. The anticipated benefits of contracts were seen to be in the creation of a structure providing a legal safeguarding of standards of service delivery, increased consumer choice and value for money. The government policy guidance document *Caring for people* (DoH, 1989) provided local authorities with guidelines for establishing and maintaining contracts. It emphasised the need for local authorities to build trust and partnerships with providers, arguing that this was essential to the creation of 'productive and innovative' relationships. Pricing of the contract was also seen as crucial.

Contracts should be for the delivery of an agreed level of service for a specified price, usually for a defined period. Agreeing prices, defining service and monitoring delivery will provide a framework within which SSDs and providers should be able to:

- live within allocated resources;
- deliver continuing improvements in cost and quality and hence in value for money;
- cope with uncertainty over pay and price levels (DoH, 1989, p 43).

However, while specific contractual agreements may seek to increase accountability on the part of providers, they may also have an inhibiting effect on the development of their services. For voluntary organisations in particular, the loss of autonomy coupled with increased administrative costs may serve to limit their ability to develop more responsive and innovative forms of provision (Knapp et al, 1994).

In addition Walsh et al (1997) drew attention to the difficulties faced by purchasers in monitoring the quality of social care provision. In particular, it may be difficult (due to the problems of observation or professional dispute) to establish the quality of outcomes achieved from a negotiated contract. Similarly, focusing on the inputs is problematic:

> It may be difficult to observe inputs to the contract, that is the 'effort' that is made by the contractor to provide an effective service. It will often be difficult to determine whether the contractors simply did not try hard enough or whether the circumstances were against them. (Walsh et al, 1997, p 36)

Walsh argues that purchasers subsequently tend to rely on the quality assurance systems that particular providers have put in place and the right to inspection in order to ensure the value of the contract. However,

Cambridge and Brown (1997) draw attention to the fact that many contracts stop short of specific procedures to measure the quality of input in terms of goods and services that adults with learning difficulties receive:

> Inspection and monitoring must therefore be sufficient to detect poor heating, food and staff cover, as well as the outcomes of teaching programmes, social contacts in the community and engagement levels. At the individual level this should include monitoring daily of weekly activity plans, and at the group level, staff meetings and the exchange of information and records. (Cambridge and Brown, 1997, p 45)

Noticeably absent from the discourse of contracts within social care is the voice of the consumer. In the absence of actual money changing hands between the consumer and the service provider for the goods or services received, the purchaser–provider contract is dominant. There is no opportunity within the contract for the individual consumer or user of services to exercise their power of 'exit' or 'voice' (Hirschman, 1970). Adults with learning difficulties then have no means to exercise any form of sanction in either the drawing up of contracts or their subsequent review (Cambridge and Brown, 1997). Instead, Community Care Plans (CCPs), in which local authorities are required to state their blueprint for the local provision of community care services, are intended to ensure that local authorities consult service users:

> Section 46 of the Act requires local authorities, in preparing CCPs, consult with DHAs, FHSAs, housing authorities, voluntary housing agencies, voluntary organisations representing service users, voluntary organisations representing carers, bodies providing housing or community services in the area.... (Secretaries of State for Health, Social Security, Wales and Scotland, 1989, p 14)

Writing on the growth of rehabilitation practice in the US, Albrecht (1992) predicted a bright future for those disabled people able to assert their rights and so control the nature and quality of services in a consumer based market:

> For those with resources and access to the system the future is bright. The emergent power of these consumers is forcing increased

bureaucratic responsiveness and accountability.... (Albrecht, 1992, p 295)

However, Albrecht was fearful on behalf of disabled adults and children who are poor and socially marginalised. He also drew attention to the growth of rehabilitation practices, servicing the needs of a range of providers and insurance companies rather than disabled people. Here, we explore whether the bright future alluded to by Albrecht is likely to be realised for adults with learning difficulties through the operation of the quasi-market in social care. Three key questions will be addressed:

1. Has the operation of a quasi-market in community care stimulated the growth of competition between service providers and choice for service users?
2. What are the effects of contractual arrangements on service provision?
3. How well are the individual needs of adults with learning difficulties met within this system?

We focus on the rural fieldwork site, which had a population of approximately 300,000. The area had suffered extensively from the running down of traditional textile based industries, increasing an already high rate of unemployment. Services for adults with learning difficulties were provided by both the local authority and a small number of voluntary organisations. According to Stalker et al (1999b), Community Care Plans in Scotland are increasingly influenced by the principles of normalisation and this was particularly evident in the following strategic objectives for adults with learning difficulties set out in the area's Community Care Plan:

• to enable people with learning difficulties to lead as normal a life as possible in the community through improving their opportunities for employment, training, education, leisure activities and holidays;
• to review and re-shape the use of residential accommodation to meet the requirements of those with greatest needs; to improve the physical accommodation and to look at alternative models of accommodation for those with limited support needs.

In terms of day services, there were four local authority ARCs, each situated in one of the larger towns. In addition, there was one large voluntary organisation providing separate day services for adults with high and low support needs. The distribution of centres meant that travel between sites was often problematic and always time consuming. Social services provision was primarily centre-based, but the local authority, in partnership with two local voluntary organisations, had recently developed a Job Coach Supported Employment programme aimed at developing training and which supported employment opportunities for adults with learning difficulties who wished to avoid or leave day services (as discussed in Chapter 6). In addition, the local further education college had developed two courses for adults with learning difficulties, a two-year vocationally based extension course primarily for school leavers and a part-time life-skills course for those with more severe learning difficulties. Vocational training was also available through specialist LEC providers and the FE college, although in practice such options tended to be reserved for the most able of those categorised as having learning difficulties rather than those in day care provision. Residential provision for adults with learning difficulties was provided by several voluntary organisations that supported both larger registered residential homes and smaller community based group homes.

The case studies presented in this chapter are of three people living in the principal market town within this area. A large voluntary organisation, founded by a religious order, was the major provider of both day and residential services for adults with learning difficulties living in the town and its locality. This organisation had undergone considerable change in the past decade with the closing of one large residential facility and the creation of 12 group homes, while retaining one large nursing home. The day services provided by the organisation had been slower to change but were also undergoing significant transformation.

Purchaser–provider perspectives

The social work department locality manager for people with learning difficulties in the area had responsibility for the commissioning of both residential and day service provision. There was a high degree of tension between the social work department and the large voluntary organisation providing residential and day services in the area. The locality manager, although quick to cite the social work department's right to seek other providers, was clear that in reality they were tied to one provider:

Interviewer:	"If someone came along and said, 'I can provide, privately, a new element of day care', you would not have the extra money for that because you're already funding the voluntary organisation?"
Locality manager:	"Yeah, but it would mean changing the contract. To do that, I mean to cater for 100 people, is a huge undertaking.... So what I prefer to do is work in collaboration so that we can change the way that the voluntary organisation meets our aspirations ... it will take some teasing out to see whether we can do that."

The locality manager was aware, however, of the voluntary organisation's reluctance, despite considerable assets tied up in property and land, to invest in new forms of community based provision. However, the director of the voluntary organisation suspected that the social work department was anxious to protect its own, in-house provision. As a result of this situation the voluntary organisation was cautious about investing in its own services, as the social work department might decide not to buy into them. A type of stalemate had thus developed. Further tension surrounded the nature of the contract between the social work department and the voluntary organisation for day service provision. The director of the voluntary organisation drew attention to the inadequacy of the block contract:

> "If you've got 123 people, 123 gets multiplied by £96 (weekly rate for day-care) ... on a staffing ratio of 1:6 and that is very convenient for a local authority to do because they just write you a cheque and say 'There you are, we'll forget about it for another year'. There's an assumption that everybody's needs are the same and they're not.... There are people who need a 1:1 or 1:3 ratio ... they need additional support and they shouldn't be treated as part of a block, they should be taken out and we should talk about their needs as individuals." (director of voluntary organisation)

The locality manger's response to this situation was to undertake a bench marking exercise that compared the cost of in-house provision with that of the voluntary organisation:

> "What I want to do is look at their costs and make comparisons. I want to look at the dependency levels of their users and make

comparisons and then look at their staff ratios and make comparisons and look at what the opportunities are for people and make comparisons and then hopefully from that come up with some form of baseline ... and then identify if there is any over-funding or under-funding." (social work locality manager)

Although also organised on the basis of a block contract, the residential services provided by the voluntary organisation were less contentious. This could largely be explained by the fact that the voluntary organisation provided only residential care as opposed to supported living. Although some group homes were supported by daily visits as opposed to 24-hour cover, all the residents living in group home provision attracted full residential rates (approximately £330 per week). Initially this might appear an expensive form of provision for the local authority to sustain, but the majority of residents in the service, having moved from the large institutional setting into smaller group homes prior to 1993, had Department of Social Security (DSS) 'preserved rights'[2]. This meant that the local authority had access to £257 of DSS funding to meet the cost (approximately £330 per week) of a residential placement with the voluntary organisation. As reported elsewhere (Simons, 1998), altering this situation would require the local authority to access new monies. In addition it would deprive the voluntary organisation of a very stable and reliable form of income. Both purchaser and provider, therefore, had an interest in the maintenance of the status quo, despite the fact that these living arrangements restricted opportunities for independent living and engagement in lifelong learning.

To summarise, the range of services for adults with learning difficulties in the particular town studied was limited to one independent provider of residential services and the same provider plus a limited range of in-house provision for day services. The introduction of quasi-market principles had failed to stimulate the entry of new providers. The local authority purchaser had no effective choice of providers and was therefore unable to buy services elsewhere in order to meet the needs of particular clients. Likewise the provider was unable to negotiate prices, since there was no other purchaser who might be interested in buying services. In the absence of effective bargaining, tensions between purchaser and provider were evident, in particular with regard to the nature of contracts. The independent day service provider was adamant their service was underfunded and as a result was hesitant to invest in service development without the assurance that the social work department would purchase places at a reasonable price. The social work department meanwhile was eager to gain an indication of the difference in costs between in-house day services and those provided by the external provider. The majority of residential service users in the local authority had DSS preserved rights. This was currently worth approximately £2 million to the local authority. This income was crucial to both the local authority and the service provider, and therefore each had an interest in preserving the status quo.

The experience of adults with learning difficulties

In the following section of the chapter we present three case studies of adults with learning difficulties in order to examine the responsiveness of this market in social care to their lifelong learning needs and the extent to which they were empowered as consumers.

Imran

Imran was a 27-year-old man with Down's syndrome. On leaving school he left his family and the city in which he grew up to move to a rural area over a hundred miles away. This was to access the services of what was seen by his family as a very progressive voluntary organisation. The local authority in which Imran lived agreed to meet the extra costs of his residential care above his DSS benefit entitlement. Imran had lived in residential accommodation provided by the voluntary organisation for approximately ten years. For the first two years of this period he lived in an adapted Victorian mansion situated several miles outside the local town. Following this period, he was deemed capable of more independent living and was moved into a large, shared house close to the centre of the town. Imran presently shared the house with four other men, all of whom had Down's syndrome. The voluntary organisation provided a high level of support for the men amounting to 23-hour live-in cover. Imran had a shared room that was very small and well below the legal size required for a double room. He was unhappy at the lack of personal space:

Interviewer: "Well do you like living in the house with other people?"

Imran: "All right."

Interviewer: "Or would you rather live by yourself?"

Imran:	"By myself."
Interviewer:	"Really?"
Imran:	"Yes. Me and Jack, we share a room, it's not fair in a big house, single room."
Interviewer:	"Do you think it should be single rooms because it's a big house?"
Imran:	"Big house. Terry has his own room."
Interviewer:	"Have you told anybody you would like your own room?"
Imran:	"Yes."
Interviewer:	"Who do you speak to about things like that?"
Imran:	"Liz."
Interviewer:	"Liz?"
Imran:	"Liz tells the managers."
Interviewer:	"And do they say anything?"
Imran:	"Nothing's happened yet."

Together with his family, Imran drew the situation to the attention of the voluntary organisation staff and the local social work department. The situation remained unresolved, with responsibility for extending the house being debated between the voluntary organisation and the local social work department.

After an initial period attending the local ARC (provided by the voluntary organisation supplying residential care), Imran became very bored and voiced his desire to leave. He then attended the local FE college and completed a two-year extension course for people with learning difficulties. This was followed by a one-year course with a local voluntary organisation providing employment opportunities. However, due to what the organisation described as the 'benefits trap' and employers' reaction to 'the way he looked', Imran's Training for Work ended without him securing a work placement. It also ended after just one year, while Imran and his care providers had thought it was a two-year course. This caused problems for Imran, who was convinced he had done something wrong. His carers were unable to replace the challenge of the Training for Work programme and Imran, reluctantly, returned to the ARC for two days a week. He was clear that he would like something different to the centre routine:

Interviewer: "What about the work in the centre?"

Imran: "The centre's all right."

Interviewer: "Just all right."

Imran: "Yes."

Interviewer: "You sound like you're a bit tired of it."

Imran: "… a bit yes, not enough staff about."

Interviewer: "How does that? Does that cause problems?"

Imran: "The staff sit down and do nothing, talking, talking, talking."

Interviewer: "Oh dear."

Imran: "They don't help us with reading, writing, money … they sit down and just talk."

Interviewer: "Do you like the staff?"

Imran: "Staff all right, need more staff."

Interviewer: "What would happen if there were more staff?"

Imran: "Work hard, reading, money, reading newspaper, writing sums and that … be better for everybody … have to be at the centre all day, not out and about."

Frustrated at not being able to work and bored with his routine, Imran had become withdrawn and depressed, causing concern to his family and carers.

Ewan

Ewan was in his mid-forties and lived in supported accommodation since leaving school. His first move from the city in which he grew up took him a hundred miles away to a small rural community where he was found supported accommodation and 'therapeutic' work on a farm. After a period of approximately 14 years this placement broke down and Ewan's social worker found him alternative residential accommodation with the voluntary organisation involved in this study.

At the time of the research he lived in a council house, shared with three other men, situated a short bus journey from the centre of the town. The men previously received a relatively high level of support but this had to be reduced due to the demand for increased staff hours in other houses within the service. When the situation improved in the other houses, however, the staff hours lost in Ewan's house were not restored to their original level as staff involved felt that the men had become more independent. Ewan required very little support, although staff commented that he sometimes '...needed some prompting to change his clothes or to shave over the weekend.' A contrary view, however, was that Ewan '...was always clean and tidy for work with his clothes washed and ironed and himself cleanly shaven'. Ewan often successfully undertook DIY tasks in the house and staff in the home said they felt confident allowing him to tackle small jobs such as leaking taps or waste blockages.

Ewan worked part-time (9.30-1pm) in a supermarket three days a week and attended an ARC for two days. His work in the supermarket was the result of a work placement found for him by a specialist training provider. The Training Agency had originally intended to place Ewan on the Employment Service Wage Subsidy Supported Employment programme but found that he was too able for the scheme, which requires an individual's level of performance to fall between 30-70% of the expected output of a non-disabled worker. Ewan's resultant placement developed into paid work that, unknown to his residential care providers, became full-time for a brief period. During this time, Ewan received full wages and even did some overtime. However, Ewan was in receipt of Income Support from the DSS (preserved rights) amounting to approximately £264 per week. Together with an additional local authority top-up, this took his benefit level to approximately £330 a week that covered the cost of his residential care. The DSS became aware of Ewan's work and notified the voluntary organisation providing his residential care that he would have to pay back to the DSS everything he earned above the £15 per week limit or face losing his Income Support. The voluntary organisation then explained the situation to Ewan, stressing that working any more than approximately 7 hours per week would not benefit him:

> "The average is about £106 to £107. [Ewan's monthly wage packet
> – gross] But I mean, like I think Ewan would work more and I think
> (the supermarket) would have him work more but it might be more
> detrimental to him so it's all explained to him so that he has a clear

understanding that he is not going to be caught any worse than he is in the poverty trap by the company saying do you want to work more hours and they don't pay him for it, that would be even worse. So he works a number of hours that he can get paid the rate for the job for and it's not worth his while working any more because it would just get taken off him pound for pound and it would just come straight into us because all he's doing is he's saving the DSS money." (voluntary organisation worker)

Ewan, trusting their guidance, reduced his hours from full-time to 7.5 hours per week. He earned approximately £26 a week gross of which he had to pay £11.68 to the DSS towards the cost of his own care. Hence his total income consisted of £15 per week from his work and £14.45 from his income support personal allowance, a total of £29.45. Ewan bought his own cigarettes and contributed to a savings plan towards his holidays. Care staff commented that he seldom went out. In order to fill Ewan's week with useful activity, his carers encouraged him to return to the ARC and the following routine emerged, remaining unchanged for several years:

Monday	Work – supermarket 0930-1300	
Tuesday	ARC – print workshop	ARC – print workshop
Wednesday	Work – supermarket 0930-1300	Visits his mother in the afternoon
Thursday	ARC – print workshop	ARC – print workshop
Friday	Work – supermarket 0930-1300	

The print workshop carried out small contract work for private individuals and local businesses. Ewan enjoyed the print workshop and was confident using both the older printing machines and the newer photocopiers.

Although sympathetic to Ewan's situation, the social work services locality manager explained the crucial contribution of his preserved rights to the overall block contract:

"I mean if Ewan could take that with him [DSS preserved rights] it would do something for Ewan but it would still leave us with the problem that the subsidy to the service is lost, there is a void and we would have to deal with that, but at the moment what we have got is a double whammy. We have Ewan needing a completely new care package, which will have to be funded, and we've got the loss of the £257 [Ewan's DSS preserved rights allowance]. At least if he had his £257 we've only got one void to deal with."

Ruth

Ruth was a woman with moderate learning difficulties in her mid-sixties. She had lived in residential care for at least 30 years with the majority of that time being spent in institutional care provided by a religious-based organisation. Having initially been raised by her father in the city, Ruth was introduced to the institution when he became ill and was unable to look after her. The institution itself was closed approximately seven years ago and Ruth was moved into community based supported accommodation. She now lives in 24-hour supported accommodation, with four other women, provided by the same organisation. Although the women knew of each other they were not involved in the decision making process that led to the establishing of their group. Ruth in particular went through a period of depression when another resident came to live in the house. The established group was given no say in this process and it quickly became apparent that Ruth and the new resident did not like each other. They quarrelled frequently with the result that Ruth was placed on a behavioural programme by the local mental health network team. She was also prescribed an anti-depressant drug that she was still taking six years after it was initially prescribed. Ruth took several drugs for a heart condition and to stabilise her blood pressure. None of the staff in Ruth's home knew the purpose of her drugs. Despite the difficulties she had encountered in her home, Ruth was often vibrant and excited about life. She often made remarks about how much her life had changed from the 'old days' and how much better it was now. Attending a local FE college was particularly important in terms of widening her social horizons and developing new skills (see Chapter 4).

At the time of the research, the college placement had just ended. Staff in Ruth's home acknowledged that she had formed new relationships at college but had reservations about enabling her to meet her friends. As the residential status of the home required the women to have 24-hour care and there was often only one member of staff on duty, the women could only go out if the whole group agreed. As a result, a trip to the nearby shops or pub was often difficult. For Ruth to visit her friends, there would have to be a dedicated member of staff to accompany her, which was not judged practical.

Ruth returned to full-time day care when her college course finished but although she enjoyed meeting others she was tired of the contract work the centre undertook for local businesses which included the production of folders for hospital case notes and the painting of small ornaments:

Interviewer: "So there will be changes here?" (Reference to apparent future reshaping of day-services)

Ruth: "Aye...."

Interviewer: "You don't know what they are?"

Ruth: "No ... what we dae or that. What we would like to do is that I was on the folders; well I'm not much on the folders now, 'cause ken me and my friends done my bit at the folding the two of us."

Interviewer: "That's the folders for the hospital?"

Ruth: "Aye and you folding them and you've got to put the lace in them and eh ...oh God when you're pulling the lace through its sare on your hands."

Interviewer: "So you do the folders?"

Ruth: "Aye I still do the folders; I give them help, say people having their babies an that. We do the pink folders that come in and you've got to concentrate an I have been doing that, but now I'm onto another job, you're polishing up the wee ornaments. They're painting it and your ... oh. Oh ... it's a dirty job."

Interviewer: "Do you not like doing it?"

Ruth: "I like it, but you've got to keep sitting all the time and polishing it up. Like the folders, like you, you can dae them and it's easy."

Interviewer: "And can you not go back and do the folders instead?"

Ruth: "Aye, eh ... Ros says that they're waiting on the man coming back to take all these folders away an he says when the other ones come in I maybe get you back onto them."

Interviewer: "So the folders are finished and now you're working on the wee dolls, or the wee ornaments."

Ruth: "I had to laugh on Wednesday, it was that funny, Trish's face got all black and I said 'oh black mamma' ken' eh.... Alexa agreed with me and said 'that's a good one'."

Discussion and conclusion

In the rural area, the social work services locality manager was the key individual purchasing services on behalf of Imran, Ewan and Ruth. However, for both day and residential services there was only one provider, and as indicated above, although it was theoretically possible to change providers, in reality the renegotiation of provision for large numbers of people was extremely unlikely. In terms of day services for Imran, Ewan and Ruth, this situation created an inappropriate and inflexible form of provision. They were restricted to attending a resource centre and participating in collective, routine, organised activities. This was particularly difficult for Imran who, after several years in further education and Training for Work, found himself back in the ARC, in the same routine that originally caused him to leave. Unable to alter the environmental circumstances contributing to his depression, it was likely that Imran's carers would refer him to his GP. Ruth too had to adapt to a full-time placement at the centre following a period in further education that increased her confidence and helped her to make new friends.

The model of day service provision accessed by Imran, Ruth and Eddie was obviously centre-based. However, more crucially, so was the contract made for their provision between the purchaser and provider. The weekly rate negotiated with the voluntary organisation was calculated on staff costs for a 1:6 ratio of staff to clients, providing little room for individual development. Activities in the centre were focused on small contract work, for which it, and not its workers, received 'real' money. Although the voluntary organisation was eager to change the nature of its provision, it was discouraged from doing so by the absence of any capital funding, and the insecurity of existing funding. Conversely, the social work department expected better value for money. The contract between the purchaser and provider effectively maintained this situation.

A similar equilibrium had been established in terms of the contract between purchaser and provider for residential service provision with severe effects on the lives of Imran, Ewan and Ruth. Ewan had been forced to give up his first full-time job due to the threat to both social work services and the voluntary organisation of losing his DSS income support. Acknowledging this possible loss as a 'double whammy', the locality manager also indicated that if Ewan were to request that he be reassessed by social work services, as he was entitled to do, he would not be placed in residential care but supported in his own tenancy. This would create a situation in which he would be able to work and which would ultimately cost the taxpayer less. Although previously securing full-time work, Ewan was likely to remain in his current situation collecting just £29 per week. For Ewan, recent work incentive measures initiated by the DSS will have no effect. Even the therapeutic earnings rule, allowing individuals to work for 16 hours per week without loss of benefit, cannot be applied to his Income Support. The apparently privileged position of having been granted preserved rights resulted in Ewan being forced into giving up full-time work to enter '...a fulfilling life with dignity'[3].

Imran was likewise prevented from working but perhaps more urgent for him was the need to have his own room. Despite the fact that he had raised the issue with management more than three years ago, and that his home, like all residential accommodation, was subject to inspection, Imran continued to share. Neither party within the purchaser-provider division would take responsibility for the capital costs involved in building an extension to the home. Absent from the terms of the contract, such costs were unlikely to be met by either party in the near future. For Ruth, the nature of the block contract for residential care had left her group home with the minimum staffing level. Managing within the available budget determined by the block contract, her residential care provider was unable to provide extra staffing to encourage Ruth's new relationships. Vernon and Qureshi (2000) identified being able to go where you want to and when you want to as one of the most important factors in any individual's overall quality of life. For both Ruth and Imran, subject to the terms of the contract to 24-hour care, this remained impossible. Ruth's increased independence since leaving institutional care had been stunted by the terms of the block contract between the social work services purchaser and her voluntary organisation provider.

Ewan, Imran and Ruth had each sought to realise very basic ambitions for lifelong learning and development within their community. However, the functioning of the quasi-market had imposed constraints on their lives that limited their autonomy. They had each become valuable commodities within a closed and prescriptive market which, in order to sustain itself, was obliged to construct and maintain their identities as adults with learning difficulties. Cambridge and Brown (1997) allude to the potential of the contracting process to build up the power base of adults with learning difficulties "...by negotiating high standards on their behalf and applying the sanctions of the market place if they are not delivered" (p 49). However, it seems that the economic disincentive to implement change remains pervasive, effectively stunting such potential. The introduction of direct payments or user advocacy in the negotiating of contracts would undoubtedly prove a catalyst for change. However, such changes required the support of the local authority that had an obvious interest in preserving the current equilibrium. Ironically, the discourses employed by the social work department and voluntary organisations advocated greater independence, choice and inclusion, but the operation of the quasi-market prevented such goals from being achieved.

The culture of contracting has centred on costs, which for convenience are negotiated as block contracts. This often has the effect of making the support available to individuals inflexible. For those dependent on Income Support, particularly those who have preserved rights, their benefits status is linked to their position as non-workers. There is little recognition that some people with learning difficulties who enter employment may still require some support in their homes. Recent government initiatives to assist disabled people into work appear to be targeted at those who have already been in employment, and offer little support to those who have never before had a job but might wish to do so. There appears to be growing salience in Albrecht's warning of the dangers in gearing policies too closely to the interests of employers and service providers rather than those of disabled people themselves:

> Although industry and government are dominant actors, recent human rights legislation and growing consumer activism are re-adjusting the dynamics of the rehabilitation business. The future of persons with disabilities rests on how well they are able to check the power of industry and government in developing programs and policies to meet their needs. Without that balance they will be forced to conform to the existing business structure, which does not always operate to their benefit. (Albrecht, 1992, p 317)

The particular dis-benefit from which the people with learning difficulties who constituted our case studies suffered was the limiting of their lives to narrow, and 'special', circuits whether residential, occupational or social. It is to try to understand this limiting that we now turn, through a discussion of the concept of 'social capital' that emerged to prominence during the course of the research.

Notes

[1] Through the requirement to spend 85% of monies transferred to local authorities from the social security budget purchasing from the independent sector.

[2] People in residential care and in receipt of DSS benefit to cover the cost of care prior to the 1993 implementation of the 1990 NHS and Community Care Act are entitled to continue to receive this benefit. The DSS benefit is not transferable to forms of provision outside of what constitutes residential care.

[3] From DSS (1998, p 51).

EIGHT

Social capital, lifelong learning and people with learning difficulties

Introduction

A recurring theme in this book has been the interconnectedness of different aspects of people's lives and the cumulative power of lifelong learning experiences to shape future life courses. School and post-school education have a powerful effect on the formation of social capital, which is subsequently reinforced by formal and informal learning opportunities in the workplace. We have already noted that people with learning difficulties are likely to be channelled into a 'special' route at an early age, thus shaping future possibilities for engaging in lifelong learning and developing social capital. In previous chapters, we discussed the way in which special schooling tends to lead into special FE or LEC provision, which in turn may lead to repeated circuits of training or placement in an ARC from which progression is unlikely. In Chapter 7, we explored the way in which particular living arrangements, and the benefits package supporting them, dictated the extent and nature of work and other activities available to individuals.

In this chapter, we develop further one of the key theoretical ideas that emerged through the process of the research and which has flowed through the account so far, the concept of social capital. Defined by Putnam (1993, p 167) as the "features of social organizations, such as trusts, norms and networks, that can improve the efficiency of society by facilitating coordinated actions", social capital is increasingly identified as the key factor contributing to the health and well-being of individuals and societies. Wilkinson (1996), for example, suggests that social capital is an essential mechanism bringing about higher levels of morbidity and mortality in more unequal societies, regardless of their average wealth. Individuals who perceive themselves as much poorer than others are likely to experience dislocated social networks, turning their anger and despair on themselves and their neighbours. Wilkinson's explanation suggests that social capital both mediates and reflects underlying patterns of wealth distribution. As we noted in Chapter 1, European governments have actively promoted the message that lifelong learning is a key transmitter of social capital, with the power to interrupt established patterns of social exclusion. They have been less keen to recognise that lifelong learning may equally well reinforce such patterns.

Social capital is now seen as just as important as financial, physical and human capital in explaining social hierarchies, variations in individual and civic health and well-being and, above all, differential national profitability. This emphasis on social capital may have particular policy implications for socially marginalised groups. If social capital has a growing influence on the distribution of economic and social goods (Field, 1998), it is clearly important to consider to what extent it is accessible to people with learning difficulties among whom there is a particular concentration of poverty. Indeed, recent policies in relation to people with learning difficulties (Scottish Executive, 2000a) may be seen as nurturing their access to social capital. Doubts remain, however, as to whether current policies have indeed succeeded in enhancing the social capital of people with learning difficulties and, more fundamentally, if lack of social capital is a cause or an effect of social oppression. In this chapter, we first discuss some key theories of social capital and its transmission, and subsequently explore the nature and effects of social capital in the lives of case study individuals.

James Coleman: reconciling neo-classical economics and social action theory

James Coleman's theory of social capital (1988, 1991, 1994) is based on the assumption that dominant human capital theories were inadequate to explain why some individuals and societies were richer than others. Gary Becker, in his exposition of a theory of human capital, was himself seeking a theory that went beyond understandings of physical capital in explaining the economic superiority of some individuals and groups. Becker (1964) uses neo-classical economic theory to explore the effects on real income of investing in people through education, training and workplace learning. He points to the conundrum that while a normal distribution of ability may be assumed (although many would disagree with this), wages are not normally distributed but are skewed towards higher earners. Having set out a complex set of equations to demonstrate the cost-benefit effects of investment in human capital both for the employer and the employee, Becker concludes that higher earners are disproportionately advantaged, not simply because of their superior ability, but also because more resources have been embedded in their personal and professional development:

> The economic incentive given abler persons to invest relatively large amounts in themselves does seem capable, therefore, of reconciling a strong positive skewness in earnings with a presumed symmetrical distribution of abilities. (Becker, 1964, p 47)

Becker's version of human capital suggests that individuals participate in education and training not primarily for its own sake, but because of its personal economic benefits. By the same token, the state, for sound economic reasons, invests in the education and training of individuals in proportion to their ability to deliver economic returns to the nation. As we have noted earlier such conceptualisations necessarily construe people with learning difficulties as being on, or beyond, the margins of rational economic investment and thus being subject to the alternative, perpetually vulnerable, discourse of welfare clienthood and burdenhood.

Many objections have been raised to Becker's arguments. For instance, it is evident that many people engage in learning not because of its economic benefits but because of their sense of its intrinsic worth. Many people such as teachers and university lecturers invest heavily in their education, training and workplace learning but do not reap extensive economic rewards. Certain groups, such as people with learning difficulties, have considerable resources invested in their lifelong learning (at least ostensibly), but this investment does not, as our case studies suggest, significantly enhance their position in the labour market.

Becker's neo-classical economic theory is clearly rooted in a functionalist and conservative view of society, based on assumptions that the prevailing social order is predominantly just, rational and necessary and that all facets of social life (including, for example, drug addiction) can be encompassed within quasi-mathematical formulae, of which the utility maximising individual is the principal term (Fine and Green, 2000). Economic elites are seen as having achieved their position because they are both the most able and the shrewdest in terms of their investment in themselves. Such views, as advanced by proponents of the free market such as von Hayek and Friedman (Deakin, 1994), profoundly influenced policies of national governments and trans-national agencies such as the World Bank and the International Monetary

Fund during the 1980s and 1990s. It had a strong impact on UK education and training policy during these decades (Riddell et al, 1998b; Fevre, 1996; Williams, 1996).

Some critics of human capital theory, including Coleman, continue to adhere to Becker's basic premise that there are rational and, implicitly, justifiable reasons for the existence of rich and poor individuals and societies. Their main quarrel with human capital theory is that it under-specifies the salience of other critical variables, particularly the quality of social capital. In his 1988 paper 'Social capital in the creation of human capital' Coleman argues that social capital should be seen as a resource available to individuals in the same way as physical, financial and human capital. It consists of three main components:

> Obligations and expectations, which depend on trustworthiness of the social environment, information-flow capability of the social structure and norms accompanied by sanctions. A property shared by most forms of social capital that differentiates it from other forms of social capital is its public good aspect: the actor or actors who generate social capital ordinarily capture only a small part of its benefits, a fact that leads to under-investment in social capital. (Coleman, 1988, p 119)

Coleman emphasises trustworthiness, so that in doing a good turn for an individual one is reasonably confident that this social debt will be repaid. In addition, trust is reinforced by sanctions that may be applied to those who flout social norms or fail in their social responsibilities. Clearly, there is an underlying assumption that access to social rights involves similar responsibilities for all, and this has implications for those who may be deemed less able to discharge their social obligations. Coleman also warns of the danger for societies who do not recharge their social capital, since this may endanger their human capital. In support of this argument, an example is provided of a middle-class household where parents are so concerned with advancing their careers that they give little attention to their children, who may fail to sustain their parents' high level of human capital into the next generation. Single parent families are seen as particularly deficient in social capital:

> Social capital within the family that gives the child access to the adult's human capital depends both on the physical presence of adults in the family and on the attention given by adults to the child. The physical absence of adults may be described as a structural deficiency

> in family social capital. The most prominent element of structural
> deficiency in modern families is the single-parent family. (Coleman,
> 1988, p 111)

Coleman's evidence is drawn largely from studies of dropout and
attainment in American public schools, although he underplays other
factors which might contribute to these high levels of dropout among
children of single parents such as poverty. Like Becker's work, there is
a tendency to circularity of argument: that those who achieve most in
society do so because of their inherent superiority in social capital which
leads to the formation of human capital and subsequently to physical
and financial capital and to success. Given the trends towards growing
numbers of single parent families and families where both parents work,
Coleman's future predictions are bleak.

> There are important implications of this public goods aspect of social
> capital that play a part in the development of children and youth.
> Because the social structural conditions that play a part in overcoming
> the difficulties in supplying these goods – that is, strong families and
> strong communities – are much less often present now than in the
> past, and promise to be even less present in the future, we can expect
> that, *ceteris paribus*, we confront a declining quantity of human capital
> embodied in each successive generation. (Coleman, 1988, p 118)

The sense of a decline in social capital in Western societies also haunts
the writing of the second seminal author on social capital, Robert
Putnam.

Robert Putnam: the decline of civic virtue

Robert Putnam, largely responsible for the current popularity of the
concept, emerged from a North American political science tradition
focused on for the role of voluntary associations in democracies. The
concept makes its first, and almost incidental, appearance at the end of
study of the effectiveness of regional government in Italy (Putnam, 1993).
In this Putnam ascribes voluntary associations with a primary role in
determining the success of the north of Italy as opposed to the south:

> Local government in Italy as a by-product of singing groups and soccer clubs, not prayer … civic associations are powerfully associated with effective public institutions. (Putnam, 1993, p 176)

Whereas regions in northern Italy have been successful in sustaining stocks of social capital such as trust, norms and networks, southern Italy has fallen prey to a culture in which individualism and family loyalty take precedence over wider civic responsibility. Networks within southern Italy tend to be vertical and based on power and deference rather than horizontal, reflecting the democratic participation of equals. Vertical networks, suggests Putnam, are far less effective than horizontal networks in building mutual trust and reciprocity, since subordinates cannot criticise superiors and the latter are unlikely to support their social inferiors. Putnam acknowledges that:

> Once established, affluence may reinforce 'civic-ness', while poverty probably discourages its emergence, in an interlocked pair of vicious and virtuous circles. Our evidence argues, however, that the 'economics-civics' loop in these interactions is not dominant. Civic norms and networks are not simply froth on the waves of economic progress. (Putnam, 1993, p 162)

The dominant argument from Putnam's initial work is thus that social capital generates human capital and economic prosperity, not the other way round.

Putnam then, in the emblematic *Bowling alone*, turns his attention to the US where he displays a sense of pessimism about the future, documenting the decline in membership of certain institutions such as churches and bowling clubs, seen as indicative of a wider decline in civic commitment (Putnam, 1995a). He initially focuses the blame for the decline in social capital, now the central concept of his work, on the advent of television since this event coincides with the decline in membership of organisations.

In his latest work, complete with dust jacket photograph of his 1955 bowling team, Putnam modifies this position in four significant ways. The blame for the decline in civic engagement in the US is more widely, and somewhat precisely, attributed (2000, pp 277-84): time and money pressures of the two career family (10%); the ecology of suburban sprawl (10%); electronic entertainment, especially television (25%); the replacement of the 'long civic generation' of publicly minded citizens born before the Second World War by the less civic baby boomers and by the anti–civic grunge of Generation X (50%). Secondly, and unusually in an argument characterised by missionary pessimism, Putnam foresees a new age of intensive social capital formation similar to that of the Progressive Era of the US around the turn of the 20th century (2000, pp 367-401).

His third development lies in the distinction between 'bonding' and 'bridging' forms of social capital. The former is "by choice or necessity, inward looking and tends to reinforce exclusive identities and homogenous groups" while the latter is "outward looking and encompass(es) people across diverse social cleavages" (Putnam, 2000, p 22). Both are necessary, the former is a 'sociological superglue' while the latter is a 'sociological WD-40' (Putnam, 2000, p 23), and any one network is a mixture of both forms of social capital. While bonding and bridging forms of social capital may reinforce and develop each in a virtuous circle there may be a direct, and antagonistic, trade off between the two forms. The examples Putnam uses to illustrate this are telling (Putnam, 2000, pp 361-3): individuals who reach out most to family and friends are often the most active in the community (a virtuous circle) whereas the public policy attempt to combat racial segregation by bussing children to schools in other areas led to damaging confrontation between bridging and bonding forms of social capital.

Finally Putnam now, and most significantly for current purposes, explicitly rejects the tendency of social capital theory to a conservative and functionalist conception of social order in which inequality is deemed predominantly just, rational and necessary. Indeed he now makes explicit "strong claims for an intrinsic and universal link between social capital and egalitarian policies", and sees "social capital as incompatible with high levels of inequality ... a complement not an alternative to egalitarian policies". This concern with power and social capital lies at the heart of the work of the final author on social capital from whose work we draw, Pierre Bourdieu.

Pierre Bourdieu: the pyrotechnics of capitals

Bourdieu's use of the concept of social capital is the earliest of the three authors, but is the most underdeveloped and most provocative. Bourdieu's work since the late 1960s has utilised a galaxy of 'capitals' (cultural, linguistic, scholastic, social, symbolic to name but a few) through which he seeks to understand the mechanisms of the reproduction of social and economic power. His focus is almost exclusively on the mechanisms by which powerful groups reproduce their position and this tends to a binary conception of the various capitals: the powerful are characterised by their possession of capitals, the less powerful by the absence of capitals rather than by the possession of different, antagonistic capitals. In this framework social capital appears as the "Diploma; old boy network" available only to the few (Bourdieu and Passeron, 1977, Figure 1, Footnote 5).

In the 1983 essay 'The forms of capital' (Bourdieu, 1997), Bourdieu brings some order to his use of the different capitals. He emphasises a materialist reading of capital: capital is "accumulated labour ... which when appropriated on a private, ie exclusive, basis by agents ... enables them to appropriate social energy in the form of reified or living labour" (Bourdieu, 1997, p 46). This accumulated labour is:

> The principle underlying the immanent regularities of the social world. It is what makes the games of society ... something other than simple games of chance ... the structure and distribution of the different types and subtypes of capital at a given moment in time represents the immanent structure of the world. (Bourdieu, 1997, p 46)

Bourdieu thus posits a unitary capital which "can present itself in three fundamental guises" (Bourdieu, 1997, p 47), economic, cultural and social, with the key theoretical question being how these different appearances of capital transform themselves into each other in order to maximise accumulation. Social capital (at last) is defined as:

> The aggregate of the actual or potential resources which are linked to possession of a durable network of more or less institutionalised relationships of mutual acquaintance and recognition ... which provides each of its members with the backing of collectively-owned capital. (Bourdieu, 1997, p 51)

For Bourdieu, social capital is not reducible to economic or cultural capital, nor is it independent of them, acting as a multiplier for the other two forms, while being created and maintained by the conversion of economic and cultural capital in the "unceasing effort of sociability" (Bourdieu, 1997, p 52). Primacy is reserved for economic capital "at the root of all other types of capital" (Bourdieu, 1997, p 54) and the home to which all accumulation eventually returns. Social capital thus interpreted is not a benign entity serving to create social harmony and economic prosperity for all; rather, it is seen as an unjust mechanism used by the middle and upper classes to secure their privileges against the perceived threat of meritocracy. Within this reading, social capital would be seen as a malign force to be dismantled in the interests of greater equality.

Theories of social capital and theories of learning difficulties

The major theorists of social capital do not make reference to issues of learning difficulties while, currently, theorists of learning difficulties do not make reference to social capital. Both theoretical streams do, however, draw from common sources. Strong parallels exist between the normative functionalist aspects of the work of Coleman and Putnam and theories of the normalisation of, or 'ordinary life' for, people with learning difficulties. The latter are the dominant framework within which policies for people with learning difficulties are framed in Britain and most of the industrialised world (Stalker et al, 1999b).

Before exploring these briefly it is worth summarising some key aspects of such normative functionalist versions of social capital. Social capital is defined as the network of social and community relations that underpin people's ability to engage in education, training and work and to sustain a healthy civic community. Key conditions for the nurturance of social capital include norms, reciprocity and trust, the imposition of sanctions when these fail, the dominance of horizontal, not vertical mechanisms for the exchange of information and support, and the willingness of the community to take on responsibility for the provision of as many social services as possible. Similarly parallels exist between theories of normalisation and the emphasis in the work of Bourdieu on the differential evaluation of cultures and networks and how these evaluation act to reproduce the dominance of the dominant.

Normalisation refers to a particular model of service delivery for people with learning difficulties that derives, *inter alia*, from Goffman's theory of stigma (1990). Wolfensberger (1972) defined normalisation as the use of cultrually normative means to establish cultrually normative behaviours.

If people with learning difficulties occupy valued social roles and merge as closely as possible with the rest of the community, they will be accorded social value and will be able to draw on and contribute to stocks of social capital. Wolfensberger emphasises the overall importance of integration and, as we have seen, suggesting that it might even be necessary for some people with learning difficulties to undergo cosmetic surgery so that they could 'pass' as normal members of the community. O'Brien (1987) maintains that services should see their principal role as assisting the social integration of people with learning difficulties.

Despite the radically different assumptions and conclusions drawn by Coleman, Putnam and Bourdieu there are key shared questions about the experience of people with learning difficulties raised by their diverse work. Putnam's recent emphasis on equality as a pre-condition for the successful formation of social capital leads us to ask if the social location of people with learning difficulties is such as to enable them to form social capital. The emphasis in Coleman and Putnam on the role of social capital in the formation and utilisation of human capital leads us to ask if the networks of which people with learning difficulties are members increase their skills in such a way as to enable them to improve their economic, and thus social, position significantly. More negatively the work of Bourdieu leads us to ask if the social capital, which the networks of people with learning difficulties do possess, is systematically devalued and treated as an absence by the culturally dominant. Finally Putnam's distinction between bridging and bonding elements of social capital leads us to ask if the forms of social capital to which people with learning difficulties do have access limit and separate them from wider forms. We address these questions to the experience of our case study individuals below.

Field, Schuller and Baron in their exploration of the relationship between human and social capital (2000, pp 243-64) suggest that the relationship between an adult learner and different forms of social capital may be envisaged as in Figure 1.

The case study analysis that follows considers the extent to which people with learning difficulties develop social capital in each of the domains indicated and its nature in terms of the 'bonding' or the 'bridging' forms of social capital.

Social capital and people with learning difficulties: evidence from case studies

Kate

Kate was 47 years old at the time of the research and lived in a small country town. She had attended a special school where her strongest

Figure 1: Sources of social capital

memory was of being tied to iron railings by a rope round her neck by another child. Kate lived in a one-bedroomed housing association flat with Robert, her husband, whom she met at the ARC that they both attended. Kate had been married for eight years and was the only case study individual to have a spouse. The flat was part of a larger complex and occupied a scenic position beside a river.

Kate's mother and three sisters lived in a nearby city and although they did not visit very often, they kept in touch by telephone. Kate was aware of family events, worrying about her nephew who had cancer. Her keyworker described her as a 'brave soul' who had not had an easy life, lacking sufficient family support. Kate left home when she was 20, many years later married Robert and moved into supported accommodation, describing this as a natural move towards greater independence from her ageing parents.

There were some financial tensions between Kate and her mother: Kate remembered being annoyed that her mother cashed her Disability Living Allowance and gave her only a small amount of pocket money. Kate's mother had also encouraged her daughter to be sterilised. Kate expressed regret over this but also some relief at not having children:

Kate: "I didnae care if I couldnae have children, it didnae bother me. They just get under your feet...."

Even though Kate was ostensibly one of the most independent of the case study individuals, she was nonetheless closely chaperoned by professionals. She had two keyworkers, one based in the ARC (Jane) and the other attached to the housing association (Maria). Maria helped Kate with budgeting and shopping and also did housing checks to make sure the flat was kept clean. She also checked up on 'social things', making sure that all was well between Robert and Kate. Robert also had support, including a 'stay back' day every Thursday which involved his keyworker providing a checklist of housework which Robert then worked through, ticking off each task when completed.

Kate's life was structured by the following timetable drawn up by the ARC keyworker:

	Morning	Afternoon
Monday	At home	Staff input from ARC
Tuesday	College till 2.30pm	Home at 4.15
Wednesday	ARC	ARC
Thursday	ARC	Housework
Friday	Day off	Day off
Saturday & Sunday	Walks, watchs TV	Walks, watch TV

Within their block, which included only two supported accommodation flats, Kate and Robert initially appeared to enjoy their independence. However, further discussion suggested that part of the reason they 'kept themselves to themselves' was because of difficulties in communicating with neighbours. Kate's main point of involvement was as secretary of the tenants' association for those in disability housing association flats. She found the job difficult but took it very seriously and had maintained her involvement for several years. Kate described the involvement thus:

Kate: "I've got a folder with documents in it, minutes and letters from tenants' meetings and agendas and items and everything.... I don't take it up with me when I go around the houses, I usually take my agenda up with me on its own with a pen when I go round all the houses. If people have nothing to say I don't pressurise them, I just put 'Nothing to say'. When it comes the time on the night of the meeting something comes up."

Interviewer: "What kinds of things do people want to talk about?"

Kate: "Holidays and having barbecues, in a week, on Saturday."

Kate and Robert invited people from the housing association and the ARC to their flat for coffee occasionally. They used to be members of the ex-servicemen's social club until Robert's membership expired. Jane, Kate's keyworker at the housing association, decided that she should investigate and renew this. As a couple Kate and Robert enjoyed going for walks and going out for a meal, but these were relatively rare activities. Occasional holidays were organised by the housing association, with residents being accompanied by members of staff.

Kate recently completed a Lifeskills course at the local FE college. In discussion with Kate, the keyworker identified the main aims of the course as "working on your independence, your independence skills and spending some time separate from Robert. And also computer skills". Despite Kate's enthusiasm to do another college course, there were no further opportunities for participation because demand from ARC clients outstripped the places available.

Kate did not see work as a priority but had been found some part-time voluntary work in a charity shop. Maria, Kate's ARC keyworker, felt it was important for her to develop some aspects of her life independently from Robert. She described the perfect future for Kate thus:

> "If I could structure her life, I'd love her to have a wee part-time job for which she'd get some pay. Also a voluntary spot as well so she's doing both those things. And perhaps going to college as well, I'd just like her to be as busy as possible doing things. I feel she could do that.... She's been saying that she'd love to be something like a speech therapist, you see. So she's not really realistic about her own abilities really. She doesn't really understand the world of work as such." (ARC keyworker)

Kate was eager to keep up her contact with the ARC and felt that working would compromise her social life at the centre that she valued. The nature of her anticipated work – just a few hours a week – would open up few alternative social possibilities.

Interviewer: "Now that you've been to college have you ever thought about getting a job? Have you ever thought about doing some work?"

Kate: "Well I'm supposed to be looking – I'm supposed to be going into shops to have a look at the clothes shops."

Interviewer: "And what's happened about that?"

Kate: "I forgot … I'm not really fussy about working."

Interviewer: "Who's been organising all this for you then?"

Kate: "My keyworker."

Interviewer: "Oh right. She thinks it would be a good idea for you to work?"

Kate: "Aye. Part-time like, not full-time."

Interviewer: "No, but you're not that fussed."

Kate: "I'm not fussed."

Interviewer: "Oh well."

Kate: "Because I canny come here and then work somewhere else."

Interviewer: "No. Would you rather come here?"

Kate: "Yes."

Interviewer: "Yeah. So why do you like coming here?"

Kate: "Company and that, all the folk."

Interviewer: "Yeah. So it's nice to see everybody, see what's going on."

Kate: "I like to know what's happening."

Fiona

Fiona was 53 and lived independently in a spacious apartment in a middle-class area of a Scottish city. She started her education in a mainstream primary school before moving to a special school at age 12. Her professional mother was infirm and lived in a home nearby and her father was dead. Her only sister had a professional job abroad, but maintained contact through annual visits and telephone calls. Fiona's mother had looked after her daughter until she had a major stroke. This meant that Fiona retained a childlike status for many years into adulthood, helping her mother with housework and sharing her mother's social life. Fiona's mother was an active church member and, following her mother's illness, Fiona was supported by her mother's old friends and was encouraged to attend events within the community where she grew up. With the support of her social worker, she also continued to be involved in National Trust and RSPB events. However, it was evident that such contacts were likely to be harder to maintain in the future as the parental friends themselves became less socially active with age and infirmity. A crisis had arisen recently when Fiona had been ill with meningitis. She had been in hospital for several weeks and there was no one available to look after her during her recuperation, since all her relatives were at a distance. Emergency care had to be arranged by the social worker.

Fiona's main base was in an ARC where the following timetable had been drawn up for her.

	Morning	Afternoon
Monday	Bowling at leisure centre	Quiz at resource centre
Tuesday	At home	Skills for Work course, FE college
Wednesday	Reminiscence group at resource centre	Community Education class
Thursday	Supported employment in city council café	Supported employment in city council café
Friday	Personal organisation, FE college	Resource centre group

Fiona was sceptical about the value of the FE college course:

Fiona: "I'm not sure we get anything out of this. We do budgeting, as if I didn't know. We do shopping, as if I didn't know, and travel, as if I didn't know."

Fiona's social worker, Maggie, was concerned about what she was getting from the resource centre, as it increasingly catered for people with higher support needs:

Maggie: "I suppose in the bigger picture I've seen the resource centre changing. I've seen people who are more disabled than Fiona being the target and Fiona will become more and more a fish out of water.... Fiona has in some ways used the resource centre and got the very best out of it, she's done all these courses and been all over the place ... I think, to be frank, she likes the staff there. I think her links are with the staff. I think she likes Jamie, in fact I think she slightly fancies Jamie, but the needs there are changing. What she gets there is changing. I think it's still helpful for them to help her access the odd course and things like that." (Fiona's social worker)

Fiona was herself aware of the shifting focus of the resource centre:

Fiona: "At the resource centre I think I've reached my limits.... The thing I like about it is the fact that I'm there among the people I've known for the last seven years and I think it's because it's home base and I know I can be happy there."

Fiona was quite dismissive of the new clients at the resource centre, seeing them as quite different from herself:

Fiona: "They came to visit and they were pathetic, in wheelchairs and blowing bubbles."

She also regarded herself as somewhat superior to others attending groups alongside her:

Fiona: "You have to watch Bryce because he's not very bright. He's OK when talking about football, but that's about it really."

Maggie, Fiona's social worker, was aware of her somewhat ambivalent attitudes towards her contemporaries:

"She hasn't got many friends of her own age and at one stage I did take her to a Monday Club. But it wasn't quite Fiona. And that really didn't work, although she did persevere, I think she went along a few times. You see Fiona is really happier with people who've got no problems and you know I feel very uneasy putting her into lots of situations that are very labelling because it's not her really." (Fiona's social worker)

An attempt to encourage a friendship between Fiona and another woman with learning difficulties had failed because Fiona felt that she was being 'crowded'.

There was uncertainty about whether Fiona should be seeking a work placement, an idea advocated by the Job Coach Supported Employment agency staff, or supported in her existing social life and involvement in her local community, the social worker's preferred course of action. Maggie, the social worker, commented:

> "She's good socially. Now, build on the positive and keep her in the area. Alan was looking at something that started at 6.00 in the morning and I said, 'Don't start her at 6.00. You're setting her up to fail and that'll really put her off'. So you know maybe I see Fiona in one way and other people see her in a different way.... I would like Alan to see her in the light of a conservative lady and not push her to great lengths.... I think he's got these links with various firms and I'd like to say, 'Stand back and forget it, forget it. Concentrate on getting her something here, something near to home'." (Fiona's social worker)

Fiona had some independent income but also received income support and Severe Disablement Allowance (SDA). She had been very upset recently when her entitlement to SDA had been questioned by the DSS. Despite the fact that she had access to greater resources, she lived very frugally, spending about £25 a week on household items. The family solicitor had power of attorney and, theoretically, could control her financial affairs. This power had never been used, but would come into play if, for instance, a major household repair was required.

Doris

Doris, aged 33, lived in a rural area with her sisters, brother and mother nearby. She had been educated in a city special school. She rented a housing association flat and was able to live independently with some support from the housing keyworker. Doris spent three days a week at the resource centre, enjoying the social contact rather than the activities. It was here that she met her boyfriend, Stephen. In addition to her time at the resource centre, Doris spent one day a week doing voluntary work, serving meals to old people, and had one day a week at home, which she spent on housework. She was employed previously in a local coffee house until it closed and she was currently looking for another part-time job. She had recently been turned down by a number of local employers including the supermarket. Because of her benefits regime, full-time work was not an option. Her social life was busy and she rejected 'special' social activities, preferring involvement in mainstream community events. She was part of the local drama group, went on theatre trips and took part in a slimming club. She also saw her mother and sisters frequently and babysat for her nieces and nephews.

Independence was a key element in Doris' life. Although she was sent to special school, she attended Brownies and Guides with her sisters and was brought up to fit in with the family and the wider community. When she left school to go to the ARC, she insisted on travelling independently rather than by special bus. Her mother commented:

> "I think she's coping very well, I really do. I find myself saying that well, we don't all go on forever and when I'm not here, she's not going to be out on to one of here sister's family. They'll always be there for her but you know, she's independent." (Doris' mother)

Stephen, Doris' boyfriend, lived at home with his mother. Although he visited Doris' flat, they tended to have little time together and were watched over closely by both families. The couple had been on holiday together, but with a social worker in attendance. Doris felt that Stephen was overprotected by his mother, describing scornfully how "his mother runs his bath for him". She was thinking about getting a bigger flat so that Stephen could move in, but Stephen's mother and social worker discouraged this. Doris' keyworker was also sceptical about whether this would work in practice:

> "I think Doris had that [a future together] in mind, but it seems to be, it's gone static. He's a friend and they come and go. That seems to be it." (Doris' housing association keyworker)

Mavis

Mavis was a 29-year-old woman who had cerebral palsy and profound learning difficulties. She spent a considerable amount of time strapped into her wheelchair. Her posture tended to be hunched and she had difficulty lifting her head. Mavis was most mobile when she was left on the floor, using her arms to pull herself around. She also used an electric wheelchair but had difficulty manoeuvring it. Mavis lived at home with her family and there appeared to be considerable tension between her parents and the ARC staff who felt that she was at best ignored and at worst abused. The staff believed that Mavis was "the principal family breadwinner":

Centre Manager:	"Unfortunately, Mavis' mother is ... I think privately, although she would never admit this, is quite ambivalent about Mavis. Mavis doesn't really signify terribly highly in the order of things, and for years Mavis has been the main breadwinner in the family but does she see any of that? No. Is she well treated? No. And I really don't know how Mavis' mother, who is an intelligent woman, actually manages to live with the problem of Mavis.... Mavis' rights being so eroded, and so at the bottom of the pecking order."
Interviewer:	"Does her mum get any help in the home, with Mavis?"
Centre Manager:	"Mavis' mum has every benefit going. I know it sounds critical ... but I don't mean it to. She has ... support, ... support, she has mobility allowance, which buys them a new car every couple of years. Mavis never goes in it, this is the kind of erosion of Mavis' rights. They have two houses that the council put together for them, one of which is in Mavis' name. She has additional heating in her house, except it's never on.... She sleeps on a ... what in other places in other families might be a futon, she has a heap of rags on the floor. Pretty basic." (ARC manager)

However, Mavis' social worker did not view the situation quite as seriously and felt that Mavis, although perhaps not having a very good quality of life, was treated no more harshly than other family members. The ARC staff, however, remain concerned and expressed strong condemnation of the family. They believed that she was not washed at home and her bed consisted of a mattress and old clothes on the floor, where she also had her food. According to their account, she was treated "worse than a dog". Social workers, however, felt that it would be too long and complex a process to make her the legal ward of the authority.

Within her ARC environment Mavis was able to make limited choices. She expressed likes and dislikes by pushing against her chair or moving her head vigorously backward and forward. In this way she was able to express a preference for playing xylophone or listening to music, but she could only differentiate between options if two distinct possibilities were presented. At mealtimes, Mavis was presented with a small sample of several meals and was able to indicate which she preferred. She was also able to express anger by violent gestures, sometimes hitting out at people with one of her arms. She became upset if her routine was broken or disrupted. The centre had developed a five-year learning programme for Mavis designed to help her make choices about her life. It involved spending more time outwith the centre and in activities she enjoyed such as music, but resources were not available to implement this programme.

Staff were confident that if a new person were admitted to the centre requiring similar levels of support, they would attract much more funding. Mavis' place at the centre was funded from a health authority budget. The social work department was contracted by the health authority to provide for 40 ARC places at a flat rate that allowed no additional support for users with high support needs. Mavis was only likely to attract extra funding, if her behaviour were to become threatening or dangerous to others. The service offered to Mavis had changed very little over a ten-year period, despite changes in the delivery and ethos of day care over this period.

Martin

Martin was educated at a special school 15 miles from his home and was very happy there. Following his Future Needs Assessment, it was decided that he should move to a Steiner community where people with learning difficulties work alongside volunteers and paid workers making crafts and food products which are sold. Martin's mother suggested that the family had been attracted to the beautiful setting and the wholesome lifestyle:

> "... It seemed ideal.... It seemed a lovely life, in fact, the sort of life we like ourselves, you know, the outdoors, the gardening and even the kitchens and sort of homely farmhouse type things and the food was very good and wholesome." (Martin's mother)

However, Martin was unhappy and his parents decided that even although other young people were leaving home at 16 or 17, Martin was too young to cope with long periods away from home. After two years, he moved back home, taking up a place at the local resource centre for people with 'mild learning difficulties'. This resource centre is regarded as one of the most innovative in the city, engaging in advocacy work and incorporating an art gallery and theatre where people with learning difficulties participate in a range of creative work. Martin took part in musical activities and classes at local FE colleges, but during the holidays preferred to stay at home rather than travel into the resource centre for social contact with other users. The centre manager was critical of what was currently on offer:

> "With FE there is more and more colleges but when you and I go to college we do a course and then we get employment – what happens with the special needs courses is you do your course but there is nothing after it, so people, some people, have been going to college for years now. Just replaced what we do in ARCs, except there is more opportunity to learn social skills in FE college because of the nature of what is going on out there." (ARC manager)

Accounts of Martin offered by the resource centre manager and his mother differ considerably. The resource centre manager emphasised his need to develop independent living skills and to think about moving into work in the future:

> "We have discussed with his folks and with Martin that he could start to look at areas of employment – I think he has definitely got the skills – he just needs to concentrate on some aspect. There could be something that Martin could do in a small way because he is kind of thorough." (ARC manager)

Martin's mother presented a less optimistic view:

Martin's mother: "There was some talk at the last meeting, perhaps finding a niche for Martin, maybe for one or two days a week working somewhere. There's one of the lads completely away from the resource centre now and he's just working in a shopping centre. I feel in a way I wouldn't want that every day, too monotonous I think and how much would he be earning? I would

> rather he had this variety he gets at the resource centre, meeting a lot more people I think anyway. But one or two mornings would be ideal doing something different, and then you'd see how he coped. ...I don't think he could cope with a permanent or long-term job." [To Martin: "Mo says she thinks you would be able to cope". To Researcher: "Depending on what he would be doing. I just think he's a bit vulnerable."]

Since Martin's sisters lived at home until they left to get married, Martin's mother considered it appropriate that he should be looked after. She knew that he could cook, although he was not allowed to use the gas or boil water in the kettle. He was left in the house by himself for two to three hours at a time, but was told not to answer the door to strangers. Martin's mother found it difficult to envisage a time when her son would become independent. After they were no longer able to look after him, her preference was for him to live with a member of the family or in supported accommodation rather than an institution. For his part, Martin said that he was very happy at home and had no desire at the moment to have his own place to live.

It was evident that Martin's family not only attended to his physical needs but also provided the major focus for his social life. Martin's mother had not worked full-time since he was born and devoted her life to doing things with him. At weekends, they went for bike rides, walks or swimming together and they were very warm and affectionate. Martin's mother described her son as a 'lovely chap' and said she really enjoyed his company. If friends came to the house for dinner or the parents were invited out, Martin always accompanied them. He did not have friends of his own age and his mother recognised that they might not have done enough to encourage this. In the place of real friendships and relationships, Martin fantasised about going out with characters from *Neighbours*. Martin himself was aware that he was different from other people. At the Research Group of people with learning difficulties that we organised (Riddell et al, 1998b), he described his feelings of unease when he sensed that people were staring at him on buses or in the street.

In many ways, Martin occupied the position of privileged and much loved youngest child in his family. His bedroom resembled that of an early teenager, with pictures of soap stars mingling with family photographs. At home, he was surrounded by people who loved him and encouraged him in his main interest, classical music. In the background, however, there was the fear and recognition that this protected existence could not go on forever and that Martin was ill-equipped to survive in the outside world. Here, many things that were not a problem within his family, such as his lack of clear spoken language, were likely to represent major barriers to social acceptance and participation.

Mick

Mick was a man of 33 years who lived at home, in comparatively straitened financial circumstances, with his widowed mother. He had an elder brother, also impaired, who worked and lived independently. Mick had Down's syndrome and attended the same flagship resource centre as Martin where he was thought to be one of the most able clients. Mick had lived in the same house for 30 years. The family had moved to this house from a much loved previous house because the neighbours mostly sent their children to high status private schools and the consequent stigma of Mick's 'special' bus:

> "We had to sit there for hours – the buses always came late. All the time you are listening to this 'and so and so has got into so and so High [school] and so and so has got into Very Posh Academy'."
> (Mick's mother)

The new house had a secluded back garden from which Mick was not allowed to wander. Mick's sibling also suffered from significant impairments. When the children were young Mike's mother found appropriate public services difficult to access. Mick first went to a mainstream nursery after a long fight for admission by his parents and then he went on to two special schools. There he progressed well academically and stood up for himself against others placed in the schools for behavioural reasons. Dissatisfied with the level of education provided for their children, both parents worked long hours to pay for private tutors to help them with their impairments. This was successful in that Mick was literate and numerate while his sibling held a 'mainstream' job, lived independently and was an activist in a local disability organisation. Mick's memory of schooling was less positive:

Researcher: " What kinds of things did you do at school?"

Mick:	"You best no to think about my past – too embarrassing."
Researcher:	"Embarrassing? What was embarrassing about it?"
Mick:	"I kicked somebody at school. With my knee."

Mick had his own room decorated with Spice Girl posters and pictures of his sporting activity that he pursued to medal level in the Special Olympics. He had a share of the domestic responsibilities.

On weekdays he attended the resource centre where he was a dominant figure, sometimes in a competitive manner, sometimes through arguing the case for the users of the centre. When the social work department "cut (the bonus) from £8 to £2 and then it was gone" Mick had been:

> "Talking about it, writing about it, all the discussions to have, talking about the bringing back the bonuses. Money. And that's been taken away.... I'm going to do something about it. I'm going to make a petition. To bring it back." (Mick)

The centre did not provide an extensive amount of activities in-house but established an individual timetable of activities, mostly 'special' activities for people with learning difficulties, in other locations. Mick had a full timetable of activities and was an active student on courses in local FE colleges. However, the sense Mick gave of at least parts of his weekly round, an evening club run a major charity, was that of resignation:

Researcher:	"What's happening at the club this week?"
Mick:	"As always. The same as usual."
Researcher:	"Do you ever get fed up of it being just the usual? Do you think they should try something different? Or do you think just the usual is best?"
Mick	"Well, it's just the usual."

There was a tension between Mick's mother and the resource centre over the expectations of independence for him. Mick's mother, talking about an incident when he had been enrolled in a 'mainstream' course on Scottish politics rather than the 'special' one and from which he had to make an embarrassing exit, said:

"I think they expect a little bit more from them than they are able for but then that is a mother talking against a professional ... they say their mothers are their biggest handicap. I think we know them best." (Mick's mother)

On the other hand the resource centre thought that Mick could be more independent but was "smart enough to know that that would be a hard option for him and why should he give up the one that he has got?" (Mick's ARC keyworker).

Mick also worked. His first job was in a sports centre but when, after two and half years, he still had not been paid, he left. He then had one paid job before the current one, a job that paid the going rate for two hours' clerical work at a large local service facility. Mick had to dress in a suit or similar for this job and his mother reported:

"His brother and father went out dressed for work and it makes him feel the part, going out like that. But having said that it means he finishes work at 11,00 and he has got to come home. He can't [go] on into the centre or the baths or something – he has got to come home and change." (Mick's mother)

Mick was clearly interested in forming relationships with women. For ten years he was interested in the sister of another person who went to the special disco and one afternoon went and bought her an engagement ring with the money carefully saved for the Special Olympics. Mick's parents intercepted, and returned, the ring:

"But we showed it to Petra and told her you had to get a father's permission to do anything like this, and all that. She was young at the time and I felt sure that she wasn't as emphatic as she might have been to put him right off.... I don't think the individual would have the capacity to have aims really. Fantasies about marrying and all that sort of thing, having children – nothing Mick would like more than for his wife to have a baby and all that sort of thing. Unrealistic, their interpretation...." (Mick's mother)

In the place of such real life relationships it appeared that Mick had a series of fantasy relationships with popular icons, The Spice Girls, Kylie Minogue and female wrestlers.

Bryce

Bryce lived in a large Scottish city. In his mid-fifties, he was a slight man who looked older than his years. He attended a special school where, during his later years, he learnt to mend shoes, a trade that he was never able to put into practice. He had never worked nor had a girlfriend, sources of great sadness to him. His retirement ambition was to get a job. Bryce lived with his mother until she died, and he then moved into accommodation under the Community Landlady scheme. His community landlady felt that his mother's death had been particularly hard for him to come to terms with because until then he had lived in a very sheltered environment. She described the way in which Bryce's sister looked after him:

> "Bryce's sister was in America but she was home when her mum was dying and we were on an outing.... I was just getting to know Bryce at this stage and we were in one of the big restaurants and she sat and she actually took Bryce's coat off him, she drew back the chair, she sat him down, pushed his chair in, put the napkin, tucked it round his neck for him and then proceeded to cut up his sausages."
> (community landlady)

When his mother died, Bryce was forced to make a sudden move out of the family home into a hostel for people with learning difficulties, where he had difficulty fending for himself in an impersonal environment. At the time of the research, Bryce had no contact with any family members. He appeared reasonably contented at the community landlady's house, although staff at the ARC thought he might be frightened by the man with whom he shared a room. The didactic nature of the relationship between the landlady and the tenants was also evident:

> "If I go to give Bryce a row, I feel very guilty because he ends up standing there like a wee ten-year-old who feels as if he is waiting to be pounced on and you can see him – his eyes, and he starts to get that stern look and his wee bottom lip starts to go and I say, 'Bryce, I am not going to pounce on you but you are wrong so you are getting a row.' Basically the things Bryce gets a row for is being unshevelled, unshaven and not keeping himself clean and tidy and it is an ongoing battle with him." (community landlady)

Part of the community landlady's job was to encourage the residents to become more independent by helping with household jobs. However, it was clear that the landlady subscribed to the view that it was inappropriate for middle-aged men to be involved in housework and that her interventions had to measured:

> "At 55 – I mean I am told that I should be involving him more in doing cooking and doing their laundry, doing their ironing – at one point I had Bryce doing his ironing and he was just a nervous wreck and I thought – I am giving this man more grief because I am told I am trying to make him better – I am actually making him worse, so I am not doing it." (community landlady)

He attended many centres and courses for people with learning difficulties around the city, and his resource centre keyworker felt the long journeys by bus and on foot were in danger of exhausting him. There was also concern that he was repeating courses rather than finding new ones that would extend him. The table below illustrates the range of activities in which he was involved:

	Morning	Afternoon
Monday	Craft activity in resource centre	Quiz in resource centre
Tuesday	FE college: Going for a walk	FE college: Going for a walk
Wednesday	Adult Basic Education class	Relaxation class in centre
Thursday	Art class at resource centre	Placement in horticultural project
Friday	Resource centre: watch videos	Group meeting with keyworker
Saturday	At home	At home
Sunday	At home	At home

Bryce had never had the opportunity to work, although in the past he had participated in a horticultural project. He believed that the reason he had never had a girlfriend was because he did not have a job and therefore had no money.

Most of Bryce's social life took place in special settings. On a number of evenings each week he was taken to and from a club in a social work minibus. His keyworker at the ARC said that although the idea of segregated social arrangements made her cringe, many people with learning difficulties enjoyed these events because of the opportunity it gave then to network. In addition to the social clubs, Bryce was taken for an outing once a week by a befriender. The centre keyworker described the purpose of the relationship in the following way:

> "They go out every Saturday together – Littlewoods for a cup of tea. In some ways having a befriender for Bryce is meeting other people and doing other things. More of an equal relationship than controlling you and telling you where to go and what to do." (resource centre keyworker)

At other times, Bryce, like other people with learning difficulties, encountered hostility in his daily routines:

> "I know from people's experiences they are not treated as adults – they get abuse every day from kids on the bus and there is stuff that goes on which is horrendous. I think we are living in a society that fears people with learning difficulties. We never see anyone with learning difficulties as sexual so there is a huge battle there." (resource centre worker)

Bryce experienced periods of anxiety and depression, triggered by traumatic life events but also due in part to the monotony of his weekly resource centre timetable. He had become very depressed after the death of his mother and a recent road accident, when he had been knocked down and had broken his leg, had again led to a sudden loss of confidence. At the time of the research, he was taking anti-depressants and was also being taught relaxation techniques at the centre.

Liam

Liam was 44 and for a few years has lived with his older brother's family in a Scottish city. Previously he stayed with his mother and father, but his mother was unable to cope after her husband died. Liam spent most of his time at the local resource centre, and recently took part in a supported employment scheme for three days a week. Reports from the placement revealed that this was not a success. He did not enjoy participating in the squad and his work rate was seen as poor. He also antagonised members of the squad by "keeping them right" and his outbursts were deemed to be alarming to the public. Liam himself felt that the work was too arduous for him and he felt exploited. The placement was eventually discontinued and Liam returned full-time to the ARC.

Liam's brother, a middle manager himself, had a scathing view of social workers, believing that their assessment of Liam's abilities was unrealistic and their promise of independent accommodation is unlikely to happen. He did, however, acknowledge that the ARCs had improved. The first centre that Liam attended when he left school was described thus:

> "He was there for four years and the staff there were just like jailers. They just kept him there and the people who ran the centres had no qualifications. It was just the dross of the social workers. They were dumb and basically they just kept them there watching videos and there was no education." (Liam's brother)

Liam's brother was anxious about the prospect of losing the ARC placement, but was also cynical about social work's ability to deliver the person-centred services in the community that they promised. Staff were described as "condescending" and "not particularly helpful".

Liam's brother had put considerable energy into arranging social activities for his brother. With a helper, he ran a social club for adults with learning difficulties in a local hall. Apart from his immediate family and workers at the resource centre, Liam had little contact with non-disabled people. His brother described the difficulties encountered:

> "You get people who cross to the other side of the street because they think they're contagious ... there's still a lot of name-calling." (Liam's brother)

Discussion and conclusion

At the start of this chapter, we outlined some central thinking of social capital theorists and considered the implications for people with learning difficulties. We noted Putnam's contention that equality is a prerequisite for the formation of social capital and Bourdieu's view that social capital, far from increasing social cohesion, is actually more likely to operate in the interests of the socially powerful to reinforce their position of privilege.

Figure 2 summarises the position of people with learning difficulties in relation to the principal sites of social capital reproduction. Strong ties, associated with Putnam's idea of bonding, often link disabled people to family, friendships and sub-cultures, voluntary organisations and initial education. However, even though these ties may be strong, the nature of the social relationships they support are fundamentally disadvantaging to the person with learning difficulties. Within the family, for example, the person with learning difficulties is likely to occupy the role of eternal child or orphan. A significant number of case study individuals experienced a catastrophic shift from the status of being a protected child to that of being an abandoned child. Bryce, for instance, was forced to make a sudden move from the family home into a bleak hostel environment. His elder sister lived overseas and broke off all contact with him. Fiona also enjoyed a relatively privileged middle-class upbringing but, at the time of the research, was living at home. She saw her sister for an annual visit, although telephone contact was maintained. Despite ongoing contact with her mother's church community, when Fiona was seriously ill there was no one to look after her. People like Mick and Martin, who were still living in the parental home, enjoyed nurturing social relationships that would inevitably be lost when their parents became infirm or died. The family was not necessarily a nurturing environment. There were also examples among our case studies of parents thought to be exploitative and abusive, for instance, those of Mavis and Greg. Overall, adults with learning difficulties were involved in strong bonding relationships with their families for much longer than other adults, as the cases of Mick and Martin illustrate. This was often because of the structural barriers to establishing independent homes. Kate and Doris had clearly succeeded in achieving some degree of independence, although their relationships and living arrangements were monitored closely by professionals. Doris was unlikely to have a child and Kate had been sterilised before marriage.

Strong friendship bonds tended to adhere to relationships based in ARCs and special social clubs. Some individuals like Fiona appeared to have stronger relationships with professionals and some contempt for users with more significant impairments. Others, however, valued their contact with other service users and valued the sense of long-established contact. While professionals looked for opportunities of moving individuals into mainstream daytime opportunities, people with learning difficulties such as Doris clearly valued the social aspect of ARCs, even if they found the activities dull and repetitive. Case study individuals experienced strong links with their primary and secondary schools, but

Figure 2: principal relationships of individuals with learning difficulties to sources of social capital

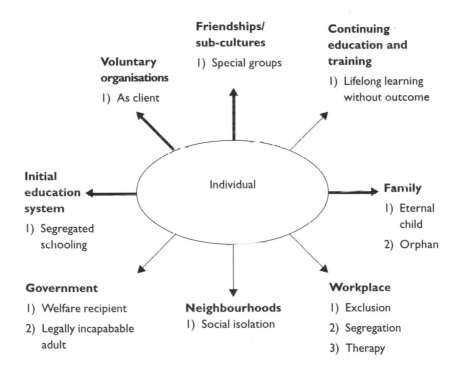

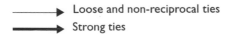

rather than providing them with social networks which could be drawn upon in later life, special schools played a major role in establishing a 'special' and exclusive identity which led into segregated post-school services removed from the labour market. Whereas many young people draw on social networks established in school to gain a foothold in the labour market, special schools provided no such valuable social links.

Loose and non-reciprocal social ties, on the other hand, existed in relation to the public spheres of education and training, the workplace, the neighbourhood and government. Rita, discussed in Chapter 4, provided an example of the difficulty in sustaining friendships developed in a one-year college course. Living in a rural area, it was impossible for her to visit her new friends independently because of lack of transport and residential staff had no time to take her on visits. Just as post-school education was fragmented and short term, so too was employment. Those participating in supported employment were often at the periphery of the workplace, spending only a few hours a week in work because of benefits regulations (as discussed in Chapter 6). In terms of engagement with governance, people with learning difficulties were often involved in users' groups in ARCs, but these tended to deal in micro-choice issues, such as arrangements for the Christmas party, rather than larger issues to do with the nature of services and the links to wider social relations. Kate was perhaps the most politically engaged, taking a leading role in a disabled people's tenants' association.

The individuals in our study appeared to have strong social networks in some social domains, but these ties tended to reinforce their position of social marginality rather than offer opportunities to challenge inequality. The weak social connections in other areas of their lives contributed to their sense of social fragmentation, but did not enable them to build bridges into new and more empowering social domains. Granovetter (1973), in his 'strength of weak ties' thesis, pointed out that weak ties, associated with bridging, were likely to be more useful in achieving economic advancement than strong ties, associated with bonding. This was particularly likely to be the case for socially disadvantaged groups, who use informal networks to gain employment. De Souza Briggs (in Putnam, 2000, p 23) made the same point, noting that bonding social capital is good for 'getting by', whereas bridging social capital is good for 'getting on'.

The strong ties of people with learning difficulties do not appear to be particularly good even at helping them to get by. The type of relationships they maintain are sometimes those of love and inter-dependency within families, but more often, and particularly once the primary bond of the family crumbles, they are more likely to involve powerlessness and dependency. Based on the experience of the case study individuals, there is much evidence to support Wolfensberger's warning that societies may base their sense of solidarity on the exclusion of those perceived as deviant, in this case people with learning difficulties who embody deep fears of the imperfect and the unknown.

Finally, people with learning difficulties illustrate the need for further development of Bourdieu's ideas. As we noted earlier, Bourdieu adopted a classical Marxist position, arguing that the economic base was ultimately deterministic and that other forms of capital were instrumental in the transmission of social advantage or disadvantage which rested on the individual's possession of wealth. However, the middle-class individuals in our study, Fiona, Martin, Imran (in Chapter 7) and Clare (whose position we analyse in Chapter 9), illustrate that the status of being a person with learning difficulties overrides the social privileges attendant on class position. Fiona and Clare, although wealthy, cannot access their money. Furthermore, their middle-class social networks have rapidly diminished as their parents have grown infirm or have died, demonstrating the fragility of their inherited social capital. Our case studies also illustrate the importance of gender in the transmission of social capital. Women, generally, had stronger social networks than men, partly because they were expected to be domestically independent and to engage in reciprocal caring relationships, babysitting for relatives or working as a volunteer in an old people's home (Elizabeth) or in a city café (Fiona). Men like Bryce were assumed to be incapable of looking after themselves, but rather than this being a privilege, it further reinforced their helplessness. In assuming that social capital is smoothly transmitted from one generation to the next, Bourdieu ignores the importance of intervening variables such as the status of learning disability and the salience of gender. Finally, in postulating a dichotomy between possessing social capital, the condition of the middle class, or lacking social capital, the position of the working class, Bourdieu ignores the fact that all social groups possess social capital. The key difference is whether it may be used to sustain or create other sorts of capital, particularly wealth, or whether it acts to reaffirm an individual's subordinate social status. It is to how the lives of the people who constituted our case studies were regulated which we now turn.

NINE

Regulated lives

In this chapter we bring together the themes of the previous eight chapters in order to offer an interpretation of the life situations of the people with learning difficulties whom we have studied. We will do this by, first, further discussing our position within the social model of disability. We will then review the development of categories and procedures in the Scottish legal system by which people have been declared incompetent in the tasks of daily life and therefore subject to special regulation. We will then analyse the position of three of our case study people, giving an extended case study of the consequences of such a classification for one woman. We will then suggest that people with learning difficulties are, due to their particular forms of, and relationships to, social capital, subject to invasive regulation by the power/knowledge of different professional groups. These discussions lead into our final chapter in which we explore the policy implications of our work.

In the first chapter we stated that we used an 'operational' rather than a 'medical' definition of learning difficulties in that we were interested in people so labelled by service providers. This is consistent with the 'social model of disability' discussed in Chapter 5 which locates disability in the barriers to full social participation experienced by people with impairments rather than in the impairment itself. For people with learning difficulties, one of the barriers is the label. The case studies provided consistent examples of how the label is flexible, contested and consequential: its flexibility is illustrated in our discussions of how it was becoming applied to increasing numbers of people, even communities, by LEC officials concerned about 'employability' (see Chapter 3) or by our account of how Ronald became (precisely) 50% disabled overnight as the public utility was groomed for privatisation (Chapter 5); its contestation is illustrated by Iona's employer firmly rejecting the imposition of the label on her chosen successor as chief cook (Chapter 4) or by Greg's father objection to his being "parried with the Mongols" (Chapter 5); its consequentiality is illustrated by

Ewan's having to give up full-time work in order to maintain the label as the warrant to his major source of income (Chapter 7) or, most starkly, by the case of Clare which we discuss later in this chapter.

In Britain there is a long history of labelling, and treating, people as legally different on the basis of imputed incompetence (Baron and Dumbleton, 2001: forthcoming; Wright and Digby, 1996). From the 13th to 19th centuries in England the *Prerogativa Regis* held that:

> He who shall be said to be an Idiot from his Birth is such a Person, who cannot account nor number twenty pence or cannot tell who is his Father or Mother, or how old he is etc. So that it may appear that he hath no understanding of Reason, what shall be to his profit or what shall be for his Loss. (Fitzherbert, 1534, quoted in Brydall, 1700)

The *Prerogativa Regis* allowed the Court of Wards to hold an inquest in which a lay jury assessed the competence of the person in question to manage their own affairs in terms of the above criteria. Neugebauer's study of the "virtually uninterrupted administrative history" from the 13th to the 19th century of this court shows that the mechanism was used not only for the upper class but also for ranks immediately below that of gentleman, but only the "occasional blacksmith or yeoman" appeared (Neugebauer, 1996, pp 23, 27). The finding of idiocy resulted in the management of the idiot's affairs being taken over by the Crown (to some profit). Less costly mechanisms, and more limited forms of guardianship, were developed from the 17th century but these, as with full guardianship, were restricted to idiots with significant assets. Poor idiots did not appear before such courts but were cared for largely by the family.

From the 17th century onwards the records of the Poor Law administration document the criteria to be used by magistrates in determining idiocy, the support given to the families of idiots and, from the 18th century onwards, the gradual incarceration of idiots into workhouses (Andrews, 1996). This marked the beginning of the 'professionalisation' of idiocy by which the definition, and increasingly the regulation and relabelling, of idiots was transferred from lay juries and the person's immediate social network to professionals. In particular, from the early 19th century the use of a jury to establish the definition of somebody as an idiot disappeared and the judgement was made on the basis of certification by two doctors; from the mid-19th century medically controlled asylums became the "natural habitat" of the idiot

(Baron and Dumbleton, 2001: forthcoming) and this lasted until the latter part of the 20th century. The decarceration of person with learning difficulties and the ensuing interprofessional struggles (especially over terminology) provided the backdrop to our fieldwork.

The development of the classification of people as incompetent, and the mechanisms for their regulation, in Scotland followed a parallel, if less well documented, path. By the 13th century the distinction between the 'fatuous' and the 'furious' was well established in old Scots law. In the former case the feudal lord assumed responsibility for the assets while in the latter case the Crown did (Baron and Dumbleton, 2001: forthcoming). From the 14th century Scots law, increasingly informed by Roman legal principles, was concerned with the personal 'tutelage' (welfare) of the fatuous as well as with the management of their material affairs. From then until the 2000 Adults with Incapacity (Scotland) Act a piecemeal system developed whereby the person with learning difficulties might be subject to the management of: a tutor-dative as personal guardian and financial manager; a curator bonis as financial manager; a statutory guardian under the 1984 Mental Health (Scotland) Act as an emergency and limited intervention; a tutor at law as personal guardian and financial manager (Ward, 1984, 1990). The tutor at law system has been in desuetude since 1924 as was the tutor-dative system until there was a test case revival in 1986. In addition there is the possibility of enduring powers of attorney being granted by a person with learning difficulties so that another person may manage their financial affairs. The overwhelming majority of people with learning difficulties are, however, not subject to special legal regulations but to:

> 'Informal voluntary arrangements' under which the problems of lack of legal capacity are solved either by agreeing to ignore the lack of legal capacity, and the resultant lack of legal validity, or by allowing someone to act for the mentally disabled person without having, strictly speaking, any authority to do so. (Ward, 1990, p 90)

In our sample of 30 case studies there was one person subject to such formal powers, one person where such powers were being held in reserve and one person where the threat of the use of such powers had been used by the local authority.

In this last case Jack, whose weekly timetable we analysed in Chapter 4, was threatened with a statutory guardianship order when social workers became concerned that he was being abused at home. Jack was 21 and lived in the rural area case study area. He was tall and energetic with disjointed conversation with almost alternate words being 'fuck'. One day when building work prevented him from gaining access to the woodwork room at the resource centre Jack became very agitated and spent some time swearing and shaking his fists at the plastic barrier erected to protect the work site. His keyworker attributed this erratic behaviour to Fragile X Syndrome. His brother also suffered from this syndrome and lived in supported accommodation nearby; staff at the resource centre describe Jack's parents as having learning difficulties. Prior to the fieldwork they had become suspicious that Jack was being emotionally and physically abused at home by, for example, being locked in his room for long periods. The keyworker and Jack reported it thus:

Keyworker: "I went through months of listening 'I don't want to be here. I hate it. I'm sore. I've got bruises ... blah, blah, blah' ... but then with a lot of work he started to get more open about it and he actually spoke to the police about it" [To Jack] Didn't you Jack? Yeah, you did.

Jack: "I did aye."

Keyworker: "So things got a lot better so I came to the conclusion."

Jack: "Things better now ... relaxed at the end of it."

Jack being an adult, the social workers and psychologists did not have the powers available had he been a child. After a period of assessment they were on the point of taking out a statutory guardianship order which would have allowed the local authority to specify where Jack should live and what activities he should attend. At this point Jack "came out and ... made that choice" (Jack's keyworker) to leave the family home and enter supported accommodation. This decision was resisted by the family who threatened legal action to challenge it. The trauma of this move and the ensuing conflict, during which Jack's clothes had to be burnt for hygiene reasons, was still evident when we conducted out fieldwork almost a year later. Shortly into the fieldwork Jack's mother died suddenly and we withdrew to avoid adding to the difficulties.

An enduring power of attorney was in operation in the case of Fiona, the middle-aged woman living in a middle-class urban area whose support by her late mother's circle of church friends we outlined in Chapter 8. Fiona is not financially dependent on benefits partly due to her inheritance and partly due to the ongoing (all-round) support of a highly paid sister living abroad. Fiona's support worker describes her as being "actually very good with money so she copes very well". Fiona has executed an enduring power of attorney in favour of a local solicitor but this is not used. It is in place in case of a major item of expenditure becoming necessary: "… a large sum of money … she wouldn't be capable of being involved in decision making about the spending of that or the repairing of the roof or things like that. Somebody needs to take over" (Fiona's home support worker).

The main legal system at the time of fieldwork for regulating the lives of people with learning difficulties was the curator bonis system. This "fragmented and outdated … inflexible" system was the mechanism available for the management of the affairs of an estimated 100,000 Scots with incapacity (Scottish Parliament, 1999, pp 1-2), and 20,000 of these people were incapacitated due to learning difficulties, being some 16% of the 120,000 Scots with varying forms of learning difficulty (Scottish Executive, 2000a, pp 5-6). The curatory process is initiated by a petition to the Sheriff Court usually by one of the near relatives, but the proceedings may be initiated by professional advisors or by the local authority or by the Mental Welfare Commission. Two medical certificates defining the person as being "of unsound mind and incapable of managing his/her affairs or of giving directions for their management" (Ward, 1990, p 98) are necessary. Unless the petition is opposed, there being no statutory provision for providing such scrutiny, the person with learning difficulties is deprived of all assets and legal capacity and become a ward of the curator bonis, in practice always a solicitor or accountant. The duties of the curator bonis are to manage the assets as the person with learning difficulties would have done had they not been of unsound mind, seeking the approval of the court for any major capital decisions. The curator bonis lodges annual accounts with an official of the Court of Session, the Accountant of Court. The curator bonis may be removed by the court, on the initiative of the Accountant of Court or any other interested party, if their execution of the duties is unsatisfactory.

In our sample of 30 people with learning difficulties there was one person who was subject to a curatory, Clare.

Clare

Clare was a woman, approaching middle age, with black hair now slowly going grey but kept in a young short style; she was short and plump but had a degree of confidence about her. She was a serious woman whose life had expanded enormously upon the death of her mother a few years previously. She had Down's syndrome and lived in a large ground floor flat in a converted Victorian house in a high status part of the rural area. The flat was tastefully decorated, filled with antique furniture and set in pleasant grounds. Clare's room contrasted with the rest of the flat. Posters of soap stars and pop bands were displayed on her bedroom wall and the floor was strewn with CDs, magazines, knitting and clothes. In contrast, the other rooms were tidy and had the appearance of not being used. Her bedroom appeared to be her den and she spent a lot of time in there watching TV. Clare lived here alone since her mother died. She was an only child and received daily visits from Geraldine, her home support worker, combined with ongoing, but distant, support from her social worker and from the family lawyer, her curator bonis. She got on well with the couple that live in the upper flat and she babysat for their young daughter. She attended a resource centre for people with learning difficulties for most of the week.

We were able to establish few details on Clare's childhood as she was very protected by her family, being 'at home'. She seemed to have had a close relationship with her father, an industrialist, but he died while she was still a young child. She then lived with her mother, a key professional within the field of services for people with learning difficulties in the area, in the family home. Clare had little to say about her past but her social worker provided this picture of Clare's earlier life:

> "She has lived a very protected life – she has been kept a child. Her father was an industrialist and when he was alive the family probably did more things, for example there were family holidays and so on. However, he died in the late 1970s and then it was just her and her mother and the balance in the family went out. Her grandfather did live with them for a while but he died in the early 1980s and then it was just her and her mother. Her mother was very old-fashioned and wanted to keep Clare a child. In an early social work case note someone has written 'the mother seems to ignore Clare but she does care deep down'. Her mother had special responsibility for assessing people with learning difficulties for benefit claims and so on.... She had a huge controlling influence over Clare." (Clare's social worker)

Clare went to a local special school and left when she was 18 or 19. She described it as a big school, which "was OK", but she then went on to say that there was a lot of bullying and sometimes she was the victim. She did not take any examinations or get any certificates. She "wasn't bothered about school really". After she left school she worked as a cleaner at a sheltered workshop. She then went to the local ARC that she still attended. She commented that it had got bigger and there were more things going on. There were some early attempts to integrate Clare into work: at one point she had a job in a café but her mother stopped this as she said it was exploiting people with learning difficulties. Later Clare worked for the café in the local church. Her mother thought this was acceptable as it was working for a charity. Clare lost this job when the café was reorganised on more businesslike lines.

Throughout this time Clare's mother would only communicate with the workers at the ARC and refused any social work involvement although the social worker did have brief case notes from the late 1970s and early 1980s. The social worker only became involved with Clare after her mother's death in the mid-1990s. Her mother was ill for a long time with cancer but did not ask for treatment or help until the last month of the illness.

Clare was made subject to a curatory order just over two years before her mother's death. The Sheriff Court records are not public and so it was not possible to establish who petitioned the court, which issued the two medical certificates, the quantity and quality of evidence presented, whether the petition was opposed and what Clare's assets were at that time. What can be noted is Ward's view that "curators are generally appointed on the flimsiest of evidence" (Ward, 1990, p 98) and that Clare's mother was professionally well connected with the local doctors who could be expected to issue such certificates.

Seven days before her death Clare's mother executed a will leaving (effectively) her whole estate for setting up a trust for Clare's lifetime benefit. On Clare's death the estate will pass to five nephews and nieces or their survivors. The trustees were her mother's sister, one nephew and the family solicitor. The clause of the will setting up the trust stipulated: "And the provision herein made for my said daughter shall be accepted by her in full satisfaction of any legal rights which she may have against my said estate". The valuation of the estate five months later was several hundred thousand pounds. Clare was thus the sole beneficiary of an estate that not only provided her with excellent accommodation but also was capable of generating a substantial annual income.

Clare was a wealthy woman but the curatory order and the terms of the will meant that she had no control over her money that was administered by a local solicitor, with distant involvement of the trustees appointed in the will. The requirements of the Accountant of Court about the activity of the curator bonis meant that receipts for every item of daily expenditure had to be obtained and logged, with prior approval of the Factor having to be obtained for the purchase of 'exceptional' items such as birthday presents for friends or a Christmas present for herself (Christmas being spent alone). The accounting requirements of the curatory system thus necessitated formal intrusion into every aspect of Clare's life.

> "What happens is I get shopping money every week and that is kept in a separate purse that I organise – write down everything, receipts for everything that gets forwarded to the lawyer." (Geraldine, home support worker)

Although the curator bonis was appointed solely to safeguard the financial affairs of the ward, there was evidence in Clare's experience of this drifting into claims to exercise control over her personal and social life. The redecoration of the flat was determined by the Factor with a choice of decor that Clare did not like; she retreated into her room that she decorated in her own style. Clare wished to join a video club in order to watch videos on a regular basis; money for this was refused on the grounds that she might rent 'blue' movies. Geraldine joined the club and gave her card to Clare, who rented the videos without supervision (and, for the curious, she had not rented blue movies).

Clare would like to have a flatmate in one of the spare rooms of the large flat so that she did not live alone; this was simply refused by the Factor. Another possibility discussed between Clare, social workers and the Factor was that the flat should be sold and the proceeds used to fund a place in supported accommodation with other people with learning difficulties. This was refused by the Factor on the grounds that Clare's mother wanted her to stay in the flat for the rest of her life, although the will does not state this.

Most significantly, Clare would like to develop an intimate relationship with Andrew, about whom she talked animatedly and fondly. She had plans to marry "sometime after next year" but it was not clear that Andrew shared such plans, or the perception of himself as the boyfriend of Clare. Conversely there was another person with learning difficulties who kept pressurising Clare to have sex with him. Her social worker described the situation thus: "He is quite pushy with her and she can't refuse. We have had to support her to say no". Clare had developed her own mechanism for dealing with the matter: displayed around the flat on yellow Post-It stickers were reminders for herself and the rules for visitors, one of which was "No more sex". Talk of the possibility of having children visibly upset Clare: "I can't have one at the minute". It would appear that Clare was sterilised shortly before her mother's death.

Clare having been declared *incapax* is in a legal and sexual limbo. Clare, Andrew and the other suitor, and anyone concerned with Clare's accommodation or welfare, would run the risk of prosecution under Section 106 of the 1984 Mental Health (Scotland) Act if they allowed (actively or passively) relationships to develop sexually or to the point of marriage. This Act makes it an offence for a person to have intercourse outside marriage with, to procure or encourage, or to allow premises to be used for such intercourse by a woman "if she is suffering from a state of arrested or incomplete development of mind which includes significant impairment of intelligence and social functioning". A marriage is not possible if the person, on medical evidence, is incapable of proper consent. As Clare had been declared 'of unsound mind' as the basis for the curator order under different legislation, it would appear that "the law does not permit mentally handicapped women who are legally incapable of marriage to experience sexual intercourse in any circumstances" (Ward, 1984, p 51).

The social workers involved with Clare expressed frustration at the wide consequences of the curator order. They saw Clare as capable of a significantly independent life and tried to support her in becoming more independent. They reported the negotiations with the Factor thus:

> "At first we had frequent meetings but he used it to pull rank over us and it was always a source of conflict which wasn't doing anyone any good so we (the social work department) have decided that we will do everything by letter and only have a meeting when we have something to discuss. The trust has total control over Clare.... As part of increasing Clare's independence we got her to write letters for things like when she needed a new toaster but the will made her *'incapax'* which means doing things like that challenge the legal definition of her ability. Every time she does something that makes her independent the lawyer argues [against it] because it would challenge the definition of being *incapax*. This is a permanent state and as far as social work can find out has only successfully been challenged in law once and that was by someone who had had an

accident and was brain damaged but who recovered enough to challenge the label." (Clare's social worker)

Clare's life situation as we have so far analysed it was one dominated by a series of legal and quasi-legal restrictions that enclosed, protected and controlled her in a manner very reminiscent of social policy for people with learning difficulties in, say, the 1950s when she was born. We have no reason to doubt the sincerity of those involved in making provision for Clare but it was clear that her potential for independence and self-fulfilment was being limited by the curatory system and its implications.

Clare however was developing techniques to negotiate these barriers herself. Her week was dominated by social work provision through the ARC: Clare attended 11 sessions (one half day or an evening), ten leisure classes and one life skills class, a week. All of these were segregated 'special' classes for people with learning difficulties. In her (real) leisure time away from the ARC, Clare worked. Two years previously, with the support of a voluntary Supported Employment agency, she applied for, and gained, an advertised job as a waitress in a large café on Sundays; at the time of the fieldwork she was in the process of starting a Saturday job in the café of a large department store in the nearby city. She had successfully held down the Sunday job and it played a key role in her life. She enjoyed the engagement with the broad range of people that the job provided; she enjoyed the (rather limited) social life of the staff outside the workplace. Clare was paid the going rate for the job that was around the national minimum wage. This money went into a bank account in her own name for which she had a cash card. This money was entirely outside the curatory ambit and Clare used it to construct her own identity. She bought the CDs, magazines, tapes and posters that littered her room from this cash and thus created her enclave in the trust-controlled flat. She used the money to rent the videos that the Factor forbade. Inverting social time by regarding the weekend as the time to work, there was a real sense of Clare taking hold of a life in which for the first 40 years she was 'kept a child'. As Geraldine, the person closest to her, said:

> "As I say, she is so independent and she knows the town better than I do. Really she is amazing. She knows exactly where she is going and what bus to take. She has all her timetables. She thinks with her head whereas you and I probably wouldn't. As I say, she is a marvel. She amazes me." (Geraldine, home support worker)

As we left the field Clare was in the process of taking on a waitressing job for three days a week – an eloquent challenge to being defined as 'of unsound mind'.

What lessons does the experience of Clare as ward of a curator bonis hold for understanding the position of people with learning difficulties in contemporary Scottish society? Clare's experience illustrates, precisely, the criticisms of the curatory system for people with learning difficulties levelled principally by Ward (1990), criticisms which have been hugely influential in the recent restructuring of the Scottish law of incapacity. There is no suggestion in our analysis of Clare's position that any of the professionals involved with her had acted in any way improperly; rather that the legal system was so structured by the assumption of a person completely without capacity living in an institution that the reasonable action of good people lead to injustice.

Clare's declaration as *incapax*, in all probability at the instigation of her mother, on the basis of the opinions of two connected professional colleagues and without a statutory requirement of independent legal representation, did not suggest an impartial procedure which took a full and sensitive view of Clare's welfare. As Ward notes:

> On the basis of no greater assessment or information that that, a fundamental change is made in the status of a mentally handicapped person, with far-reaching consequences for that person and for family and carers. Moreover the change is likely to be lifelong; there is no requirement for review. There is not requirement for any other professional assessment, such as the assessment by a Mental Health Officer in statutory guardianship procedure. (Ward, 1990, p 98)

There is an arguable case that Clare is one of the 'inappropriate curatories' of which Ward writes. The decision to declare Clare *incapax* and to deprive her of legal capacity was total: the court was faced with only a binary decision between Clare being of legal capacity or not. That we have not been allowed access to the relevant court documents and records further reinforces the impression of a system which is arbitrary and not open to scrutiny.

Once subject to the curatory Clare was enmeshed in an administrative system that celebrates "meticulous accounting for accounting's sake" (Ward, 1990, p 94). With every daily item having to be documented in a manner which we personally would neither accept nor be able to sustain, the possibility of Clare developing life skills and a money culture within (what we assume to be) the normal range is remote: having to ask the 'icey' at the ice cream van for a receipt securely marks people out as different and questionable. The curatory was felt by the social work staff to be inhibiting Clare's every movements towards independence: as Ward points out this is a consequence of the system which emphasises meeting set basic needs rather than being proactive in defining and meeting new needs. Fear of scrutiny by the Accountant of Court can lead an expansion of financial control into areas of personal development so that reasonable developmental needs are denied, membership of a video club being one example in Clare's case. Clare's Factor did meet with her from time to time and so is not liable to the criticism of many Factors that their remoteness and insensitivity is "cruelly distressing" (Ward, 1990, p 95).

Whether the system was serving Clare well financially is also open to question. The accounts of the trust are not open to public scrutiny but to regulation by the Accountant of Court, a system which emphasises the minutiae and "does not always guarantee that there will not be serious mismanagement" (Ward, 1990, p 95). According to Ward, the system may lead to an undue emphasise on the inheritance rights of those entitled to succeed on the death of the person with learning difficulties. What is undeniable is that the reasonable professional fees allowed by the Accountant of Court for the detailed accounting of expenditure represents a significant drain on the assets of the person with learning difficulties. In 1990 Ward estimated a minimum estate of £50,000 below which the costs of the curatory would have an overwhelming impact on the available income. As trust accounts are not open to public scrutiny it is not possible to take a view on the operation of Clare's. What may unambiguously be supported from her case are Ward's conclusions (Ward, 1990, pp 103-6) that "mentally handicapped people to whom curators have been appointed have not been able to draw the attention of the courts to the injustices described" and that "the main qualification for appointment should be understanding of the handicapped person's capabilities, disabilities and potential".

Ward's conclusion on the curatory system is pertinent to Clare:

> So the mentally handicapped person who requires a curator bonis because some of his affairs are complex, becomes legally disqualified from transacting any business however simple. That is the result even though by the law's own tests he might otherwise have been legally capable of those simple transaction. It is said that wealth does not guarantee happiness! In the case of the mentally handicapped, wealth may result in the severe penalty of deprivation of all legal

capacity, even of those who without such wealth would have at least partial capacity. (Ward, 1984, p 39)

The Adults with Incapacity (Scotland) Act came into force in autumn 2000. It was informed by the principles that anything done under the law for an adult with incapacity will have to:

* benefit the adult;
* take account of the adult's wishes and those of the nearest relative, primary carer and guardian or attorney, if appointed;
* be the least restrictive of the adult's freedom while achieving the desired purpose.

Anyone authorised or appointed to intervene in the adult's affairs will have to encourage the adult to use their existing skills and acquire new skills where possible. Incapacity will continue to be determined on the basis of medical reports, although the spirit of the law is to encourage adults to exercise as much capacity as they can. Individuals will be able to make plans for their future by granting a power of attorney to a person of their choice, who will then be able to deal with whatever welfare, medical treatment or financial matters the person granting the power has specified. Hospitals and care home managers will be allowed to manage the funds of patients and residents who lack capacity to do so, but will be stringently monitored. Doctors and other healthcare professionals will have a general authority to treat adult patients who are unable to give their consent and to conduct research relevant to their treatment. The Sheriff Court will be able to make one-off orders, on the application of relatives or other interested parties, to deal with specific decisions faced by adults with incapacity such as selling a house or signing an important document. The court will also be able to appoint a longer-term guardian to deal with any combination of welfare, medical treatment or financial matters. The new kind of guardian will replace curators bonis, tutors and Mental Health Act guardians, all of whom are currently appointed to take decisions on behalf of adults with incapacity. The courts will be able to intervene in how guardians and attorneys use their powers. The Public Guardian, a new office within the court system, will keep public registers of attorneys, intervention orders and guardians and will supervise those with financial powers. Registration and Inspection teams in local authorities and health boards will inspect accounts where these are managed by residential and nursing home managers. The Mental Welfare Commission will monitor attorneys and guardians with welfare powers and carry out investigations where something appears to be wrong.

At the time of writing, the extent to which these new measures will significantly improve matters for people with learning difficulties who happen to be wealthy is a moot point. It is evident that, once a person has been certified as an incapable adult, the Sheriff Court and guardian will have very significant powers, as will healthcare professionals, in carrying out medical treatment, including sterilisation, without the person's consent. While tighter accountability procedures have been put in place, it is not difficult to imagine circumstances in which the basic rights of a person with learning difficulties might be unreasonably curtailed and their wealth controlled by those who may not always have their best interests at heart.

Clare, as we have noted, was fighting back by inverting social time, spending her weekends as a waitress in a 'real job'. This inversion gives us a clue into the regulation of the lives of people with learning difficulties who are not subject to the medical definition as *incapax* and the legal processes of a curatory (and its successor). The complex web of laws regulating these lives is summarised in Appendix 2. It is to these wider regulatory processes to which we now turn.

That Clare was the only person in our sample of 30 case studies who was subject to a curatory was not surprising. Currently there are some 1,400 curatory orders active in Scotland. Separate classification of the cause of the 'unsound mind' is not performed but staff at the Accountant of Court's office believe (personal communication) that the 'vast majority' of cases are due to dementia, with people with learning difficulties constituting about 2% of cases (about 30 curatory orders for people with learning difficulties in Scotland). If we apply the overall number of curatory orders to the Scottish Executive's estimates (Scottish Parliament, 1999, p 1) of the number of adults with incapacity in Scotland (100,000, of whom 20,000 are incapacitated due to learning difficulties) then we would expect one in every 71 incapable adults to be subject to an order, with some 282 orders for people with learning difficulties. While it must be emphasised that the figures from both the Accountant of Court and the Scottish Executive are estimates they suggest that only one tenth of the people with learning difficulties who we might expect to be wards through a curatory order are in fact so subjected. The majority of people with learning difficulties, as Ward notes above, are thus regulated through informal means. It is to this informal regulation of people with learning difficulties, in all aspects of their lives, to which we now turn.

The case of Clare's apron is instructive. The café where Clare works at the weekend was not happy with the apron in which she appeared for work one day. It was not entirely clean and appeared crumpled. The supervisor spoke to her and also contacted the voluntary organisation that supported Clare in her work. They spoke to Geraldine, the home support worker, and she and Clare arranged for the regular laundry and ironing of the aprons. The matter was resolved and the problem has not re-emerged.

If we think about this incident in the terms of social capital that we developed in the last chapter, we see the undifferentiated bonding social capital norm of the employer (all employees should be clean and tidy for waitressing) being applied to Clare. As well as speaking with Clare directly, the employer called upon the bridging social capital of the voluntary organisation and of the home support worker to try to ensure that the bonding norm was met. Geraldine, on the basis of the reciprocal relationship between herself and Clare, was able to support Clare in meeting the expectations of the workplace.

In this moment we see in play social capital processes of everyday life (employer norms) being supplemented by social capital processes specific to people with learning difficulties (a voluntary organisation and a home support worker) to the benefit, we suggest, of all including Clare for whom maintaining her job was a high priority. With a prevailing policy ethos of seeking 'ordinary lives' for people with learning difficulties Clare's apron represents a small example of integration being supported and advanced. Is this interlocking of different forms of social capital typical of the rest of Clare's life and of those of the other people who constituted our case studies?

In order to address this we now develop the argument about the relationship of people with learning difficulties to forms of social capital proposed in Chapter 8 by applying it by way of summary to the case study individuals of the research.

Family, domestic arrangements and neighbourhood

The family of origin provides the centre of developing networks for people as they grow from childhood to adulthood and it introduces the child to sets of norms and the sanctions that impose them. As we have argued elsewhere (Baron et al, 1999) leaving home is one of the key moments in the transition to adulthood. This process is highly significant in the person gaining access to different networks and to different normative systems through which they can negotiate identities and establish eco-niches. For many young people the local neighbourhood provides the context for developing these networks.

The evidence of our case studies is that this process is significantly delayed or prevented in the case of people with learning difficulties with 17 out of the 30 still living in the family of origin. Significantly, four of the 11 people over the age of 40 years were still in their family of origin while four were in various forms of special accommodation. Two people over the age of 40 years from relatively wealthy backgrounds were living in the now inherited family home, while only one person over the age of 40 had been able to establish their own home. This person was the only one in our sample to have formed an enduring intimate personal relationship. We found only little evidence of our case study people having links into their neighbourhoods and some evidence of feelings of rejection and hostility.

The consequences of such a pattern of domestic arrangements are twofold. Firstly, the person with learning difficulties is held within the ambit of strong familial bonding social capital often until, in middle age, death deprives them of parents. While these ties are reciprocal in many ways (the son's or daughter's benefits were crucial to the domestic economy of some families) there was strong evidence that people were being held in the dependent position of childhood and not being enabled to develop their potential for independent living. Secondly, when the people with learning difficulties did leave home of origin through choice or, more usually, through necessity they transferred to locations dominated by 'special', bonding, forms of social capital: specially registered bed and breakfast accommodation, group homes, supported living in flats or houses shared with other people with learning difficulties. Access to more broadly based forms of domestic bridging social capital which enable young people to move from home of origin, often through some form of elective flat sharing, to independent living was conspicuously absent in the lives of our case study people.

The initial education system and peers

The initial education system can be seen as helping form both bonding and bridging forms of social capital for the young people passing through it. It provides bridging social capital in the sense of the school standing at the centre of a network of other institutions, especially further education and training and work, to which the school leaver has systematic (but not unconditional) access. Schools also provide the ground on, and against, which the strong forms of bonding social capital of youth culture and peer groups in part occur. The latter can act as a crucial support mechanism for the young person as they leave the home of origin and develop their independent life.

All of our sample had either been subject to special schooling in one form or another and/or had a history of breakdown of placements in ordinary schools. A constant theme in the experience of our case study people of school was of separation from others of the same age and the failure to develop networks with them. Separate institutions clearly imply this but such isolation was also present in those of our sample who had attended mainstream schools: special units having different timetables and locations or strong peer cultures of conformity to a norm of normality were examples of how some case study people became differentiated and excluded from mainstream networks. Loneliness and rejection haunt the accounts of initial schooling that we gathered. If access to young people's forms of bridging social capital was difficult it does not seem to have been complemented by the development of a bonding social capital among those subject to special education. There was little evidence, even among our recent school leavers, of lasting friendships having been made in, or maintained after, special education. While initial education seems to have bound our case study people into its difference it does not appear to have used this separate space to develop any sense of solidarity and identity among the people with learning difficulties.

The consequences of such systems for the young school leavers in our sample were clear. They had a clear image of themselves as different and being a 'problem' of one type or other. Their social circles were very limited and they had been passed on from special schools or equivalent to further forms of special provision in Local Enterprise Company Skillseekers programmes, in the special programmes departments of FE colleges or in ARCs. There was little evidence of them having been able to form, or utilise, bridging social capital which would enable them to explore life possibilities outwith the circuit of special provision. The biographies of our older case study individuals documented lifetimes of limited peer group engagement and of moving from one special provision to another, albeit with some having had a period of work, which ended with the closure of traditional manufacturing plants in the 1980s. It is to the relationship of our case study people with learning difficulties to the world of work that we now turn.

Work

In this chapter we have already shown the centrality of work to Clare in her creation of her own space and identity outside the confines of the trust. Such an experience is, as we would expect given the research literature over the past 30 years on work as the 'main reality', contrary to the postmodernist challenge, determining life chances and forming identities. Work gives access to forms of social capital in three main ways: it is one of the major encounters with the normative orders of contemporary Scottish society; it provides the context in which networks may develop among the workers, providing not only social contact but also group solidarity which may challenge and re-form normative orders; it provides one of the pillars of the labour process which not only develops personal qualities and identity but also provides an income through which other aspects of personal development can be funded. None of these in the crisis-ridden state of Scottish capitalism is, to say the least, 'unproblematic', but exclusion from such encounters is a key to social subordination.

As we have noted in Chapter 5, people with disabilities in general, and people with learning difficulties in particular, have been squeezed out of the open labour market in the past 20 years. Some of our older case study people had worked when they were younger but had lost their jobs when plants shut and they had not been able to regain work. At the time of fieldwork none of the sample was working a full week in an open labour market job. The one person who had been doing this recently had been forced to become 'disabled' and only work for 15 hours a week in order to maintain the benefits which paid for accommodation. Another person had been presented with the choice between becoming precisely 50% disabled (and thus subsidised) or dismissal; two others held stable part-time jobs. Otherwise, the experience of work of our sample ranged from full-time supported employment with employers to various special work lookalike schemes. What was striking was that those with a connection to work in open or near open labour market schemes organised their time and identities around the connection; many of those who did not have such a connection felt the deprivation across a similar range of their lives.

Twenty-six of our 30 case study individuals did not have such a connection and spent their time in education, training or quasi-work.

Continuing education, voluntary organisations and government

Participation in continuing education and in voluntary organisations are taken by many writers on social capital to be key indicators of the active citizenry necessary to produce, and keep in check, good government (Baron et al, 2000). Similarly in recent years with the development of the 'knowledge economy', participation in continuing education has become one of the touchstones of the 'Learning Society'. At first glance most of our 30 case study individuals fulfil such criteria.

Some form of continuing education or training was a significant part of the week for the people who did not have a connection with the open labour market. Timetables of different classes in resource centres and colleges filled each day (and often evening) of the working week. The subject matter of this provision ranged from training for work (particularly in horticulture and catering) to leisure classes (photography or karaoke for example). In the rural area most of our case study people had contact only with the charity that provided accommodation and day services for the local council. In the urban area there was a rich diversity of voluntary organisations and, again, the majority of our case study people had contact with one or more such body.

As we have suggested the people with learning difficulties appear, at one level, to be pioneers of the continuous educational engagement of learning society; if we analyse these relationships in terms of the forms of social capital that underpin them, then a different picture emerges. The value attributed to participation in continuing education and voluntary organisations by writers on social capital lies largely in terms of the reciprocal formation of bridging social capital: active citizenry as the building of links between groups through dialogue, particularly about the public good. The relationship of our case study people to continuing education and voluntary organisations was dominated by bonding and non-reciprocal social capital. There was little evidence of our case study people, caught within special classes, forming links with a wider circle of people and substantial evidence that the voluntary organisations and continuing education served to bind them into the limited circuit of special provision. There was little evidence of people with learning difficulties having an impact on the operations and policy of the organisations with which they dealt; there was significant evidence of such organisations making provision to meet their own needs and priorities rather than those of the case study people.

By way of summary we suggest that across the different aspects of life analysed in this book and this chapter people with learning difficulties are systematically excluded from the normal circuits of social capital: they are often kept at home in a child-like relationship until middle age; they do not, on the whole, form a network of relationships in their neighbourhood; once the family origin becomes non-viable as a home they tend to move into special accommodation with other people with learning difficulties; initial schooling tends neither to enable them to participate in a mainstream peer group nor to form a lasting alternative peer group; schools tend to direct people with learning difficulties onto special programmes post-school; open labour market work is elusive and work substitutes dominate their weekly timetables; participation in continuing education and voluntary organisations does not provide the bridging social capital and active citizenry which the literature would suggest but rather further encompassing by strong and non-reciprocal ties of bonding social capital.

As we have outlined above the majority of our case study people were not subject to the formal mechanisms of legal regulation of a curator bonis and so on. Our analysis of their relationship to forms of social capital suggests that they are excluded from the normal, informal mechanisms of social regulation through networks and their imposition of norms. This means that people with learning difficulties are in something of a regulatory void: excluded from normal circuits of social capital they not only lack the informal regulation of networks but they also lack the ability to move between networks in order to find the most congenial form of regulation, and they lack the ability to alter such regulation through their participation in the networks. Into this regulatory void in the past 20 years have stepped a variety of social welfare professionals using the mechanisms of 'rights' and 'an ordinary life'.

Appendix 2 contains a synopsis of the current legal framework for people with learning difficulties in Scotland taken from the recent Review of Services for People with Learning Disabilities. The overwhelming thrust of the various pieces of legislation is to give people with learning difficulties rights to assessments of needs and access to services. This is as it should be at one level, but our analysis of the exercise of these rights as realised in the assessment of needs and the delivery of such services suggests that the services act more to regulate and contain people with learning difficulties within an enclosed circuit of special places and events than to define and meet needs in a developmental way which would see them moving out and into mainstream social contexts and activities.

Across the sites analysed above the lives of people with learning difficulties were subject to professional regulation. Domesticity in special accommodation was regulated through the inspection and registration activities of the two social work departments, with detailed manuals defining an hotel vision of 'normality' and an accountancy version of quality of life; those living with their family of origin or in their own homes were subject to more sporadic, but no less intrusive, professional scrutiny of their personal lives. Timetables constructed by professionals dominated the lives of our case study individuals with rounds of training and leisure activities lasting all day and into many of the evenings of the week. Outcomes of such activity in terms of progression to applying skills in more open social contexts were rare: one of the older case study individuals was about to 'retire' from the training round, without ever had the opportunity to put the training into practice, onto which the younger case study individuals were about to embark. Our case study people were held under professional surveillance and control just as securely as were the prisoners in Bentham's Panopticon (Foucault, 1991): an 'ordinary life' thus constructed is truly 'extra-ordinary'.

Some of these issues have been recognised in recent Scottish policy debates. One of the first actions of the Scottish Executive was to conduct a review of services for persons with learning disabilities, the results of which were published in 2000 (Scottish Executive, 2000a). In the Ministerial Foreword Iain Gray writes:

> I particularly welcome the opportunities for people to have more say and more control over their lives. Professionals need to acknowledge their limits and the rights of others. Using *direct payments, brokerage* and advocacy services more will help people have more influence. (Scottish Executive, 2000a, p iv, emphasis in original)

The review undertook a substantial consultation exercise that included people with learning difficulties and their carers (for stylistic consistency we will continue to use the term 'learning difficulties' as opposed to the review's 'learning disabilities'). Their message was clear, and consistent with our research findings. People with learning difficulties in Scotland want: to be included in the community; to have more control over their lives; to work; to have the chance to learn and develop and to have a wider social life; to have the information and support necessary for these.

As highlighted in the Ministerial Foreword particular emphasis is placed on direct payments, brokerage and advocacy whereby people with learning difficulties can buy the services which they deem necessary using, if necessary, the support of a citizen advocate. This lay volunteer would owe primary allegiance to the person with learning difficulties and would act to ensure that their interests were the guiding principle of the services purchased rather than those of the professionals providing the services.

This is a very welcome emphasis and holds out the possibility of a significant change in the power relations between professionals and people with learning difficulties. Two major obstacles inhibit this: firstly, as our research suggests, alternative services and activities on which the hoped for choices depend simply do not exist for most people with learning difficulties; secondly the thrust of the rest of the Review of Services for people with learning difficulties, and of other Scottish Executive policy is firmly towards an increasing professionalisation of the field of learning difficulties. It is on this that we now focus.

Health authorities and local authorities are required to produce joint plans for services for their areas including how they are to classify individuals, define needs and commission services to meet these needs. In this vision four pages are devoted to details of inter-professional relations; two lines are devoted to advocacy and the role of service users and carers. The keyworker in the delivery of services will be an area coordinator whose main tasks will be to link 50 people with learning difficulties with appropriate local services. Such coordinators will be responsible to a joint management committee of the local authority, health boards, voluntary organisation 'as well as local users and carers' (Scottish Executive, 2000a, p 20). The area coordinators will have a budget with which to meet the needs they identify. That the perspectives of people with learning difficulties are not central to this system is acknowledged by the perceived needs for advocates as well as the area coordinator. Moreover each person with learning difficulties 'who wants it' will be subject to a 'personal life plan' (Scottish Executive, 2000a, p 21) not as a self-generated autobiographical act but as a professional 'assessment' done to the person (who must be informed that it is being done). Respite, education, work, housing, transport needs must all be assessed by the area coordinator and a copy given to the person and their carers in the hope that they will 'also own the plan' (Scottish Executive, 2000a, p 22).

This trend to the further professionalisation of learning difficulties is reinforced by the 1999 White Paper, *Aiming for excellence* (Scottish Office, 1999) and the subsequent Policy Position Paper *The way forward for care* (Scottish Executive, 2000b). Following a public scandal about the appalling circumstances of the death of Miss McCabe in the Glengova Home, a new system of regulating social care is being developed. A Scottish Commission on the Regulation of Care will replace the registration and inspection functions of 32 local authorities and 15 health boards with one central body to ensure standardisation of care. The definition of the 'care' to be regulated is considerably expanded from residential homes to include, *inter alia*, anyone offering psychological support as a service to another "such as reminding someone to carry out daily activities such as washing and eating"; similarly any activities which are intended to promote the "social, educational or employment opportunities" of a person with learning difficulties are subject to regulation (Scottish Executive, 2000b, paras 28, 31).

Inter-linked with this system for the regulation of services are the proposals for the regulation of the workforce through a Scottish Social Services Council to "strengthen and support the professionalism of the workforce" (Scottish Executive, 2000b, para 99). Starting with priority groups of staff the regulation of the council will roll out across the social care workforce, defined to include short-term volunteers including citizen advocates. Key to personal registration (and thus activity) is the attainment of nationally defined qualifications which are still being drafted but which are highly prescriptive about the 'values' to which workers must subscribe. The professionalisation of the workforce is thus increasingly surrounding the person with learning difficulties with a set of people, including lay advocates, with a uniform approach to the issues of learning difficulties and the mandate to define needs and appropriate services accordingly. While these services may vary from those currently on offer the informal regulation of people with learning difficulties seems set to increase as 'joined-up policy' impacts on their lives.

Conclusion

In this chapter we have argued that people with learning difficulties are characterised by lives that are highly regulated. Formal regulation through declaration as a ward of a curator bonis is relatively rare but highly intrusive if declared. The new dispensation under the 2000 Adults with

Incapacity (Scotland) Act seeks to develop less blunt instruments of formal regulation but it is not at all clear that these will benefit people with learning difficulties significantly. Deprived of access to, and mobility between, mainstream forms of social capital and their different normative orders, people with learning difficulties inhabit a separate social world peopled largely by other people with learning difficulties. The normative order of this world revolves around timetables of training and leisure activities the nature of which are determined by a variety of professionals. Recent policy, rightly concerned with the string of scandals that have emerged in Scottish social care, seeks to enhance the choice and social integration of people with learning difficulties but does so in a manner that will increase their regulation.

Despite overt policies of 'rights' and an 'ordinary life' the trend of policy is thus for people with learning difficulties to lead lives of extra-ordinary regulation. It is the significance of this for understanding of a 'learning society' to which we turn in the final chapter.

TEN

Conclusion: Implications of different versions of the Learning Society for people with learning difficulties

Introduction

In Chapter 1 of this book, we set out three key versions of the Learning Society which are in play in official policy talk and are also reflected in services delivered by a range of agencies. These were the human capital, the social capital and the social control versions of a Learning Society. Having explored lifelong learning in relation to post-school education, training, employment and benefits regimes, we consider the extent to which each of these versions of a Learning Society is in evidence and its implications for people with learning difficulties. We conclude by suggesting some more fruitful directions for the Learning Society of the future that might enable it be an inclusive rather than an exclusive force.

The human capital version of the Learning Society

As we suggested earlier, this essentially economic version of the Learning Society has become the dominant model and appears to be capable of uniting, at least at a superficial level, a wide variety of interest groups. Official policy documents routinely assert that investment in human capital is essential to beat off competitors in the global jungle. Thus the introduction to the Scottish White Paper on lifelong learning asserts:

> We ignore the economic importance of lifelong learning at our peril. There is a very positive message for individuals and employers that

> sustained investment in learning opportunities and training is the key to personal and business success. (Scottish Office, 1998a, p 2)

The consequences of this economic justification of lifelong learning are different for different groups. People in work are likely to find growing opportunities for formal and informal learning at work, as initiatives such as Investors in People, the University for Industry and Individual Learning Accounts support individuals in upgrading their skills. Entry to programmes providing employment-orientated skill formation is likely to be restricted to more able individuals who will produce the best economic return on investment.

For people with learning difficulties, however, the consequences of a Learning Society driven by human capital rhetoric are likely to be very restrictive. As we noted in Chapter 3, the passage of the 1992 Further and Higher Education (Scotland) Act, which obliged colleges to 'have regard' for the needs of disabled students, ostensibly produced a massive expansion of provision, but this was almost exclusively of a segregated nature which reinforced the separate identity of people with learning difficulties, excluding them from the labour market rather than providing bridges into it.

Local Enterprise Companies (LECs), providers of post-16 training programmes, also strongly reflected a human capital approach in their mode of delivery and underlying assumptions. Whereas some LECs provide training for those with learning difficulties (although they use the blanket term 'additional needs'), the majority maintain that this group are unlikely to be economically active and are therefore the responsibility of social services. The funding system, offering remuneration to trainers on the basis of the number of people gaining Level 2 vocational qualifications and finding jobs, clearly reflects a human capital perspective and illustrates powerfully the way in which such an approach may mitigate against the interests of people with learning difficulties in term of accessing education and training, since they are likely to be expensive to train and may find difficulty in gaining qualifications and finding employment. Most Employment Service programmes operate outcome criteria which exclude disabled people. There is also evidence that when public spending is squeezed, training programmes and, to an even greater extent, supported employment schemes designed for people with learning difficulties, are particularly vulnerable to cuts (Riddell et al, 1993). Indeed, despite growing interest in supported employment for people with learning difficulties, it is evident that opportunities for this type of involvement in the labour market are scarce, due to lack of funding rather than difficulties in locating suitable employers or individuals' capacity to participate.

Even if people with learning difficulties invest in their education and training, they are very likely to experience difficulties obtaining work due to structural changes within the labour market as well as a reluctance to invest in their training. May and Hughes (1985), in a three-year study of the post-school experiences of young people from special schools and units for young people with moderate learning difficulties in one Scottish region, demonstrated that the employment prospects for this group had deteriorated markedly since the mid-1970s. They cited evidence that in the 1940s, 80% of youngsters 'graduated' from Glasgow's special schools into open employment but, by the mid-1980s, the disappearance of unskilled manual work had eroded their chances of employment, so that in 1986 only 5% found employment on leaving school. The authors commented:

> Where once they might have expected to find jobs of one sort or another eventually, and with them some measure of economic independence, now it would seem that the best they can expect in the short and intermediate term at least, is a series of short-lived placements on various government sponsored schemes of dubious meaning and value, punctuated by successive and growing periods of unemployment as they move further beyond the range of the emergency measures set up to assist the post-school transition. (May and Hughes, 1985, p 158)

Currently, the dominance of human capital thinking has very negative consequences for people with learning difficulties, particularly those with the most significant problems. The limited opportunities available reflect the perception that investment in training and employment for this group does not pay. It is worth noting, however, that earlier generations used utilitarian thinking to justify a minimal level of investment in disabled people's education and training to prevent them being a 'burden on the state'. The disability movement has also used economic arguments to justify investment in training for disabled people, maintaining that benefits to the individual and the Treasury outweigh the programmes' costs.

The social capital version of the Learning Society

While mainstream education and training is informed by human capital thinking, policy for people with learning difficulties, reflected in recent policy documents such as the Learning Disabilities Review, is strongly influenced by the principles of normalisation. In its focus on the importance of social networks in valorising individual lives and producing social stability, normalisation has much in common with social capital theory, although the two bodies have developed independently. Developed by Wolfensberger (1972) and O'Brien (1987) normalisation reflects an assumption that, on humanitarian grounds, adults with learning difficulties should be fully integrated into mainstream society. According to O'Brien, services for adults with learning difficulties should be geared towards: presence in the community; supporting choice; developing competences; affording respect; ensuring social participation. Insofar as gaining employment might contribute to the social inclusion of adults with learning difficulties, then work should be valued, although the worth of other means of social valorisation, such as independent living, should also be recognised. Education and training, within the principles of normalisation, should be geared towards enabling disabled people to gain access to social networks so that they can function as valued citizens The principles of normalisation have been criticised by social model writers such as Oliver (1990), who see them as conservative and restrictive.

Much of the education and training delivered to people with learning difficulties is informed by both normalisation and social capital thinking. Programmes delivered in day centres, FE colleges and by Community Education have a major focus on social and life skills. Even supported employment programmes, supposedly aimed at getting 'real jobs', are often reframed as a form of therapy, designed to foster meaningful relationships with co-workers rather than to earn money Within community care discourse, 'mainstream daytime opportunities' are seen as infinitely preferable to incarceration in long-stay institutions. While the demise of such institutions is universally welcomed, the type of lifelong learning available to people with learning difficulties may actually offer a new form of segregation. Our analysis of the type of social capital available to people with learning difficulties suggested that, to use Putnam's (2000) terminology, bonding networks tended to fix them in powerless and dependent relationships. There were few opportunities to develop bridging or inclusive networks that might open up the possibility of reciprocal relationships essential to a more independent life.

Socially cohesive societies may base their solidarity on the exclusion of deviant groups, as noted by Wolfensberger:

> When we review society's efforts to handle deviancy, we can readily classify these efforts into four categories: Destruction of deviant individuals, their segregation, reversal of their condition, or prevention thereof. In the past, some kinds of deviance were seen to be the work of the devil or other malignant forces. As such, the deviant person was seen as evil too, and was persecuted and destroyed in order to protect society. As a more human alternative to destruction, the deviant person who is perceived as being unpleasant, offensive or frightening can be segregated from the mainstream of society and placed at its periphery. Deviance can be seen as someone's fault or perhaps a sign that the deviant person's parents had sinned and were therefore being punished by the Lord. The belief that blemished offspring is a punishment for parental wrongdoing appears to be deeply ingrained in the consciousness of the people. (Wolfensberger, 1972, p 24)

While welcoming current moves to nurture the social capital of people with learning difficulties, it is important to be mindful of the danger that 'mainstream daytime opportunities' may be a euphemism for new forms of segregation.

On the other hand, if social capital is construed in terms of including all members of the society, then this might have very positive implications both for people with learning difficulties and those regarded as non-disabled. The entry of people with learning difficulties into the workplace might be seen as an opportunity for increasing the circulation and accumulation of social capital; the personal and shared basis of instrumental skills would have to be made explicit and the collective normative order of the workplace would similarly have to be questioned and subject to conscious review. The questioning of what was previously taken for granted might well be to the benefit of all.

The social control version of the Learning Society

In Chapter 9, we discussed the ways in which the lives of people with learning difficulties are regulated by the state. Appendix 2 provides a summary of the statutory framework of this regulation. Defenders of these statutes would maintain that they are there to protect the interests of a group of people who are inherently vulnerable. However, it is clear that, whatever the intentions of the legislators, the effects of these laws are not to open up opportunities but to foreclose on them. Being identified as requiring special education is likely to lead to endorsement by the Careers Company as being in need of a special college course, which may then lead on to a special training programme. This in turn is likely to lead to placement in a day centre, from which the only escape routes are more segregated education, training or employment programmes. Normalisation for people with learning difficulties is often shorthand for recycling through circuits of training that take them further away from the labour market and the opportunity to establish independent relationships. This may be seen as exemplifying profoundly dystrophic effects of a Learning Society, where education and training are used to produce docile bodies and minds and to compensate for the lack of more purposeful activity.

The way forward

At the present time, both human and social capital versions of the Learning Society appear to operate as controlling mechanisms, restricting rather than enhancing the life chances of people with learning difficulties. In this final section, we summarise the key points emerging from earlier chapters, suggesting the type of social policy shifts which might open up new opportunities for people with learning difficulties.

1. There is a need to dissolve the binary divide, expounded in the DSS's Green Paper (DSS, 1998), between work for those who can and security for those who cannot. Most people with learning difficulties fall into the latter category and the configuration of disability benefits they receive prevents them from engaging in the type of learning that will lead to employment. Furthermore, even if a job is found, working hours are greatly restricted so that little financial or social benefit may accrue from employment. Flexible working should be possible without endangering benefits status.
2. More direct intervention in the labour market by the government would begin to cancel some of the disadvantages experienced by people with learning difficulties as a result of their impairment. The post-war wage subsidy scheme, for example, enabled people with

learning difficulties to enter the labour market on more equal terms. Treating all workers equally simply reinforces existing inequalities.

3. The government has set performance targets in many areas of social policy. Setting inclusion targets for educators, trainers and employers in both public and private sectors might be a powerful means of pushing for change and 'naming and shaming' those who reinforce social exclusion.

4. Attention should be paid to ensuring that the benefits paid to disabled people are sufficient to banish poverty, the underlying reason for loss of social power.

5. There is a need to rethink the meaning of work in post–industrial societies. Castells (2000) argues that consumption is as important as production in the regeneration of wealth. The notion of inter-dependency (Shakespeare, 2000) focuses attention on the important role of those with the most significant needs in creating employment for others. Direct payments, rarely used by people with learning difficulties, provide them with the opportunity to fulfil the role of the employer, engaging others to facilitate access to education, training and employment as well as providing personal assistance.

A large part of the argument of this book has been that, for people with learning difficulties, lifelong learning has failed to deliver social inclusion. However, we still believe that there are ways of envisioning a Learning Society for people with learning difficulties that offers:

> A high quality general education, appropriate vocational training and a job (or series of jobs) worthy of a human being while continuing to participate in education and training throughout their lives. (Coffield, 1994)

References

Abberley, P. (1987) 'The concept of oppression and the development of a social theory of disability', *Disability, Handicap and Society*, vol 2, no 1, pp 5-21.

Abberley, P. (1998) 'The spectre at the feast: disabled people and social theory', in T. Shakespeare (ed) *The disability reader*, London: Cassell.

Albrecht, G. (1992) *The disability business – rehabilitation in America*, London: Sage Publications.

Andrews, J. (1996) 'Identifying and providing for the mentally disabled in early modern London', in D. Wright and A. Digby (eds) *From idiocy to mental deficiency: Historical perspectives on people with learning disabilities*, London: Routledge.

Arthur, S., Corden, A., Green, A., Lewis, J., Loumidis, J., Sainsbury, R., Stafford, B., Thronton, P. and Walker, R. (1999) *New Deal for Disabled People: Early implementation*, Social Security Research Report No 106, London: DfEE.

Ball, S.J., Macrae, S. and Maguire, M. (1999) 'Young lives at risk in the "futures" market: some policy concerns from ongoing research', in F. Coffield (ed) *Speaking truth to power: Research and policy on lifelong learning*, Bristol: The Policy Press.

Barnes, C (1990) *'Cabbage syndrome': The social construction of dependence*, London: The Falmer Press.

Barnes, C. (1991) *Disabled people in Britain and discrimination: A case for anti-discrimination legislation*, London. Hurst Calgary.

Barnes, C. (1996) 'Disability and the myth of the independent researcher', *Disability and Society*, vol 2, no 1 pp 107-11.

Barnes, C. (2000) 'A working social model? Disability, work and disability politics in the 21st century', *Critical Social Policy*, vol 20, no 4, pp 421-44.

Barnes, M. (1997) *Care communities and citizens*, London: Longman.

Baron, S. (1989) 'Community education: from the Cam to the Rea', in S. Walker and L. Barton (eds) *Politics and processes of schooling*, Milton Keynes: Open University Press.

Baron, S. and Dumbleton, P. (2001: forthcoming) *The politics of learning disability*, Basingstoke: Palgrave.

Baron, S., Field, J. and Schuller, T. (eds) (2000) *Social capital: Critical perspectives*, Oxford: Oxford University Press.

Baron, S., Gilloran, A. and Schad, D. (1995a) 'Collaboration in a time of change: from subjects to collaborators', *Social Sciences in Health*, vol 1, no 3, pp 175-88.

Baron, S., Gilloran, A. and Schad, D. (1995b) 'Collaboration in a time of change: blocks to collaborators', *Social Sciences in Health*, vol 1, no 4, pp 195-205.

Baron, S., Riddell, S. and Wilson, A. (1999) 'The secret of eternal youth', *British Journal of the Sociology of Education: Special Issue on Youth and Social Change*, vol 20, no 4, pp 483-99.

Baron, S., Stalker, K., Wilkinson, H. and Riddell, S. (1998) 'The Learning Society: the highest stage of human capitalism?', in F. Coffield (ed) *Learning at work*, Bristol: The Policy Press.

Beck, U. (1992) *The risk society*, London: Sage Publications.

Becker, G. (1964) *Human capital: A theoretical and empirical analysis with special reference to education*, Princeton NJ: Princeton University Press.

Beresford, P. (1996) 'Poverty and disabled people: challenging dominant debates and policies', *Disability and Society*, vol 11, no 4, pp 553-69.

Beyer, S., Goodere, L. and Kilsby, M. (1996a) *The costs and benefits of supported employment agencies*, DfEE Research Studies RS37, London: The Stationery Office.

Beyer, S., Goodere, M. and Sproston, K. (1996b) *The Access to Work Programme: A survey of recipients, employers, Employment Service managers and staff*, London: Social and Community Planning Research.

Beyer, S., Kilsby, M. and Shearn, J. (1999) 'The organisation and outcomes of supported employment in Britain', *Journal of Vocational Rehabilitation*, vol 12, no 3, pp 137-47.

Booth,T. (2000) 'Inclusion and exclusion policy in England: who controls the agenda?', in F.Armstrong, D.Armstrong and L.Barton (eds) *Inclusive education*, London: David Fulton Publishers.

Booth, T. and Booth, W. (1993) 'Accentuate the positive: a personal profile of a parent with learning difficulties', *Disability and Society*, vol 8, no 4, pp 377-92.

Bourdieu, P. (1997) 'The forms of capital', in A.H. Halsey, H. Lauder, P. Brown and A. Stuart Wells (eds) *Education: Culture, economy, society*, Oxford: Oxford University Press.

Bourdieu, P. and Passeron, J.-C. (1977) *Reproduction in education, culture and society*, London: Sage Publications.

Brown, H. and Smith, H. (eds) (1992) *Normalisation. A reader for the nineties*, London: Routledge.

Bynner, J. (1991) 'Controlling transition', *Work, Employment and Society*, vol 5, no 4, pp 645-58.

Cambridge, P. and Brown, H. (1997) 'Making the market work for people with learning disabilities', *Critical Social Policy*, vol 51, no 17, pp 27-52.

Carnoy, M. (1995) *Encyclopaedia of economics of education*, Oxford: Pergamon Press.

Castells, M. (1996) *The information age: Economy, society and culture. Volume 1: The rise of the network society*, Malden, MA: Blackwell Publishers.

Castells, M. (2000) 'Information technology and global capitalism', in W. Hutton and A. Giddens (eds) *On the edge: Living with global capitalism*, London: Jonathon Cape.

CCCS (Centre for Contemporary Cultural Studies) (1981) *Unpopular education: Schooling and social democracy in England since 1944*, London: Hutchinson.

Christie, N. (1992) 'Six ways of dealing with stigma: in defence of the ghetto', in S. Baron and J.D. Haldane (eds) *Community, normality and difference*, Aberdeen: Aberdeen University Press.

Clarke, J. and Newman, J. (1997) *The managerial state*, London: Sage Publications.

Closs, A. (ed) (1993) *Special educational needs beyond 16 ...*, Edinburgh: Moray House Publications.

Coffield, F. (1994) *The Learning Society: Knowledge and skills for employment research specification for the ESRC Programme*, Swindon: ESRC.

Coffield, F. (1999) 'Breaking the consensus: lifelong learning as social control', *British Educational Research Journal*, vol 25, no 4, pp 479-501.

Coffield, F. (2000) 'Introduction: The structure below the surface: reassessing the significance of informal learning', in F. Coffield (ed) *The necessity of informal learning*, Bristol: The Policy Press.

Coleman, J.S. (1988) 'Social capital in the creation of human capital', *American Journal of Sociology*, vol 94 (Supplement), pp 95-120.

Coleman, J.S. (1991) 'Prologue: constructed social organisation', in P. Bourdieu and J.S. Coleman (eds) *Social theory for a changing society*, Oxford: Westview Press.

Coleman, J.S. (1994) *Foundations of social theory*, Cambridge: Belknap Press.

Corker, M. (1997) *Deaf and disabled or deafness disabled*, Buckingham: Open University Press.

CSJ (Commission on Social Justice) (1994) *Social justice: Strategies for national renewal*, London: Vintage.

Deakin, N. (1994) *The politics of welfare: Continuities and change*, London: Harvester Wheatsheaf.

DES (Department of Education and Science) (1978) *Special educational needs* (Warnock Report), London: HMSO.

DES (1999) *Adult education in an era of lifelong learning*, Dublin: DES.

DfEE (Department for Education and Employment) (1998) *The learning age: A renaissance for a new Britain*, London: The Stationery Office.

DfEE (1999) *Learning to succeed: A new framework for post-16 learning*, Cm 4392, London: The Stationery Office.

Disability Alliance (1991) *A way out of poverty and disability: Moving towards a comprehensive disability income*, London: Disability Alliance.

DoH (Department of Health) (1989) *Caring for people: Community care in the next decade and beyond*, London: DoH.

DoH (1992) *The health of the nation*, London: DoH.

DoH (1998) *Independent inquiry into inequalities in health* (Acheson Report), London: The Stationery Office.

Drake, R. (2000) 'Disabled people, New Labour, benefits and work', *Critical Social Policy*, vol 20, no 4, pp 421-44.

DSS (Department of Social Security) (1998) *New ambitions for our country: A new contract for welfare*, London: The Stationery Office.

Durkheim, E. (1938, reprinted 1982) *The rules of sociological method*, Houdsmill: Macmillan.

Dutch Ministry of Education and Science (1998) *Lifelong learning: The Dutch initiative*, Amsterdam: Dutch Ministry of Education and Science.

EC (European Commission) (1996) *White Paper on Education and training, teaching and learning: Towards the learning society*, Luxembourg: Office for Official Publications for the European Communities.

Egerton Commission (1889) *Report of the Royal Commission on the Blind, the Deaf, the Dumb and Others of the United Kingdom*, 4 vols, London: HMSO.

Espie, C., Curtice, L., Morrison, J., Dunnigan, M., Knill-Jones, R. and Long, L. (1999) 'The role of the NHS in meeting the health needs of people with learning disabilities', Paper to the Scottish Executive, Glasgow, University of Glasgow.

Fairley, J. (1992) 'Scottish local authorities and Local Enterprise Companies: strategic issues', *Local Government Policy-Making*, vol 19, no 1, pp 38-45.

FEFC (Further Education Funding Council) (1996) *Inclusive education: Report of the learning difficulties and/or disabilities committee* (Tomlinson Report), London: HMSO.

Fevre, R. (1996) 'Some sociological alternatives to human capital theory and their implications for research on post-compulsory education and training', Paper presented to the European Conference on Educational Research, University of Seville, 25-28 September.

Field, J. (1998) 'Informal learning and social capital', Paper presented to the ESRC Learning Society Programme Conference on Informal Learning, Bristol, 3 June.

Field J., Schuller T. and Baron S. (2000) 'Social capital and human capital revisited', in S. Baron, J. Field and T. Schuller (eds) *Social capital: Critical perspectives*, Oxford: Oxford University Press.

Finch, J. (1984) *Education as social policy*, London: Longman.

Fine, B. and Green, F. (2000) 'Economics, social capital and the colonization of the social sciences', in S. Baron, J. Field and T. Schuller (eds) *Social capital: Critical perspectives*, Oxford: Oxford University Press.

Fitzherbert, A. (1534) *New natura brevium*, quoted in J. Brydall (1700) *Non compis mentis*, London: Richard and Edward Atkins.

Finkelstein, V. (1980) *Attitudes and disabled people: Issues for discussion*, New York, NY: World Rehabilitation Fund.

Ford, J. (1969) *Social class and the comprehensive school*, London: Routledge and Kegan Paul.

Foucault, M. (1991) *Discipline and punish*, Harmondsworth: Penguin.

Fraser, N. (1997) *Justice interruptus: Critical reflections on the post-socialist condition*, London: Routledge.

French, S. and Swain, J. (1997) 'Changing disability research: participatory and emancipatory research with disabled people', *Physiotherapy*, vol 83, no 1, pp 26–32.

Fukuyama, F. (1999) *The great disruption: Human nature and the reconstruction of social order*, Bury St Edmunds: Profile Books.

Giddens, A. (1989) *Sociology*, Cambridge: Polity Press.

Glasgow City Council (2000) *Achieving partnership: Services for people with learning disability in Glasgow City*, Draft Joint Strategy 2000-2003, Glasgow: Glasgow City Council.

Goffman E. (1990) *Stigma*, Harmondsworth: Penguin.

Goldberg, D. (1999) 'Mental health', in D. Gordon, M. Shaw, D. Dorling and G. Davey Smith (eds) *Inequalities in health: The evidence presented to the Inquiry into Inequalities in Health, chaired by Sir Donald Acheson*, Bristol: The Policy Press.

Gowans, F. and Hulbert, H. (1983) 'Self-concept assessment in mentally handicapped adults: a review', *British Institute of Mental Handicap*, vol 11, pp 121–3.

Gramsci, A. (1971) *Selection from the prison notebooks*, London: Lawrence and Wishart.

Granovetter, M. (1973) 'The strength of weak ties', *American Journal of Sociology*, vol 78, no 4, pp 1350–80.

Gray, J. (1992) *The moral foundations of market institutions*, London: Institute of Economic Affairs.

Griffiths, R. (1988) *Community care: Agenda for action*, London: HMSO.

Hancock, R. and Sutcliffe, J. (1995) 'Choice and change: opportunities and issues in continuing education for adults with learning difficulties', in T. Philpot and L. Ward (eds) *Values and visions: Changing ideas in services for people with learning difficulties*, Oxford: Butterworth Heinmann.

Harris, P. (1995) 'Who am I? Concepts of disability and their implications for people with learning difficulties', *Disability and Society*, vol 10, no 3, pp 341-53.

Hartmann, H. (1981) 'The unhappy marriage of marxism and feminism: towards a more progressive union', in L. Sargent (ed) *The unhappy marriage of marxism and feminism: A debate on class and patriarchy*, London: Pluto Press.

Hirschman, A. (1970) *Exit, voice and loyalty*, Cambridge, MA: Harvard University Press.

Humphries, S. and Gordon, P. (1992) *Out of sight: The experience of disability 1900-1950*, Plymouth: Northcote House Publishers.

Hyde, M. (1998) 'Sheltered and supported employment in the 1990s: the experiences of disabled workers in the UK', *Disability and Society*, vol 13, no 2, pp 199-217.

Hyde, M. (2000) 'From welfare to work: social policy for disabled people of working age in the United Kingdom', *Disability and Society*, vol 15, no 2, pp 327-341.

Jahoda, A., Markova, I. and Cattermole, M. (1988) 'Stigma and the self-concept of people with a mild mental handicap', *Journal of Mental Deficiency Research*, vol 32, pp 103-15.

Jacoobs R. and Van Doorsslaer, J. (2000) *Het Ponphuis van de 21ste Eeuw. Educatie in de Actieve Welvaarsstaat*, Amsterdam: EPO.

Keep, E. and Mayhew, K. (1996) 'Towards a learning society: definition and measurement', *Policy Studies*, vol 17, no 3, pp 25-32.

Knapp, M., Wistow, G., Forder, J. and Hardy, B. (1994) 'Markets for social care: opportunities barriers and implications', in W. Bartlett, C. Propper, D. Wilson, and J. Le Grand (eds) *Quasi-markets in the welfare state*, Bristol: SAUS Publications.

Kregel, J. (1997) 'Supported employment', *Remedial and Special Education*, vol 18, no 4, pp 194-6.

Kregel, J., Wehman, M. and Banks, P.D. (1989) 'The effects of consumer characteristics and type of employment model on individual outcomes in supported employment', *Journal of Applied Behavioral Analysis*, vol 22, pp 407-15.

Lash, S. and Urry, J. (1993) *Economies of signs and space*, London: Sage Publications.

Le Grand, J. (1991) 'Quasi-markets and social policy', *Economic Journal*, vol 101, pp 1256-67.

Levitas, R. (1996) 'The concept of social exclusion and the new Durkheimian hegemony', *Critical Social Policy*, vol 15, no 1, pp 5-20.

Lonsdale, S. (1986) *Work and inequality*, Harlow: Longman.

Lonsdale, S. (1990) *Women and disability: The experience of physical disability amongst women*, London: Macmillan.

Lugnaris-Kraft, B., Rule, S., Salzberg, C. and Stowitschek, J.J. (1988) 'Social vocational skills of workers with and without mental retardation in two community employment sites', *Mental Retardation*, vol 26, pp 297-306.

McKay, C. and Patrick, H. (1995) *The law and your rights to community care in Scotland*, Glasgow: Enable and SAMH.

Macintyre, S. (1999) 'Geographical inequalities in mortality, morbidity and health-related behaviour in England', in D. Gordon, M. Shaw, D. Dorling and G. Davey Smith (eds) *Inequalities in health: The evidence presented to the Inquiry into Inequalities in Health, chaired by Sir Donald Acheson*, Bristol: The Policy Press.

Mank, D., Cioffi, A. and Yovanoff, P. (1997) 'Analysis of the typicalness of supported employment jobs, natural supports and wage integration outcomes', *Mental Retardation*, vol 35, no 3, pp 185-97.

Marx, K. (1973) *Grundrisse*, Harmondsworth: Penguin.

Marx, K. (1976) *Capital*, Harmondsworth: Penguin.

Maudslay, E. and Dee, L. (1995) 'Beyond the "inclusionist" debate', in E. Maudslay and L. Dee (eds) *Redefining the future: Perspectives on students with learning difficulties and disabilities in further education*, London: Institute of Education.

May, D. and Hughes, D. (1985) 'The prospects on leaving school for the mildly mentally handicapped', *British Journal of Special Education*, vol 12, no 4, pp 151-8.

Merrill, B. (2000) 'The community education and social inclusion research agenda: Europe', Paper presented to the ESRC seminar *Lifelong Learning and Social Equity Agenda*, 23 May, University of Leeds.

Neugebauer, R. (1996) 'Mental handicap in medival and early modern England: criteria, measurement and care', in D. Wright and A. Digby (eds) *From idiocy to mental deficiency: Historical perspectives on people with learning disabilities*, London: Routledge.

O'Brien, J. (1987) 'A guide to lifestyle planning: using the activities catalogue to integrate services and natural support systems', in B.W. Wilcox and G.T. Bellamy (eds) *The activities catalogue: An alternative curriculum for youth and adults with severe disabilities*, Baltimore: Brookes, pp 175-89.

Oliver, C (1986) 'Self-concept assessment: a case study', *Mental Handicap*, vol 14, pp 24-5.

Oliver, M. (1990) *The politics of disablement*, Basingstoke: Macmillan.

Oliver, M. (1992) 'Changing the social relations of research production?', *Disability, Handicap and Society*, vol 7, no 2, pp 101-14.

Oppenheim, S. and Harker, L. (1996) *Poverty: The facts* (updated 3rd edn), London: Child Poverty Action Group.

OECD (Organization for Economic Co-operation and Development) (1998) *The knowledge based economy*, Paris: OECD.

Parent, W., Kregel, J. and Johnson, A. (1996) 'Consumer satisfaction: a survey of individuals who receive supported employment services', *Focus on Autism and Other Developmental Delays*, vol 11, pp 207-21.

Phillips, A. (1997) 'From inequality to difference: a severe case of displacement?', *New Left Review*, vol 224, pp 143-53.

Putnam, R.D. (1993) *Making democracy work: Civic traditions in modern Italy*, Princeton, NJ: Princeton University Press.

Putnam, R.D. (2000) *Bowling alone: The collapse and revival of American community*, New York, NY: Simon & Schuster.

Rawls J. (1972) *A theory of justice*, Oxford: Oxford University Press.

Rees, T. and Bartlett, W. (1999) in F. Coffield (ed) *Why's the beer always stronger up North?: Studies of lifelong learning in Europe*, Bristol: The Policy Press.

Riddell, S. and Tett, L. (eds) (2001: forthcoming) *Education, social justice and inter-agency working: Joined-up or fractured policy?*, London: Routledge.

Riddell, S., Baron, S. and Stalker, K. (1995) 'The meaning of the learning society for adults with learning difficulties; a proposal to the ESRC', Stirling: University of Stirling.

Riddell, S., Baron, S. and Wilkinson, H. (1998b) 'Training from cradle to grave: social justice and training for people with learning difficulties', *Journal of Education Policy*, vol 13, no 4, pp 531-44.

Riddell, S., Baron, S. and Wilson, A. (1999) 'Social capital and people with learning difficulties', *Studies in the Education of Adults*, vol 31, no 1, pp 49-66.

Riddell, S., Ward, K. and Thomson, G.O.B. (1993) 'The significance of employment as a goal for young people with special educational needs', *British Journal of Education and Work*, vol 6, no 2, pp 57-72.

Riddell, S., Wilkinson, H. and Baron, S. (1998a) 'From emancipatory research to focus group: people with learning difficulties and the research process', in P. Clough and L. Barton (eds) *Articulating with difficulty: Research voices in inclusive education*, London: Paul Chapman Publishing.

Riddell, S., Adler, M., Farmakopoulou, N. and Mordaunt, E. (2000) 'Special educational needs and competing policy frameworks in England and Scotland', *Journal of Education Policy*, vol 15, no 6, pp 621-35.

Riddell, S., Stalker, K., Wilkinson, H. and Baron, S. (1997a) *The meaning of the Learning Society for adults with learning difficulties: Report of phase 1 of the study*, Glasgow: Glasgow University.

Scottish Enterprise (1997) *Annual Report 1996/97*, Glasgow: Scottish Enterprise.

Scottish Executive (1999a) *Social justice: A Scotland where everyone matters*, Edinburgh: The Stationery Office.

Scottish Executive (1999b) *Implementing inclusiveness, realising potential* (Beattie Committee Report), Edinburgh: Scottish Executive.

Scottish Executive (2000a) *The same as you? A review of services for people with learning disabilities*, Edinburgh: The Stationery Office.

Scottish Executive (2000b) *The way forward for care*, Edinburgh: The Stationery Office.

Scottish Office (1998a) *Opportunity Scotland: A paper on lifelong learning*, Cm 4048, Edinburgh: The Scottish Office.

Scottish Office (1998b) *The future of community education in Scotland* (Osler Report), Edinburgh: The Scottish Office.

Scottish Office (1999) *Aiming for excellence: Modernising social work services in Scotland*, White Paper, Edinburgh: Scottish Office.

Scottish Parliament (1999) *Adults with Incapacity (Scotland) Bill: Policy memorandum*, Edinburgh: Scottish Parliament.

Secretaries of State for Health, Social Security, Wales and Scotland (1989) *Caring for people: Community care in the next decade and beyond*, London: HMSO.

Shakespeare, T. (1996) 'Doing disability research: rules of engagement', *Disability and Society*, vol 11, no 1, pp 115-21.

Shakespeare, T. (2000) *Help*, London: Verso.

Simons, K. (1998) *Home, work and inclusion: The social policy implications of supported employment for people with learning disabilities*, York: Joseph Rowntree Foundation.

Skeggs, B. (1997) *Formations of class and gender*, London: Sage Publications.

Sly, F. (1996) 'Disability and the labour market', *Labour Market Trends*, December, pp 439-59.

Stalker, K. (1997) 'Choices and voices: a case study of a self-advocacy group', *Health and Social Care in the Community*, vol 5, pp 246-54.

Stalker, K. (1998) 'Some ethical and methodological issues in research with people with learning difficulties', *Disability and Society*, vol 13, no 1, pp 5-19.

Stalker, K. and Hunter, S. (1999) *Resettlement of people with learning disabilities from Scottish hospitals*, Edinburgh: Scottish Executive.

Stalker, K., Baron, S., Riddell, S. and Wilkinson, H. (1999b) 'Models of disability: the relationship between theory and practice in non-statutory organisations', *Critical Social Policy*, vol 9, no 1, pp 5-31.

Stalker, K., Cadogan, L., Petrie, M., Jones, C. and Murray, J. (1999a) *'If you don't ask you don't get', Review of services to people with learning disabilities: The views of people who use services and their carers*, Edinburgh: Scottish Executive Central Research Unit.

Stone, D.A. (1984) *The disabled state*, Basingstoke: Macmillan.

Taylor, M. and Hoggett, P. (1994) 'Quasi-markets and the transformation of the independent sector', in W. Bartlett, C. Propper, D. Wilson and J. Le Grand (eds) *Quasi-markets in the welfare state*, Bristol: SAUS Publications.

Thornton, P., Sainsbury, R. and Barnes, H. (1995) *Helping disabled people to work: A cross national study of Social Security: A report for the Social Security Advisory Committee*, York: Social Policy Research Unit.

Tomlinson, S. (1982) *A sociology of special education*, London: Routledge.

Townsend, P. (1999) 'A structural plan needed to reduce inequalities of health', in D. Gordon, M. Shaw, D. Dorling and G. Davey Smith (eds) *Inequalities in health: The evidence presented to The Independent Inquiry into Inequalities in Health*, chaired by Sir Donald Acheson, Bristol: The Policy Press.

Townsley, R. (1995) 'Avon calling', *Community Care*, January, pp 12-18.

Vernon, A. and Qureshi, H. (2000) 'Community care and independence: self-sufficiency or empowerment', *Critical Social Policy*, vol 20, no 1, pp 255-67.

Walmsley, J. (1994) 'Learning disability: overcoming the barriers?', in S. French (ed) *On equal terms: Working with disabled people*, London: Butterworth Heinemann.

Ward, A. (1984) *Scots law and the mentally handicapped*, Glasgow: Scottish Society for the Mentally Handicapped.

Ward, A. (1990) *The power to act*, Glasgow: Scottish Society for the Mentally Handicapped.

Walsh, K., Deakin, N., Smith, P., Sourgen, P. and Thomas, N. (1997) *Contracting for change: Contracts in health, social care and other local government services*, Oxford; Oxford University Press.

Wehman, P. and Kregel, J. (1995) 'At the crossroads: supported employment a decade later', *Journal of the Association for Persons with Severe Handicaps*, vol 20, no 4, pp 286-99.

Whittaker, J. (1995) 'Does your college of further education have learning difficulties?', in E. Maudslay and L. Dee (eds) *Redefining the future: Perspectives on students with learning difficulties and disabilities in further education*, London: Institute of Education.

Whittaker, J., Gardner, S. and Kershaw, J. (1990) *Service evaluation by people with learning difficulties*, London: The Kings Fund.

Whitty, G., Aggleton, P., Gamarnikow, E. and Tyrer, P. (1999) 'Education and health inequalities', in D. Gordon, M. Shaw, D. Dorling and G. Davey Smith (eds) *Inequalities in health: The evidence presented to the Inquiry into Inequalities in Health, chaired by Sir Donald Acheson*, Bristol: The Policy Press.

Wilkinson, R. (1996) *Unhealthy societies: The affliction of inequality*, London: Routledge.

Wilkinson, R. (1999) 'The social environment', in D. Gordon, M. Shaw, D. Dorling and G. Davey Smith (eds) *Inequalities in health: The evidence presented to the Inquiry into Inequalities in Health, chaired by Sir Donald Acheson*, Bristol: The Policy Press.

Williams, S. (1996) 'Educating for flexibility: the political economy of lifetime learning in the UK', Paper presented to the European Conference on Educational Research, University of Seville, 25-28 September.

Wilson, A., Lightbody, P. and Riddell, S. (2000) *A flexible gateway to employment? An evaluation of Enable Service's traditional and innovative forms of work preparation*, Glasgow: Strathclyde Centre for Disability Research.

Wolfensberger, W. (1972) *The principle of normalisation in human services*, Toronto, Canada: National Institute on Mental Retardation.

Wolfensberger, W. (1983) 'Social role valorisation: a proposed new term for the principle of normalisation', *Mental Retardation*, vol 21, no 6.

Wright, D. and Digby, A. (1996) *From idiocy to mental deficiency: Historical perspectives on people with learning disabilities*, London: Routledge.

Young, I.M. (1990) *Justice and the politics of difference*, Princeton, NJ: Princeton University Press.

Zarb, G. (1992) 'On the road to Damascus: first steps towards changing the relations of research production', *Disability, Handicap and Society*, vol 7, no 2, pp 125-38.

Appendix I
Researching the lives of people with learning difficulties: lessons from the research process

Disabled people, identities and the research process

Research is clearly not a neutral activity, but may be used to support or subvert dominant social discourses. In Oliver's view, research in the area of disability has hitherto been a conservative rather than a radical force. He comments:

> Disabled people have come to see research as a violation of their experience, as irrelevant to their needs and as failing to improve their material circumstances and quality of life. (Oliver, 1992, p 105)

In developing a more democratic disability research paradigm, two strands have emerged, participatory and emancipatory research. The distinction between these is not altogether clear; sometimes the terms are used interchangeably and at other times participatory research is seen as a stepping-stone towards emancipatory research. French and Swain (1997), for example, argue that the key difference lies in their contrasting relationship with the social model of disability:

> Emancipatory research espouses a social model of disability where the foci for research are the physical and social barriers within society that prevent disabled people leading full and active lives. Although participatory research may give support to the social model of disability, it is not inherently associated with it. In emancipatory research the research processes themselves and the outcomes of research are part of the liberation of disabled people – that is part of the process of changing society to ensure their full participation and citizenship. This is not just a process of empowerment as in

participatory research, where research participants may be given
opportunities to tell their own stories and analyse their own situation,
but in terms of disabled people taking control of the research processes
which shape their lives. The processes and products of emancipatory
research are used by disabled people as tools towards the achievement
of their liberation. Emancipatory research is thus a form of
educational and political action. (1997, p 28)

Stalker (1998) summarises the main beliefs of emancipatory and
participatory research thus:

First, that conventional relationships, whereby the researcher is the
'expert' and the researched merely the object of investigation, are
inequitable; secondly, that people have the right to be consulted
about and involved in research which is involved in issues affecting
their lives and, thirdly, that the quality and relevance of research is
improved when disabled people are closely involved in the process.
(1998, p 6)

Fulfilling all three criteria in action research with physically disabled
people is imaginable and such research has provided the model for all
disability research. Attempting to fulfil these criteria with other groups,
in our case, people with learning difficulties, is more complex: the
expertise of the researcher (presumably the warrant for any research
activity) is not transmissible to some people with cognitive impairments;
the involvement of people with learning difficulties in the process of
the research may similarly be limited; current models of the consultation
and involvement of people with learning difficulties in issues affecting
their lives suggest that the pulls either to the trivial or to the professionally
stage-managed are hard to resist.

According to Stalker, adopting a more democratic research paradigm
with people with learning difficulties is potentially problematic for
academics because such research, when done properly, is likely to take
longer and lead to different forms of dissemination and publication.
These requirements run counter to the current intensification of research
production, demanding that work is conducted more rapidly and that
publications should be in the most prestigious academic journals rather
than those aimed at non-academic audiences. The following questions
concerning power differentials, Stalker suggests, should be tackled by all
those doing disability research but will be particularly tricky for those
working with people with learning difficulties:

How much does – or can – most research 'empower' people with
learning difficulties, and in what ways? How many people want to
be empowered by research? Or is it the researcher who is empowered,
if the study yields more publications or leads to another grant?
(Stalker, 1998, p 6)

These questions are challenging not only for those who perhaps do not
make great claims for their work in terms of its empowering properties,
but also for those who might be tempted to make glib assertions that
their work is 'giving disabled people a voice', without considering
whether this is in their gift, whether disabled people wanted it in the
first place and what the nature of the gift relationship is. We explore
such issues of involving disabled people in the next section.

Activism and the academy: involving disabled
people in research

If, as French and Swain suggest, the social model of disability is associated
with emancipatory research, it is perhaps not surprising that the examples
of full participation following the removal of barriers generally relate to
those with physical and not intellectual impairment. For instance, Zarb
(1992) describes an investigation into a self-operated care scheme in
which the Greenwich Association of Disabled People played a central
role throughout the research, recommending methods of investigation,
commenting on research instruments, contributing to the analysis of
the data and finally scrutinising the research report. The involvement of
the group, according to Zarb, was both 'daunting and exciting'. They:

> Challenged almost every aspect of the report – interpretation and
> inferences, the language used, and even the ordering of the authors'
> names on the cover.

Zarb's comments raise important questions in relation to the involvement
of disabled people, including those who are multiple disadvantaged, in
research. What happens, for example, when researchers and disabled
people disagree about the conduct and meaning of research? Do non-
disabled researchers ever have the right to disagree with disabled people
over how data should be read?

Unsurprisingly, researchers have come up with different answers to
these questions. For Barnes (1996) the independence of the researcher

must always take second place to the promotion of arguments in support of the struggle of disabled people against oppression, the nature of which he takes to be unproblematic:

> If disability research is about researching oppression, and I would argue that it is, then researchers should not be professing 'mythical independence' to disabled people, but joining with them in their struggles to confront and overcome this oppression. Researchers should be espousing commitment, not value freedom, engagement, not objectivity, and solidarity, not independence. (Barnes, 1996, p 110)

Shakespeare (1996), on the other hand, sees a separate role for activists and researchers because of the different nature of political and sociological knowledge:

> Disability Studies is an academic investigation of the social world, and as such is more than simply common sense (Giddens, 1989). Sociological discourse is a critical discourse, but also a reflective discourse, because it is critical upon itself. In this, it differs from political language. (Shakespeare, 1996, p 118)

Because of the distinction between academic work and political struggle, Shakespeare maintains that he feels accountable to his research subjects in terms of honesty about research intentions and methods, but not to the British Council of Organisations of Disabled People, to local self-organised groups or to other organisations within the movement.

In relation to people with learning difficulties, a particular form of accountability is advocated by Booth and Booth (1993). Their version of accountability is closer to the position of Barnes than Shakespeare, in that responsibility to research participants as well as the wider disability movement is acknowledged. Nonetheless, the type of research described by Booth and Booth does not involve people with learning difficulties in its conduct or in the development of theory. A biographical profile is presented of Molly Austin, a mother with learning difficulties. Molly lives with her two children and her partner Kevin in a dreary and uncomfortable caravan and is about to sign over responsibility for the children to her husband. The authors present two contrasting accounts of Molly, one based on a deficiency and the other on a capacity perspective. Seen through a deficiency lens, Molly appears "incapable of living up to her responsibilities as a mother or of putting her children's needs before her own". (Booth and Booth, 1993, p 388). Adopting a capacity perspective, on the other hand, reveals Molly as lacking motivation rather than skills, an understandable response to "the daily grind of a life cramped by poverty." (Booth and Booth, 1993, p 390). Support from health and social services is sparse and crisis-orientated. In sum, it is not so much that Molly has failed as that she has not been given a chance to succeed. Given the growing number of parents with learning difficulties, the authors suggest that health and social services must avoid the presumption of incompetence, the mistake of false attribution and the tendency to blame the victim. By highlighting the differing interpretations arising from a capacity as opposed to a deficiency perspective, the authors alert researchers to the dangers of adopting the latter uncritically and suggest that a capacity perspective is more likely to encourage the growth of services that support rather than punish. The work of Tim and Wendy Booth, highlighting barriers rather than individual deficits, appears to be compatible with the social model of disability, although it does not involve disabled people as researchers. Nonetheless, as we shall see in the following section, some commentators would see such work as falling short of the ideal, in which disabled people control all aspects of the research process.

People with learning difficulties and the research process

Stalker (1998), citing Walmsley (1994), refers to the vision created by the social model of disability in which people with learning difficulties oversee a research project from beginning to end, taking the lead role in design, conduct, analysis and dissemination in the same way as the Greenwich Association of Disabled People, referred to above. According to the social model, this should be possible if certain disabling barriers are overcome. In the literature, however, it is evident that there are still few examples of research that has begun to move in this direction, let alone achieve this goal. Here, we consider some recent accounts of the involvement of people with learning difficulties in research projects and the significance of the nature of their inclusion and exclusion.

Townsley (1995), for example, described the way in which researchers at the Norah Fry Research Centre involved a group at a resource and activity centre in an investigation of issues around gender in service provision. Assisted by a group worker and a researcher from the centre, the group devised questions for a questionnaire survey and were involved in the administration of the questionnaire and the collation of findings, which were subsequently presented at a dissemination conference. Similarly, direct involvement of adults with learning difficulties in service evaluation is reported by Whittaker, Gardner and Kershaw (1990). A researcher from the King's Fund Centre (Andrea Whittaker) worked with two consultants (Simon Gardner and Joyce Kershaw) from People First, an organisation run by and for people with learning difficulties with a strong commitment to self-advocacy. Interviews with service users were conducted by Gardner and Kershaw, assisted by Whittaker, who endeavoured to support the consultants without influencing the substance of the researchers' questions or the service users' responses. It is interesting that both these examples focus on concrete issues to do with service delivery, where people with learning difficulties will clearly have an active involvement, rather than more abstract or theoretical ideas that might, for example, form the basis of an ESRC research project. Nonetheless, they have little to say about the process of data analysis, in particular the way in which a narrative emerged from the interview transcripts. Nor are we told of any problems that might have arisen during the course of the work concerning the relationship between the supporter and the consultants. Did everyone involved in these projects share similar views of the project, how much of a steering role did the supporters take and to what extent was the work judged by the academic criteria of 'accuracy, effectiveness and consistency' to ensure 'quality and integrity' (Shakespeare, 1996, p 117)?

Stalker (1998) points out that when researchers encounter difficulty in involving people with learning difficulties in aspects of academic research, there may be a temptation to 'rubbish' research. For example, Minkes et al (1995) maintain that it is important to focus on issues from service users' point of view and not "some hidden agenda of ivory towered scientific rigour." Stalker comments:

> There are some interesting unspoken assumptions underlying this statement. While few would disagree with the first part of it, there is an anti-intellectualism or anti-academicism within the second part which gives pause for thought. Good research is rigorous. It does not follow that rigour is incompatible with a focus on users' viewpoints. (Nor am *I* implying that research carried out in non-academic settings is less than rigorous.) (1998, p 16)

Stalker describes in some detail the power relations inherent in her own research; she highlights the points at which involvement of people with learning difficulties was successful and the reasons why, on occasion, it failed. In a research advisory group on a study of the exercise of choice by service users, for example, she comments on the problems encountered by the people with learning difficulties in contributing to discussions. Academic debate on methodological issues, a perfectly legitimate topic for the advisory committee (of which two of the current authors were members), was impenetrable not only to the two consumer representatives but, it later transpired, to the local authority officer as well. It was also difficult for the disabled people to comment on practical aspects of the research since it was not being conducted in an environment with which they were familiar. The presence of a supporter to intervene on their behalf, with the aim of interpreting and refocusing the discussion, might have proved a significant help in removing barriers. The lessons from this experience, suggests Stalker, illustrate certain steps that researchers could take to involve people with learning difficulties in research, but also indicate that there may be aspects of research in which not everybody has the necessary knowledge and skill to play a role. If people with learning difficulties are to be involved in the research, then it should be in ways that draw on their expertise and specialist knowledge, with accountability remaining a guiding principle. Certain types of theorising may be difficult to engage with, but this is an argument not for ditching the theory (she makes the telling point that both the social model and normalisation have made a significant contribution to the improvement of disabled people's lives), but for thinking through where involvement is possible and fruitful and in addition, what is the likely impact of the development of certain theories on people's lives.

To summarise thus far, it is evident that there is currently much debate in the area of disability over power relations in research. Parallels with the development of feminist research have been drawn, with the suggestion that the loss of confidence in meta-narrative and the identity politics and research accompanying this may have limited the power of the women's movement as a political force. Within discussions of disability research, it is often suggested that disabled people should ideally control all aspects of the research process, with researchers putting their knowledge and skills at the disposal of disabled people rather than acting independently. The possible implications of this for people with learning difficulties have been flagged up: if people's intellectual impairment means that their involvement in research, in particular abstract theorising, is limited, does this mean that the activity should be abandoned and would this contribute to the social marginalisation of this group? It was with the commitment to involve people with learning difficulties in research, but with reservations about the simple empowerment model, that we formed a research group as part of an ESRC funded project. Let us now look at what happened in practice.

The research project and the research group

The project, entitled 'The meaning of the Learning Society for adults with learning difficulties', part of the ESRC *Learning Society Programme*, aims to map the education, training and employment opportunities for people with learning difficulties in Scotland, to explore the professional discourses of a range of providers and to understand the perspective of service users of different ages and in urban and rural settings. In order to pursue the latter aim, 30 case studies of people with learning difficulties in two local authorities, involving ten visits to each person, were planned. Central theoretical concerns were the operation of markets and choice, the nature of adult status and the barriers to full social participation. In our proposal we recognised the importance of the involvement of adults with learning difficulties in the research process and undertook to explore "creative and multiple ways in which this can happen" (Riddell et al, 1995). Because of the difficulties discussed above in attempting to include people with learning difficulties in a project advisory group (Stalker, 1998), we decided that we would involve a small number of case study participants in the conduct of the research.

There were a number of different ways in which we could have involved adults with learning difficulties and we spent a considerable amount of time thinking through the various possibilities. One possibility was to train people with learning difficulties to act as interviewers, but there were a number of problems with this. Our methodology did not involve the use of a one-off structured interview, but rather a series of ethnographic interviews entailing progressive focusing. In the tight timetable to which we were committed, we did not have enough time to train people with learning difficulties to act as interviewers and also were uncertain about the implications of using people with learning difficulties in this way. Certainly we did not wish to assume that there was some essential quality in having an intellectual impairment that specifically enabled people with learning difficulties to empathise with each other in a way that others could not. The work involved an ongoing process of theorisation that any inexperienced interviewer would have found difficult to undertake. Within the context of this project, then, we could see few benefits and a number of significant disadvantages in involving people with learning difficulties in the wider fieldwork.

Another possibility, the one we finally pursued, was to bring together a group of people with learning difficulties who had already participated in the case studies and involve them in discussion of the initial research findings and of key themes within the research. Rather than considering the abstract concepts referred to above, we decided to focus on lower order constructs arising from our initial inductive analysis of the qualitative data. These were broadly connected with various life experiences including childhood and going to school, leaving school and moving on, work, money, homes and housing, and relationships. Although much less ambitious than some of our earlier plans, this nonetheless proved both difficult to implement and rewarding. The achievements and difficulties of the Research Group are discussed below.

The group consisted of six people, two women and four men aged between 19 and 59, who had participated in the case studies. They all lived in a large Scottish city and meetings of the group were held in an ARC on a two weekly basis. At the time of writing, seven meetings of the group had taken place and more were planned. Getting all six people together proved to be difficult. Each was travelling to the centre from a different location using public transport and so times of arrival were unpredictable. The people who attended the Research Group were involved in a range of other activities that sometimes took priority. The effect of this was that most meetings lacked one or two participants. Most people in the group knew each other either from school or from attending events for people with learning difficulties; this familiarity produced a relaxed atmosphere, but also led to the surfacing of some long-established tensions. The group was convened and supported by Heather Wilkinson with Sheila Riddell acting as observer.

There was some uncertainty, reflected in frequent discussion at team meetings, of the priority that should be accorded to the work of the group and how it should relate to the main body of the research. In the event, we invested a considerable amount of the project's resources in the Research Group, spending one day a week of the Research Fellow's time in coordinating and convening the group over a 12-month period. Most of the case study individuals in the first stage of the ethnographic work participated in the Research group and in this sense there was a sense of continuity between its activities and the main research project. At the same time, however, we were conscious of a permanent state of tension between the amount of time we were able to dedicate to the group and the rest of the study. Group members made it clear that they would have welcomed the opportunity to meet up with the researcher on an ongoing and regular basis, and again there were tensions between individuals' need for friendship and the nature of the research relationship. Some of the less secure group members asked the researcher frequently if it would be possible to get together outwith the planned research meetings and it was difficult to explain that this was not possible.

The ideal referred to earlier, where people with learning difficulties decide on an issue which needs to be researched and convene a group of researchers to help them in this task, was far from the reality of this research group. In formulating our proposal to the ESRC to undertake research as part of the *Learning Society Programme*, we had drawn on ongoing work with people with learning difficulties (Baron et al, 1995a, 1995b; Stalker, 1997). However, as it did not then exist, the Research Group had not been involved in the formulation of the project and the research questions, and so it was not surprising that they regarded the research as our project in which they were temporarily involved. They were happy to come along to the meetings because they enjoyed the interaction with the researchers and each other, but they expected the researchers to structure what happened when they arrived. They also made it clear that they expected the sessions to be reasonably entertaining and not too much like hard work. They were not keen on interviewing each other because they preferred the discussion to be coordinated by the researchers, whom they regarded as new and interesting people in their social world. This was not to imply that they accepted passively the direction suggested by the researchers; if they felt the topic was boring or irrelevant they would steer the conversation back to an area of greater interest. They also reminded the researchers of their relatively privileged position. For instance, it was suggested to Heather Wilkinson that she was very lucky having her job because it appeared to be well paid and spending time talking to them was scarcely difficult.

Learning difficulties and theory

As indicated earlier, we wished to explore the extent to which people with learning difficulties were able, within the context and limitations of our project, to participate in theory generation. Based on our knowledge of the people who attended the Research Group and our reading of others' experiences, we did not seek directly their views on the nature of choice, the meaning of adult status or their views of themselves as users and consumers of services. Rather, we engaged in a discussion of their common sense theories and the implications of these for the provision of education, training and employment services. As well as listening to their views, we told them about some of the ideas emerging from the data and they in turn commented on these. In the following sections, we discuss two major areas where the Research Group contributed to the generation of theory.

The identity of people with learning difficulties

The focus of our research is the experience of people with learning difficulties as members of what is optimistically termed a learning society. Our definition of people with learning difficulties is deliberately fuzzy, based on operational definitions employed by service providers including government agencies, voluntary organisations and user groups. One of the aims of the Research Group was to encourage those within it to reflect on their collective experience as people with learning difficulties. However, it became apparent that the subjectivity of group members was not based on the idea of being a person with learning difficulties and indeed this was not an identity they welcomed.

This rejection of the term was first apparent in early discussions as to who should be invited to the group. Fiona, one of the participants, expressed opposition to including two of the men because they could not read and write and therefore would not be able to make a valid contribution. Rejection of the identity of a person with learning difficulties was evident throughout Fiona's discussion of her educational experiences. She described how she had enjoyed her first primary school where she had learnt to write, won prizes for Bible work and joined in playground games. Then she had moved to a special school that she described as:

> "The type of school where you didn't have a lot of friends."

> "I felt they were all special needs, I didn't have any friends as such ...
> I felt different to the others and when I got my first job I can
> remember thinking, 'Oh great!'"

She said she had no choice in the change of school and the reason for the move was because she was assessed as having "high frequency deafness". She also explained that the reason she got into trouble for her needlework was because:

"I couldn't concentrate because I've got a lazy eye and I just couldn't seem to keep the neatness straight."

Fiona's sister Shona who attended an independent school in the city, was described as 'awf'y brainy', as if Fiona wished to retain a sense of herself as the norm and her sister as abnormally bright. Despite this, Fiona was clearly making an unfavourable comparison between herself and her sister:

"Shona did OK, she was very good at school and she made some good friends at school and has kept in touch with some of them."

Other group participants described the reason for their having been placed in a special school in terms of some other trait rather than having an intellectual impairment. Mick, for instance, said that the reason he was placed in a special school was because of his violence and then described an escape from school:

"I was a violent boy ... I remember I was determined to get over the primary school wall ... I got over the netting ... and I jogged and ran home ... I never went back ... some kids got onto me."

As researchers who had brought the group together to explore their collective identity, we were unsure how to proceed. Given the negative connotations that the group attached to learning difficulties, we felt that we should not impose on them an identity that they themselves were rejecting. At the same time, we were struck by the extent of the denial, silence and subterfuge surrounding intellectual impairment in which professionals and voluntary organisations were complicit. Throughout their education, training and social activity, these people were grouped together on the implicit understanding that they had certain common characteristics and required particular types of provision. However, the basis of their social grouping and the attributed social identity that flowed from it appeared not to have been discussed by parents and professionals with those whose lives it concerned. It appeared that intellectual impairment, for from being celebrated, was too shameful to be discussed openly even with those who were being consigned to this category. The contrasting experience of, for example, deaf people is evident. Although deafness may at times be associated with damaged social identity, deaf people themselves celebrate their culture, using this as the basis for opposing disabling barriers (Corker, 1997). It is now associated with a rich culture of its own and difficulties which deaf people encounter in participating in mainstream society are attributed to social and economic barriers rather than individually based deficits (Corker, 1997). There is evidence that although intellectual impairment is used to justify social segregation, its existence is denied by professionals who identify it and individuals who are thus labelled.

This denial of intellectual impairment is noted by Harris (1995). He refers to Gowans and Hulbert's (1983) review of studies measuring the self-concept of people with intellectual impairment, which confirms that they prefer not to identify with 'mentally handicapped' others. Oliver (1986) using a repertory grid technique to assess the self-concept of a girl with Down's syndrome found that she did not wish to identify with mentally handicapped others. Jahoda et al (1988) also reported that people with 'mild mentally handicap' were likely to define themselves as essentially the same as other 'non-handicapped people' rather than essentially different. Their mothers, on the other hand, tended to see their sons and daughters as essentially different. Jahoda et al concluded from this that people with learning difficulties recognise the stigma attached to intellectual impairment and do not automatically internalise this sense of negative worth, rather rejecting the negative label. A problem with this, of course, is that rejecting intellectual impairment as part of one's subjectivity may leave an absence of identity rather than a positive sense of self. Harris points to tentative evidence that people with learning difficulties who participate in self-advocacy groups may have higher self concepts than others. Given that the system of education, training and employment is premised on the segregation of people with intellectual impairment from others and the imposition of special status, it would appear that this is likely to produce spoiled identities. There is clearly a need for work that explores the uses of self-advocacy to develop a positive sense of self without disavowing central elements of identity. The refusal of the identity and label 'learning difficulties' has significant political implications. Although sharing the same or similar material locations, the people in the Research Group displayed little consciousness of these and how they might seek to alter them. It is to competing understandings of this material base to which we now turn.

The material basis of social inclusion

Following European social theorists such as Beck (1992), it has been suggested that life chances and experiences may no longer be determined by an individual's relationship to the economic base, but rather to the individualised negotiation of risk. Beck concedes that risk is not randomly distributed and that Western societies display "an amazing stability" (Beck, 1992, p 91), with wealth protecting some people against life hazards and poverty exposing others to "an abundance of risk". Such theories have wide implications for disabled people including those with learning difficulties. In our project we wished to consider the extent to which intellectual impairment exposes people to an abundance of risk and whether disability has an effect independent of social class. At the level of social policy, there is a current focus on the centrality of employment to social inclusion. New Labour's Welfare to Work policy is firmly rooted in notions of the redemptive power of employment; those who cannot participate will have their basic needs met but will be excluded from civil society. Given these theoretical and policy concerns with the relationship between access to financial resources and social inclusion, we were curious to know how people with learning difficulties construed their situation.

The male members of the group were very clear that the development of social relationships was contingent on access to employment. Bryce, a man who was approaching retirement but had never had a job, felt the lack of employment keenly:

Bryce: "You need money to take your girlfriend out.... Women should have jobs as well so they can go to the dances and enjoy themselves."

The type of job people would do in order to be paid differed. Mick described with distaste a job at a leisure centre where he was meant to tidy up equipment but was also asked to clean the toilets. Bryce disagreed with him:

"I wouldn't mind cleaning the toilets. It saves you wandering the streets. I wouldn't mind doing a scaffy's [street sweeper's] job. The job's dirty but the money's clean!"

There was also recognition of the link between an independent household and an intimate relationship. Mick, a young man who had recently left school, rejected the type of independent living available to those ascribed special status:

Mick:	"My mum, she wants me to go into a hostel. I don't like it. My mum thinks it might be a good idea and I don't want to."
Interviewer:	"Have you been to look at a hostel?"
Mick:	No. "I don't want it. I just want to get married."
Interviewer:	"What d'you think the hostel would be like?"
Mick:	"Very soor."
Interviewer:	"Soor? What's that?"
Mick:	"One, you don't get help, two, you would be left in the lurch.... I would prefer to get married.... It's the best chance for me."

Mick perceives accurately that the type of independent living available in a hostel with other disabled people is different from that associated with the acquisition of one's own home in the context of the formation of adult social relationships. In the absence of this possibility, his preferred solution is to remain at home with his mother.

Conclusion

Whereas some have maintained that the social model implies research directly controlled by disabled people, we point out the difficulties that might arise in relation to people with learning difficulties if this principle were to be enforced. In the context of the research project, we aimed to include people with learning difficulties in aspects of the data collection but for a range of reasons our original plans were scaled down. This, of course, is not to suggest that involvement of people with learning difficulties in the research process must inevitably be limited; greater involvement in the formulation of the project from the outset might have produced stronger links between the main research project and the Research Group. Furthermore, the type of research demanded by the ESRC is not necessarily compatible with time-consuming work of building research relationships with people with learning difficulties.

Despite these limitations, the Research Group suggested important themes and provided a commentary on ideas emerging from preliminary data analysis. The researchers were pushed into clarifying their emerging theories by explaining them in a straightforward manner to group participants. For instance, we had to find direct ways of asking people about the identification and negotiation of risk and whether the barriers to full social participation they encountered were cultural or material in origin. Furthermore, we had to think through the contradictions of inviting people to discuss the barriers associated with intellectual impairment, when it was apparent that they did not see themselves as people with learning difficulties. It seemed to us that there was a need for the further development of the type of self-advocacy promoted by groups like People First, which sees learning difficulties as associated with barriers to understanding and communication in a world which places great store by intellectual and verbal dexterity, but at the same time acknowledges the wealth of ability and potential which people with learning difficulties nonetheless possess and is committed to dismantling the social and economic barriers they encounter.

Our awareness of the dangers of exploitation in research relationships made us question what was gained by those who participated in the Research Group. The fact that they attended for almost a year, making considerable efforts to be there, suggested that they saw it as an enjoyable and worthwhile experience, but also, less positively, that for many there were no more pressing demands on their time as would have been the case for most adults with work and family commitments. Despite the fact that their lack of social involvement was not of our making, nonetheless their desire for ongoing contact with the researchers underlined their vulnerability and marginalisation. This made it all the more important for us to address issues of accountability and we were guided by Booth and Booth's (1993) ideas of what accountability in research with people with learning difficulties may mean. Although our research was not formulated by people with learning difficulties, we felt compelled to ensure that, as far as this were possible, our work would be supportive of, rather than damaging to, the lives of those who participated in it. While supporting attempts to involve disabled people in research, and acknowledging that we have much to learn about how best to do this, we ultimately believe that research should be judged on its rigor, its ability to make sense of diverse experience and its capacity to make suggestions about the conditions which might improve people's lives.

Appendix 2
The statutory framework

The main legal requirements for local authorities and health boards to provide social, health, housing, education, employment and services for people with learning disabilities are set out below.

1968 Social Work (Scotland) Act

Section 12

This places a general duty on every local authority to promote social welfare by making advice, guidance and help available on a scale appropriate for their area.

Section 12A

This was added by the 1990 National Health Service and Community Care Act (see section 55). The 1968 Social Work (Scotland) Act was also amended by the 1995 Carers (Recognition and Services) Act. This places a duty on the local authority to carry out community care assessments and then decide whether to provide services.

Section 14

This places a general duty on every local authority to provide domiciliary services for households where there are people in need. It also gives the power to provide laundry facilities for these households.

1972 Chronically Sick and Disabled Persons (Scotland) Act

This Act extends sections 1 and 2(1) of the 1970 Chronically Sick and Disabled Persons Act to Scotland.

Section 1 (of the 1970 Act)

This places a duty on every local authority (which has a role under section 12 of the 1968 Act) to know about the numbers of disabled people living in their area and the need to make arrangements for these people. Every local authority should publish general information about the services they provide. They are also to let disabled people know about relevant services that they know others provide.

Section 2(1) (of the 1970 Act)

This lists the arrangements that can be made to help disabled people. These include:

- Practical help for that person in his or her home
- Getting, or helping someone to get a radio, TV, phone, or specialist equipment to be able to use a phone
- Help in using library, recreational or educational facilities
- Providing facilities to and from home, or helping with travel
- Adaptations to the home
- Holidays
- Meals.

Section 21

This is the Orange Badge Scheme of parking concessions for disabled and blind people.

1973 Employment and Training Act (as amended by the 1993 Trade Union Reform and Employment Rights Act)

This sets out the duty of the Secretary of State for Scotland to provide relevant services for helping people in education to decide on future employment, and what training may be necessary to fit them for this employment.

Sections 10(1) and 10(2)

These say "in doing so the Secretary of State shall have regard to the requirements of disabled persons."

1980 Education (Scotland) Act

Section 1

This places a general duty on education authorities to provide adequate and efficient school education for their area. This must include special educational needs, which covers those with learning difficulties that may arise from a disability.

Section 60(2)

So that education authorities can fulfil their duties in terms of special educational needs, they must find out which children belonging to their area (who are two years old or over but under 16) have obvious, specific or complex special educational needs which need to be reviewed. They must open and keep a Record of Needs for any children who, following assessment, have these needs. They also have the power to carry out these functions for children aged between 16 and 18 who are still at school.

Section 65B

This places a duty on the education authority to provide a future needs assessment for any child with special educational needs so that children may benefit from local authority services after leaving school.

1984 Mental Health (Scotland) Act

Sections 2 to 6

These provide for the Mental Welfare Commission for Scotland whose main function is to use their general protective functions for people with mental disorders. This includes those with learning disabilities. The Commission's powers cover people in the community as well as those in hospital or other care settings.

Sections 7 and 8

These give power to local authorities to make arrangements for providing services for people with mental disorders. This includes accommodation for those not in hospital, and, in particular, after-care services for those who are or have been suffering from mental disorders.

Section 11

This says local authorities must provide training and jobs for people with learning disabilities.

Sections 17-35

These cover care and treatment of patients with mental disorders in hospital.

Section 17 sets out the conditions for going into hospital.

Sections 35A to 35K

These sections were introduced by the 1995 Mental Health (Patients in the Community) Act. They cover community care orders for people who have left hospital, to make sure they receive the services they need while in the community. (However, they do not allow for compulsory treatment in the community.)

Sections 36-52

These cover guardianship for people with mental disorders if this is appropriate. The guardian may be the local authority or an individual.

Sections 60-76

These set out conditions relating to hospital orders and restriction orders for people with mental disorders who have been charged with offences. They also cover transferring prisoners with mental disorders to hospital where appropriate.

Section 94

This covers managing the property of patients who are receiving treatment in hospital for mental disorders (whether or not they are formally held under the Act) and who cannot manage their own affairs.

Part X covers treating mental disorders of patients who are held to whom Part X applies. In particular, it regulates certain treatments (at present electro-convulsive therapy, drug treatment for more than three months, psychosurgery and implanting hormones). Part X1 covers other conditions including offences against people with mental disorders. Part XI contains offences against people with mental disorders (particularly section 106, which regulates sexual relationships with women with learning disabilities). It places a duty on professionals to give information to relatives and carers of patients under guardianship. It grants powers to Mental Health Officers and the police to intervene if people with mental disorders are neglected or abused, or need care in a public place.

1986 Disabled Persons (Services, Consultation and Representation) Act

Section 4
This places a duty on the local authority to decide whether the needs of a disabled person call for a range of services in line with section 2(1)

of the 1970 Act if the disabled person, his or her representative or carer ask for this.

Section 8 (1)

This places a duty on the local authority to take account of the ability of the carer to continue to provide care.

Section 13

This deals with disabled people leaving special education in Scotland. Under this section local authorities have a duty to assess the needs of disabled children in relation to providing services in accordance with the welfare enactments, and for that assessment to be carried out.

1987 Housing (Scotland) Act

Section 1

This places a duty on local authorities to consider the housing needs of their area, and in doing so, take account of the needs of chronically sick or disabled people.

Section 236

This gives local authorities the power to pay improvement grants to, among others, disabled occupants.

1990 National Health Service and Community Care Act

Section 47 (2)

This says that if, during an assessment of need, a person appears to be disabled, the local authority will move automatically to make a decision on services.

Section 55

This added a new section 12A into the 1968 Act under which the local authority would carry out assessments of needs and would then decide whether these needs call for services.

1990 Enterprise and New Towns Act (as amended by the 1993 Trade Unions Reform and Employment Rights Act)

Section 2(3)

This deals with Training for Work. It says that Scottish Enterprise and Highlands and Islands Enterprise must each make appropriate arrangements for helping people to train so that they may get and keep suitable jobs.

Section 2(4)

This says that the above should include arrangements for encouraging more opportunities for (and types of) employment and training that are available to disabled people.

1992 Further and Higher Education (Scotland) Act

Section 1

This says the Secretary of State has a duty to "secure adequate and efficient provision of further education in Scotland". Further education that this duty applies to is described in the Act as amended by Schedule 5, paragraph 8, of the 1996 Education (Scotland) Act. In carrying out his duty, the Secretary of State "shall have regard to the requirements of persons over school age who have learning difficulties". The term learning difficulties is used in the Act in its broad sense to include difficulties in learning and barriers to learning.

1995 Carers (Recognition and Services) Act

Section 2 (1)

This changes section 12A of the 1968 Act to make an independent assessment of carers' needs when they ask for this. However, this only applies if the care they offer is substantial and regular.

1995 Disability Discrimination Act

Section 19

This makes it illegal for anyone providing services to discriminate against a disabled person in relation to access, for example, how information is used and how communication is used.

Part V

This is a matter for the Westminster Parliament and covers regulations to set minimum conditions for providing access for disabled people to public transport vehicles. Rail Vehicle Accessibility Regulations came into force on 1 January 1999. Regulations on access to buses, coaches and taxis are at various stages of being prepared.

The 1995 Children (Scotland) Act

Section 22
This places a duty on local authorities to protect and promote the welfare of children in need in their area.

Section 23

This introduces a new legal framework for assessment, services, and support to children with disabilities, children affected by disabilities and their families. The principle behind this is that services are designed to reduce the negative effect of the child's disability and improve the child's opportunity to lead as normal a life as possible.

Section 24

In carrying out an assessment to decide on the needs of a disabled child the local authority must assess a carer's ability to provide, and to continue to provide, care for that child.

1995 Criminal Procedure (Scotland) Act

Sections 52 to 63
These cover putting people accused of offences in hospital if they have mental disorders.

Sections 60 to 76 of the 1984 Act set out the conditions relating to hospital orders and restriction orders for people with mental disorders who have been charged with offences. They also cover transferring prisoners with mental disorders to hospitals where appropriate.

1996 Direct Payments Act
This amends the 1968 Social Work (Scotland) Act, section 12B and section 12C.

The 2000 Adults With Incapacity (Scotland) Act

This Act replaces current arrangements for curators bonis, tutors, tutors dative and guardians appointed under the 1984 Mental Health (Scotland) Act. All of these office holders can currently make decisions about either the finances or the welfare of people who do not have the ability legally to make their own decisions.

Standards in Scotland's Schools Bill

This will mean local authorities must provide pre-school education for every three- and four-year-old whose parents want a place. Children with learning disabilities stand to benefit from this duty no less than others.

Index

NOTE: Page numbers followed by *Ap* indicate information is in the Appendices; page numbers followed by *n* indicate information is in a note.